SEVEN TYPES *Of* AMBIGUITY

William Empson

DP DOABA PUBLICATIONSS

Price:
₹395/- $7.99/- £6.99/-

ISBN : 9789367216521

First Edition **2025**

Published by
DOABA PUBLICATIONSS
Shanti Mohan House, 16 Ansari Road, Daryaganj
New Delhi – 110002
www.doabapublications.com
www.doababooks.com

sales@doababooks.com

Typeset at:
MB Graphics, Delhi

Printed in New Delhi

PREFACE TO THE SECOND EDITION

The first and only previous edition of this book was published sixteen years ago. Till it went out of print, at about the beginning of the war, it had a steady sale though a small one ; and in preparing a second edition the wishes of the buyers ought to be considered. Many of them will be ordering a group of books on this kind of topic, for a library, compiled from bibliographies; some of them maybe only put the book oil their list as an awful warning against taking verbal analysis too far. Anyway, such a buyer wants the old book, not a new one, even if I could make it better. On the other hand, there was obviously room to tidy up the old one, and I would not want to reprint silently anything I now think false.

It seemed the best plan to work the old footnotes into the text, and make clear that all the footnotes in this edition are second thoughts written recently. Sometimes the footnotes disagree with the text above them; this may seem a fussy process, but I did not want to cut too much. Sir Max Beerbohm has a fine reflection on revising one of his early works ; he said he tried to remember how angry he would have been when he wrote it if an elderly pedant had made corrections, and how certain he would have felt that the man was wrong. However, I have cut out a few bits of analysis (hardly ever without a footnote to say so) because they seemed trivial and likely to distract the reader's attention from the main point of the passage; I have tried to make some of the analyses clearer, and occasionally written in connecting links; the sources of the quotations needed putting in; there were a lot of small proof corrections to make; and some of the jokes which now seem to me tedious have gone. I do not think I have suppressed quietly any bit of analysis which would be worth disagreeing over. There is now an index and a summary of chapters.

I was surprised there was so little of the book I should prefer to change. My attitude in writing it was that an honest man erected the ignoring of 'tact' into a point of honour. Apart from trailing my coat about minor controversies, I claimed at the start that I would use the term 'ambiguity' to mean anything I liked, and repeatedly told the reader that the distinctions between the Seven Types which he was asked to study would not be worth the attention of a profounder thinker. As for the truth of the theory which was to be stated in an irritating manner, I remember saying to Professor I.A Richards in a 'supervision' (he was then my teacher and gave me crucial help and encouragement) that all the possible mistakes along this line ought to be heaped up and published, so that one could sit back and wait to see which were the real mistakes later on. Sixteen years later I find myself prepared to stand by nearly the whole heap. I have tried to clear the text of the gratuitous puzzles of definition and draw attention to the real ones.

The method of verbal analysis is of course the main point of the book, but there were two cross-currents in my mind leading me away from it. At that time Mr. T. S. Eliot's criticism in particular, and the Zeitgeist in general, were calling for a reconsideration of the claims of the nineteenth-century poets so as to get them into perspective with the newly discovered merits of Donne, Marvell, and Dryden. It seemed that one could only enjoy both groups by approaching them with different and incompatible presuppositions, and that this was one of the great problems which a critic ought to tackle. My feeling now is not so much that what I wrote about the nineteenth century was wrong as that I was wrong in tackling it with so much effort and preparation. There is no need to be so puzzled about Shelley. But I believe that this looking for a puzzle made me discover something about Swinburne, and I did not treat the Keats *Ode to Melancholy* as a dated object.

The second cross-current was the impact of Freud. Some literary critics at the time were prepared to 'collaborate' with the invading psycho-analysts, whereas the honest majority who were prepared to fight in the streets either learned fire- watching technique or drilled with the Home Guard. This problem, too, I think, has largely settled itself in the intervening years, and I can claim that my last example of the last type of ambiguity was not concerned with neurotic disunion but with a fully public theological poem. However, I want now to express my regret that the topical interest of Freud distracted me from giving adequate representation in the seventh chapter to the poetry of straightforward mental conflict, perhaps not the best kind of poetry, but one in which our own age has been very rich. I had not read Hart Crane when I published the book, and I had had the chance to. Mr. T. S. Eliot, some while ago (speaking as a publisher), remarked that poetry is a mug's game, and this is an important fact about modern poets. When Tennyson retired to his study after breakfast to get on with the *Idylls* there had to be a hush in the house because every middle-class household would expect to buy his next publication. I believe that rather little good poetry has been written in recent years, and that, because it is no longer a profession in which ability can feel safe, the effort of writing a good bit of verse has in almost every case been carried through almost as a clinical thing; it was done only to save the man's own sanity. Exceedingly good verse has been written under these conditions in earlier centuries as well as our own, but only to externalise the conflict of an individual. It would not have been sensible to do such hard work unless the man himself needed it. However, if I tried to rewrite the seventh chapter to take in contemporary poetry I should only be writing another book.

I want here to consider some theoretical points which have been raised in criticisms of the book; and I am sorry if I have missed or failed to keep some powerful attack which ought to be answered. I have remembered a number of minor complaints which I have tried to handle in the textual corrections or the footnotes. The fundamental arguments against my approach, I think, were all put briefly and clearly by Mr. James Smith in a review in the *Criterion* for July 1931; so it is convenient to concentrate on that article, though many other critics expressed similar views. To some extent I think these objections were answered in the text, but obviously they were not answered clearly or strongly enough, and if I have anything fresh to say I ought to say it now.

He made objections to my uses of the term 'ambiguity' which I have tried to handle in re-editing; but I have also to answer this sentence: 'We do not ordinarily accuse a pun, or the better type of conceit, of being ambiguous because it manages to say two things at once; its essence would seem to be conciseness rather than ambiguity.' We call it ambiguous, I think, when we recognise that there could be a puzzle as to what the author meant, in that alternative views might be taken without sheer misreading. It a pun is quite obvious it Would not ordinarily 'Be called ambiguous, because there is no room for puzzling. But if an irony is calculated to deceive a section of its readers I think it would ordinarily be called ambiguous, even by a critic who has never doubted its meaning. No doubt one could say that even the most obvious irony is a sort of playing at deception, but it may imply that only a comic butt could be deceived, and this makes a different sort of irony. Cardinal Newman found Gibbon ambiguous, we must suppose, because some remarks by the Cardinal imply that he did not know that Gibbon meant to be ironical. But most readers would consider the ironies of Gibbon unambiguous, though possessed of a 'double meaning,' because they would feel that no one could be deceived by them. Thus the criterion for the ordinary use of the word is that somebody might be puzzled, even if not yourself. Now I was frequently puzzled in considering my examples, though not quite in this way. I felt sure that the example was beautiful and that I had, broadly speaking, reacted to it correctly. But I did not at all know what had happened in this ' reaction ' ; I did not know why the example was beautiful. And it seemed to me that I was able in some cases partly to explain my feelings to myself by teasing out the meanings of the text. Yet these meanings when teased out (in a major example) were too complicated to be remembered together as if in one glance of the eye ; they had to be followed each in turn, as possible alternative reactions to the passage ; and indeed there is no doubt that some readers sometimes do only get part of the full intention. In this way such a passage has to be treated as if it were ambiguous, even though it may be said that for a good reader it is only ambiguous (in the ordinary sense of the term) while he is going through an unnecessary critical exercise. Some critics do not like to recognise this process because they connect it with Depth Psychology, which they regard with fear. But it is ordinary experience that our minds work like this ; that we can often see our way through a situation, as it were practically, when it would be extremely hard to separate out all the elements of the judgment. Most children can play catch, and few children are good at dynamics. Or the way some people can do anagrams at one shot, and feel sure the letters all fit, is a better illustration; because there the analytic process is not intellectually difficult but only very tedious. And it is clear that this process of seeing the thing as a whole is particularly usual and important in language; most people learn to talk, and they were talking grammar before grammarians existed.

This is not to argue that some elemental and unscholarly process is what is in question, nor that what has to be explained always happens in a rapid glance of the eye. Indeed, what often happens when a piece of writing is felt to offer hidden riches is that one phrase after another lights up and appears as the heart of it; one part after another catches fire, so that you walk about with the thing for several days. To go through the experience in question is then slower, not quicker, than the less inspiriting process of reading an analysis of it; and the fact that we can sometimes grasp a complex meaning quickly as a whole does not prove that a radically different mode of thought (an intrusion of the lower depths) is there to be feared.

This is meant as a sketch of the point of view which made 'ambiguity' seem a necessary key word; of course, I do not deny that the term had better be used as clearly as possible, and that there is a use for a separate term ' double meaning,' for example when a pun is not felt to be ambiguous in effect, but it could be argued that, until you have done your analysis of the ambiguities, you cannot be sure whether the total effect is ambiguous or not; and that this forces you in some degree to extend the meaning of the term. I wanted in any case to put such a sketch before giving a longer quotation from Mr. James Smith's review, in which his objections are more fundamental. As the book went on, he said, there was an increasing proportion of examples from plays :

> The effect of the dramatic upon the poetic scale is almost sure to be unfortunate. The first business of the student of drama, so far as he is concerned with ambiguity, is historical ; he records that situations are treacherous, that men are consciously or unconsciously hypocritical, to such or such a degree. The student of poetry, on the other hand, has as his first business the passing of a judgement of value. It is not his main, or even his immediate, concern that a word can be interpreted, that a sentence can be construed, in a large number of ways; if he make it his concern, there is a danger that, in the enumeration of these ways, judgements of value will be forgotten. And unless they are put in at the beginning of an analysis they do not of their own account emerge at the end. Quite a number of Mr. Empson's analyses do not seem to have any properly critical conclusion ; they are interesting only as revelations of the poet's, or of Mr. Empson's, ingenious mind. Further, some of Mr. Empson's analyses deal, not with words and sentences, but with conflicts supposed to have raged within the author when he wrote. Here, it seems to me, he has very probably left poetry completely behind. . . .

There are a number of irrelevancies in Mr. Empson's book, and as in a measure they derive from, so probably in a measure they increase, his vagueness as to the nature and scope of ambiguity. Finding this everywhere in the drama, in our social experience, in the fabric of our minds, he is led to assume it must be discoverable everywhere in great poetry. I doubt whether the reader who remembers his Sappho, his Dante, or the Lucy poems of Wordsworth is even prepared to be convinced of this ; but even if he were he could not be so until Mr. Empson had made his position much clearer. Is the ambiguity referred to that of life — is it a bundle of diverse forces, bound together only by their co-existence? Or is it that of a literary device — of the allusion, conceit, or pun, in one of their more or less conscious forms? If the first, Mr. Empson 's thesis is wholly mistaken ; for a poem is not a mere fragment of life ; it is a fragment that has been detached, considered, and judged by a mind. A poem is a noumenon rather than a phenomenon. If the second, then at least we can say that Mr. Empson 's thesis is exaggerated.

I thought this ought to be reprinted with the book, if only because it puts clearly what many readers will feel. Other reviewers made an illustrative point along the same line of objection : that in learning a foreign language the great thing is to learn to cut out the alternative meanings which are logically possible ; you are always liable to bring them up till you have 'grasped the spirit' of the language, and then you know they aren't meant. Of course, I don't deny that the method could lead to a shocking amount of nonsense ; in fact, as a teacher of English literature in foreign countries I have always tried to warn my students off the book. It is clear that we have to exercise a good deal of skill in cutting out implications that aren't wanted in reading poems, and the proof of our succecs is that we are actually surprised when they are brought out by a parody. However, I recognised in the book that one does not want merely irrelevant ambiguities, and I should claim to have had some success in keeping them out. To be sure, the question how far unintended or even unwanted extra meanings do in fact impose themselves, and thereby drag our minds out of their path in spite of our efforts to prevent it, is obviously a legitimate one ; and some of the answers may be important. But it is not one I was much concerned with in this book.

In the same way, when Mr. James Smith said that I often left out the judgment of value he was of course correct. Many of the examples are only intended to show that certain techniques have been widely used. Even in the fuller examples, where I hope I have made clear what I feel about the poem as a whole, I don't try to ' make out a case ' for my opinion of its value. The judgment indeed comes either earlier or later than the process which I was trying to examine. You think the poem is worth the trouble before you choose to go into it carefully, and you know more about what it is worth when you have done so. It might be argued that a study of the process itself is not really 'criticism' ; but this change of name would not prove that there is any fundamental fallacy in trying to study it. No doubt the study would be done badly if there were wrong judgments behind it, but that is another thing.

The distinction made by Mr. James Smith between the dramatic situation and the judgment of the poet is, therefore, a more fundamental objection. It seems to me one of those necessary simplifications, without which indeed life could not go forward, but which are always breaking down. Good poetry is usually written from a background of conflict, though no doubt more so in some periods than in others. The poet, of course, has to judge what he has written and get it right, and his readers and critics have to make what they can of it too. When Mr. James Smith objected to my dealing with 'conflicts supposed to have raged within the author' I think he was overplaying his hand very seriously; he was striking at the roots of criticism, not at me. If critics are not to put up some pretence of understanding the feelings of the author in hand they must condemn themselves to contempt. And besides, the judgment of the author may be wrong. Mr. Robert Graves (I ought to say in passing that he is, so far as I know, the inventor of the method of analysis I was using here) has remarked that a poem might happen to survive which later critics called 'the best poem the age produced/ and yet there had been no question of publishing it in that age, and the author had supposed himself to have destroyed the manuscript. As I remember, one of the best-known short poems by Blake is actually crossed out by the author in the notebook which is the only source of it. This has no bearing on any 'conflict' theory; it is only part of the difficulty as to whether a poem is a noumenon or a phenomenon. Critics have long been allowed to say that a poem may be something inspired which meant more than the poet knew.

The topic seems to me important, and I hope I may be allowed to digress to illustrate it from painting. As I write there is a grand semi-government exhibition of the painter Constable in London, very ample, but starring only two big canvases, both described as 'studies.' Constable painted them only as the second of three stages in making an Academy picture, and neither could nor would ever have exhibited them. I do not know how they survived. They are being called by some critics (quite wrongly, I understand) the roots of the whole nineteenth-century development of painting. It seems obvious to many people now that they are much better than Constable's finished works, including the two that they are 'studies' for. However, of course, nobody pretends that they were an uprush of the primitive or in some psychological way 'not judged' by Constable. When he got an idea he would make a preliminary sketch on the spot, then follow his own bent in the studio (obviously very fast), and then settle down on another canvas to make a presentable picture out of the same theme. 'My picture is going well,' he remarks in a letter, 'I have got rid of most of my spottiness and kept in most of my freshness.' You could defend the judgment of Constable by saying that he betrayed his art to make a living, but this would be absurdly unjust to him; at least Constable would have resented it, and he does not seem to have had any gnawing conviction that the spottiest version was the best one. Of course, the present fashion for preferring it may be wrong too ; the point I am trying to make is that this final 'judgment' is a thing which must be indefinitely postponed. Would Mr. James Smith say that the 'study,, which is now more admired than the finished work, was a noumenon or a phenomenon ? I do not see any way out of the dilemma which would leave the profound truths he was expressing much importance for a practical decision.

The strongest point of Mr. James Smith's criticism, I felt, was the accusation that, owing to my vagueness about ambiguity, I supposed it to exist everywhere in great poetry, whereas this would obviously be false about Sappho, Dante, and Wordsworth on Lucy. Oddly enough among the other reviewers at the time, one chose a passage from Dante and another from Wordsworth on Lucy to make a rather different point. They used the lines they quoted as examples of the real ambiguity of great poetry, a thing, they said, which underlay the superficial and finicking ambiguities I had considered, and gave them whatever value they had. These views are perhaps not really very unlike, though I would feel more at home with the second. But it seems clear that I ought to try to answer a question: What claim do I make for the sort of ambiguity I consider here, and is all good poetry supposed to be ambiguous ?

I think that it is ; but I am ready to believe that the methods I was developing would often be irrelevant to the demonstration. As I understand it, there is always in great poetry a feeling of generalisation from a case which has been presented definitely; there is always an appeal to a background of human experience which is all the more present when it cannot be named. I do not have to deny that the narrower chisel may cut more deeply into the heart. What I would suppose is that, whenever a receiver of poetry is seriously moved by an apparently simple line, what are moving in him are the traces of a great part of his past experience and of the structure of his past judgments. Considering what it feels like to take real pleasure in verse, I should think it surprising, and on the whole rather disagreeable, if even the most searching criticism of such lines of verse could find nothing whatever in their implications to be the cause of so straddling a commotion and so broad a calm.

CONTENTS

I

An ambiguity, in ordinary speech, means something very pronounced, and as a rule witty or deceitful. I propose to use the word in an extended sense, and shall think relevant to my subject any verbal nuance, however slight, which gives room for alternative reactions to the same piece of language[1]. Sometimes, especially in this first chapter, the word may be stretched absurdly far, but it is descriptive because it suggests the analytical mode of approach, and with that I am concerned.

In a sufficiently extended sense any prose statement could be called ambiguous. In the first place it can be analysed. Thus, ' The brown cat sat on the red mat' may be split up into a series : ' This is a statement about a cat. The cat the statement is about is brown,' and so forth. Each such simple statement may be translated into a complicated statement which employs other terms ; thus you are now faced with the task of explaining what a 'cat' is; and each such complexity may again be analysed into a simple series; thus each of the things that go to make up a 'cat' will stand in some spatial relation to the 'mat.' 'Explanation,' by choice of terms, may be carried in any direction the explainer wishes; thus to translate and analyse the notion of ' sat ' might involve a course of anatomy; the notion of 'on' a theory of gravitation. Such a course, however, would be irrelevant not only to my object in this essay but to the context implied by the statement, the person to whom it seems to be addressed, and the purpose for which it seems to be addressed to him; nor would you be finding out anything very fundamental about the sentence by analysing it in this way; you would merely be making another sentence, stating the same fact, but designed

1 In the first edition I made it ' adds some nuance to the direct statement of prose.' This, as was pointed out, begs a philosophical question and stretches the term ' ambiguity ' so far that it becomes almost meaningless. The new phrase is not meant to be decisive but to avoid confusing the reader ; naturally the question of what would be the best definition of ' ambiguity '(whether the example in hand should be called ambiguous) crops up all through the book.

for a different purpose, context, and person. Evidently, the literary critic is much concerned with implications of this last sort, and must regard them as a main part of the meaning. There is a difference (you may say that between thought and feeling) between the fact stated and the circumstance of the statement, but very often you cannot know one without knowing the other, and an apprehension of the sentence involves both without distinguishing between them. Thus I should consider on the same footing the two facts about this sentence, that it is about a cat and that it is suited to a child. And I should only isolate two of its 'meanings,' to form an ambiguity worth notice; it has contradictory associations, which might cause some conflict in the child who heard it, in that it might come out of a fairy story and might come out of Reading without Tears.

In analysing the statement made by a sentence (having, no doubt, fixed on the statement by an apprehension of the implications of the sentence), one would continually be dealing with a sort of ambiguity due to metaphors, made clear by Mr. Herbert Read in English Prose Style because metaphor, more or less far-fetched, more or less complicated, more or less taken for granted (so as to be unconscious), is the normal mode of development of a language. 'Words used as epithets are words used to analyse a direct statement,' whereas 'metaphor is the synthesis of several units of observation into one commanding image; it is the expression of a complex idea, not by analysis, nor by direct statement, but by a sudden perception of an objective relation.' One thing is said to be like another, and they have several different properties in virtue of which they are alike. Evidently this, as a verbal matter, yields more readily to analysis than the social ambiguities I have just considered; and I shall take it as normal to the simplest type of ambiguity, which I am considering in this chapter. The fundamental situation, whether it deserves to be called ambiguous or not, is that a word or a grammatical structure is effective in several ways at once. To take a famous example, there is no pun, double syntax, or dubiety of feeling, in

Bare ruined choirs, where late the sweet birds sang,

but the comparison holds for many reasons; because ruined monastery choirs are places in which to sing, because they involve sitting in a row, because they are made of wood, are carved into knots and so forth, because they used to be surrounded by a sheltering building crystallised out of the likeness of a forest, and coloured with stained glass and painting like flowers and leaves, because they are now abandoned by all but the grey walls coloured like the skies of winter, because the cold and Narcissistic charm suggested by choir-boys suits well with Shakespeare's feeling for the object of the Sonnets, and for various sociological and historical reasons (the protestant destruction of monasteries ; fear of puritanism), which it would be hard now to trace out in their proportions; these reasons, and many more relating the simile to its place in the Sonnet, must all combine to give the line its beauty, and there is a sort of ambiguity in not knowing which of them to hold most clearly in mind. Clearly

this is involved in all such richness and heightening of effect, and the machinations of ambiguity are among the very roots of poetry.

Such a definition of the first type of ambiguity covers almost everything of literary importance, and this chapter ought to be my longest and most illuminating, but it is the most difficult. The important meanings of this sort, as may be seen from the example about the cat, are hard to isolate, or to be sure of when you have done so ; and there is a sort of meaning, the sort that people are thinking of when they say ' this poet will mean more to you when you have had more experience of life,' which is hardly in reach of the analyst at all. They mean by this not so much that you will have more information (which could be given at once) as that the information will have been digested; that you will be more experienced in the apprehension of verbal subtleties or of the poet's social tone; that you will have become the sort of person that can feel at home in, or imagine, or extract experience from, what is described by the poetry; that you will have included it among the things you are prepared to apprehend. There is a distinction here of the implied meanings of a sentence into what is to be assimilated at the moment and what must already be part of your habits; in arriving at the second of these the educator (that mysterious figure) rather than the analyst would be helpful. In a sense it cannot be explained in language, because to a person who does not understand it any statement of it is as difficult as the original one, while to a person who does understand it a statement of it has no meaning because no purpose.

Meanings of this kind, indeed, are conveyed, but they are conveyed much more by poets than by analysts; that is what poets are for, and why they are important. For poetry has powerful means of imposing its own assumptions, and is very independent of the mental habits of the reader; one might trace its independence to the ease with which it can pass from the one to the other of these two sorts of meaning. A single word, dropped where it comes most easily, without being stressed, and as if to fill out the sentence, may signal to the reader what he is meant to be taking for granted; if it is already in his mind the word will seem natural enough and will not act as an unnecessary signal. Once it has gained its point, on further readings, it will take for granted that you always took it for granted ; only very delicate people are as tactful in this matter as the printed page. Nearly all statements assume in this way that you know something but not everything about the matter in hand, and would tell you something different if you knew more; but printed commonly differ from spoken ones in being intended for a greater variety of people, and poetical from prosaic ones in imposing the system of habits they imply more firmly or more quickly.

As examples of the things that are taken for granted in this way, and assume a habit, rather than a piece of information, in the reader, one might give the fact that a particular section of the English language is being used; the fact that English is being used, which you can be conscious of if you can use French; the fact that a European language is used, which you can be conscious of if you can use Chinese. The first of these 'facts' is more definite than it sounds ; a word in a speech which falls outside the expected vocabulary will cause an uneasy stir in all but the soundest sleepers; many sermons use this with painful frankness. Evidently such a section is defined by its properties rather than by enumeration, and so alters the character of the words it includes; for instance, one would bear it in mind when considering whether the use of a word demands that one should consider its derivation. Regional or dialect poets are likely to use words flatly from that point of view. No single example of so delicate and continuous a matter can be striking; I shall take one at random out of the Synge Deirdre to make clear that a word need not be unpoetical merely because its meaning has been limited :

> Deirdre. ... It should be a sweet thing to have what is best and richest, if it's for a short space only.
>
> Naisi. And we've a short space only to be triumphant and brave.

The language here seems rich in implications ; it certainly carries much feeling and conveys a delicate sense of style. But if one thinks of the Roman or medieval associations of triumphant even of its normal use in English, one feels a sort of unexplained warning that these are irrelevant; the word here is a thin counter standing for a notion not fully translated out of Irish;

it is used to eke out that alien and sliding speech-rhythm, which puts no. weight upon its single words.[2]

The process of becoming accustomed to a new author is very much that of learning what to exclude in this way, and this first of the three 'facts,' hard as it may be to explain in detail, is one with which appreciative critics are accustomed to deal very effectively. But the other two are more baffling; one can say little about the quality of a language, if only because the process of describing it in its own language is so top-heavy, and the words of another language will not describe it. The English prepositions, for example, from being used in so many ways and in combination with so many verbs, have acquired not so much a number of meanings as a body of meaning continuous in several dimensions; a tool-like quality, at once thin, easy to the hand, and weighty, which a mere statement of their variety does not convey. In a sense all words have a body of this sort ; none can be reduced to a finite number of points, and if they could the points could not be conveyed by words.

Thus a word may have several distinct meanings; several meanings connected with one another; several meanings which need one another to complete their meaning ; or several meanings which unite together so that the word means one relation or one process. This is a scale which might be followed continuously. 'Ambiguity' itself can mean an indecision as to what you mean, an intention to mean several things, a probability that one or other or both of two things has been meant, and the fact that a statement has several meanings.[3] It is useful to be able to separate these if you wish, but it is not obvious that in separating them at any particular point you will not be raising more problems than you solve. Thus I shall often use the ambiguity of 'ambiguity,' and pronouns like ' one,' to make statements covering both reader and author of a poem, when I want to avoid raising irrelevant problems as to communication. To be less ambiguous would be like analysing the sentence about the cat into a course of anatomy. In the same way the words of the poet will, as a rule, be more justly words, what

2 Not a clear example, and I am not sure that what I said is true ; but a borderline example was needed here to show that fine shades can be concerned.

3 It would seem pedantic to alter the phrase ' has several meanings,' but it is treacherous. If the simplest statement has a subject find a predicate it may be said to include two meanings. There would be no point in calling it ambiguous unless it gave room for alternative reactions.

they represent will be more effectively a unit in the mind, than the more numerous words with which I shall imitate their meaning so as to show how it is conveyed.

And behind this notion of the word itself, as a solid tool rathe. than as a collection of meanings, must be placed a notion of the way such a word is regarded as a member of the language ; this seems still darker and less communicable in any terms but its own. For one may know what has been put into the pot, and recognise the objects in the stew, but the juice in which they are sustained must be regarded with a peculiar respect because they are all in there too, somehow, and one does not know how they are combined or held in suspension. One must feel the respect due to a profound lack of understanding for the notion of a potential, and for the poet's sense of the nature of a language.

These examples of the 'meanings' of an English sentence should make clear that no explanation, certainly no explanation written in English, can be conceived to list them completely ; and that there may be implications (such as I should call meanings) of which a statement would be no use. Neither of these are objections to my purpose, because I can assume that my readers already understand and enjoy the examples I shall consider, and I am concerned only to conduct a sufficient analysis of their enjoyment to make it seem more understandable.

It is possible that there are some writers who write very largely with this sense of a language as such, so that their effects would be almost out of reach of analysis. Racine always seems to me to write with the whole weight of the French language to remind one always of the latent assumptions of French in a way that I am not competent to analyse in any case, but that very possibly could not be explained in intelligible terms. Dryden is a corresponding English figure in this matter; Miss Gertrude Stein, too, at this point, implores the passing tribute of a sigh. To understand their methods one might have to learn a great deal about the mode of action of language which is not yet known, and it might always be quicker to use habit than analysis, to learn the language than to follow the explanation.

I propose, then, to consider a series of definite and detachable ambiguities, in which several large and crude meanings can be separated out, and to arrange them in order of increasing distance from simple statement and logical exposition. There is much danger of triviality in this, because it requires a display of ingenuity such as can easily be used to escape from the consciousness of one's ignorance; because it ignores the fact that the selection of meanings is more important to the poet than their multitude, and harder to understand; and because it gives no means of telling how much has been done by meanings latent in the mode of action of the language, which may be far more elaborate and fundamental than those that can be written up. My methods can only be applied at intervals; I shall frequently pounce on the least interesting aspect of a poem, as being large enough for my forceps ; and the atoms which build up the compounds I analyse will always be more complex than they. But in so far as anything can be said about this mysterious and important matter, to say it ought not to require apology.

I shall almost always take poems that I admire, and write with pleasure about their merits ; you might say that, from the scientific point of view, this is a self-indulgence, and that as much is to be learnt from saying why bad poems are bad. This would be true if the field were of a known size ; if you knew the ways in which a poem might be good, there would be a chance of seeing why it had failed. But, in fact, you must rely on each particular poem to show you the way in which it is trying to be good ; if it fails you cannot know its object ; and it would be trivial to explain why it had tailed at something it was not trying to achieve. Of course, it may succeed in doing something that you understand and hate, and you may then explain your hatred; but all you can explain about the poem is its success. And even then, you can only have understood the poem by a stirring of the imagination, by something like an enjoyment of it from which you afterwards revolt in your own mind. It is more self-centred, therefore, and so less reliable, to write about the poems you have thought bad than about the poems you have thought good.

But, before I start to do this, I must consider two fundamental objections to my purpose, which many critics would raise; the objection that the meaning of poetry does not matter, because it is apprehended as Pure Sound, and the objection that what really matters about poetry is the Atmosphere. These two opinions are very similar, but are best answered in different ways.

The main argument for Pure Sound is the extreme oddity if the way poetry acts ; the way lines seem beautiful without reason ; the way you can decide (or at any rate people in practice do decide) whether a poem deserves further attention by a mere glance at the way it uses its words. This certainly is an important piece of evidence, and makes one feel that very strange things may be true about the mode of action of poetry, but it shows very little as to what these things may be. I shall myself try to bully my readers into a belief in the importance of ambiguity, for just this same reason.

There was a period of the cult of Pure Sound when infants were read passages from Homer, and then questioned as to their impressions, not unlike Darwin playing the trombone to his French beans. And, indeed, conclusive evidence was collected in this way that a vague impression as to the subject of a poem may be derived from a study of its reciter ; one can only question how far this is relevant to the question at issue. There is a crux here (to revive a rather stale controversy) which makes experiment difficult; on the one hand, it is no use telling a person who does not know Greek to read Homer for himself, because he does not know how to pronounce it (even if he knows how to pronounce the words, he will not pronounce them as a sentence) ; on the other hand, if you tell him how to pronounce the sentence, it is impossible to be sure you have not told him how to feel about it by the tone of your voice. Certainly it is no use denying that feelings can be conveyed, even between animals of different species, by grunts and screams; and there are those who say that language itself was at first a self-explanatory symbolism, based on these expressions of feeling, on onomatopoeia, and on that use of the tongue to point at matters of interest, or to imitate and so define a difficult action, which may be seen in a child learning to mite. Certainly, too, one would expect language in poetry to retain its primitive uses more than elsewhere. But this sort of thing is no use to the admirers of Pure Sound in poetry, because a grunt is at once too crude and too subtle to be conveyed by the alphabet at all. Any word can be either screamed or grunted, so if you have merely a word written on paper you have to know not only its meaning but something about its context before it can tell you whether to grunt or to scream. Most admirers of Pure Sound, indeed, will admit that you have to be experienced in the words used by a poet before their sound can be appreciated, and evidently this admission makes all the difference.

They are the more willing to admit this because they are usually appreciative critics, persons of an extreme delicacy of sensibility who have to guard this delicacy in unusual ways. A first-rate wine-taster may only taste small amounts of wine, for fear of disturbing his palate, and I dare say it would really be unwise for an appreciative critic to use his intelligence too freely; but there is no reason why these specialised habits should be imposed on the ordinary drinker or reader. Specialists usually have a strong Trades Union sense, and critics have been perhaps too willing to insist that the operation of poetry is something magical, to which only their own method of incantation can be applied, or like the growth of a flower, which it would be folly to allow analysis to destroy by digging the roots up and crushing out the juices into the light of day. Critics, as ' barking dogs,' on this view, are of two sorts : those who merely relieve themselves against the flower of beauty, and those, less continent, who afterwards scratch it up. I myself, I must confess, aspire to the second of these classes; unexplained beauty arouses an irritation in me, a sense that this would be a good place to scratch; the reasons that make a line of verse likely to give pleasure, I believe, are like the reasons for anything else; one can reason about them; and while it may be true that the roots of beauty ought not to be violated, it seems to me very arrogant of the appreciative critic to think that he could do this, if he chose, by a little scratching.

One reason, by the way, that the belief in Pure Sound is plausible seems interesting; it is that people often test it by experiments within their own family of languages. They know, say, a novel-reading amount of French, a public-school amount of Latin, half-forgotten, and a smattering of Italian ; they try reading the Oxford Book of Spanish Verse and are impressed by the discovery that they can get a great deal of pleasure out of individual lines without understanding the 'meaning' at all. Now such poetry is in a tradition to which they are accustomed ; they know roughly what to look for in the poetry of a Latin language ; they know what the syntax connecting one or two large words is likely to be ; and they are almost sure to know the root meaning (though not the precise meaning) of the one or two large words . It seems to be true that with this equipment one has a very fair chance of seeing what I may call the ' lyrical point ' of one or two lines. This may be an important piece of evidence about the mode of action of poetry, but as far as it concerns Pure Sound one must remember that such people will be pronouncing the lines entirely wrong. (And Vergil remains the most melodious of poets through all the vagaries of official pronunciation.)

Such points would be admitted by most reasonable people, and it may seem an evasion on my part to attack Pure Sound as a defence of the opposite fallacy of Pure Meaning. But the situation about Pure Sound is like that about crude materialism ; both beliefs lead a sort of underground existence, and at a low level of organisation have much vitality. Crude materialism is the first rough idea that people tumble into when they are interested in the sciences. In the same way, if you ask people in general about the interpretation of poetry, they are likely to say that it is no use talking because what they like is the sheer beauty of the sound.

The official, and correct, view, I take it, is that ' the sound must be an echo to the sense,' that we do not know what this condition may be, but that if we knew a great deal it could be analysed in detail. Thus

> Tendebantque manus ripae ulterioris amore
>
> (Aenid vi.)

(the stock line to try on the dog) is beautiful because ulterioris the word of their banishment, is long, and so shows that they have been waiting a long time; and because the repeated vowel sound (itself the moan of hopeless sorrow) in oris amore connects the two words as if of their own natures, and makes desire belong necessarily to the unattainable. This I think quite true, but it is no use deducing from it Tennyson's simple and laborious cult of onomatopoeia. Once you abandon the idea that sounds are valuable in themselves you are thrown far towards the other extreme ; you must say that the sounds are valuable because they suggest incidental connections of meaning. If this be true, one can do a great deal to make poetry intelligible by discussing the variety of resultant meanings, without committing oneself very deeply as to how they have been suggested by the sounds.

In claiming so much for analysis I shall seem to be aligning myself with the 'scientific' mode of literary criticism, with 'psychological' explanations of everything, and columns of a reader's sensitivity-coefficients. There is coming into existence a sort of party-system among critics; those critics will soon be considered mere shufflers who are not either only interested in Truth or only interested in Beauty; and Goodness, the third member of that indissoluble trinity, has somehow got attached only to Truth, so that aesthetes are expected to profess a playful indifference to the principles on which they in fact (one is to assume) order their own lives. It is odd, and I think harmful, that this fin-de-siecle squabble is still going on. Somewhere in the eighties of the last century the idea got about that Physics, and those sciences that might be conceived as derivatives of Physics, held a monopoly of Reason ; aesthetes had therefore to eschew Reason. Now there are serious difficulties about applying the scientific view of truth to the arts; I shall attempt to restate them in my last chapter. But the belief that Reason can be applied to the arts is as old as criticism, and fundamental to it; there is no more materialism about it than there is about Aristotle. And if one is to be forced to take sides, as a matter of mere personal venom, I must confess I find the crudity and latent fallacy of a psychologist discussing verses that he does not enjoy less disagreeable than the blurred and tasteless refusal to make statements of an aesthete who conceives himself to be only interested in Taste.

Johnson's remarks about the correspondence theory are not to be despised, particularly in the 92nd Rambler:

> There is nothing in the art of versifying so much exposed to the power of imagination as the accommodation of the sound to the sense. It is scarcely to be doubted that on many occasions we make the music that we imagine ourselves to hear, that we modulate the poem by our own disposition, and ascribe to the numbers the effects of the sense.

But on the other hand :

> The measure of time in pronouncing may be varied so as very strongly to represent, not only the modes of external. Motion, but the quick or slow succession of ideas, and consequently the passions of the mind.

His examples certainly show very clearly that there is no single mode of correspondence ; that very similar devices of sound may correspond effectively to very different meanings. And often enough in Milton, for instance, it is the opposite of onomatopoeia which is employed ; thus in the lines about Vulcan –

> thrown by angry Jove
>
> Sheer o'er the crystal battlements; from morn
>
> To noon he fell, from noon to dewy eve,

> A summer's day ; and with the setting sun
>
> Dropped from the zenith –

Milton is extremely cool about the matter; one is made to sit with him pleasantly in the shade, all day long, needing no further satisfaction; it is delightfully soothing to feel that the devil is all the time falling faster and faster. But this is only to say that a sound effect must be interpreted. I think myself its most important mode of action is to connect two words by similarity of sound so that you are made to think of their possible connections.

Another of Johnson's remarks brings up some questions which deserve mention :

> Dionysius himself tells us, that the sound of Homer's verses sometimes exhibits the idea of corporal bulk: is not this a discovery nearly approaching to that of the blind man, who, after long enquiry into the nature of the scarlet colour, found that it represented nothing so much as the clangour of a trumpet?

The blind man seems to have anticipated Miss Sitwell, who has actually used this comparison, I think very justly. She also writes

> The light is braying like an ass,

which of course depends for its effect on the whole scene described. In such cases, apprehension in terms of one of the senses is described in terms of, or compared with, one of the others; this has been called synaesthesia, and is clearly sometimes effective. It throws back the reader upon the undifferentiated affective states which are all that such sensations have in common; perhaps recalls him to an infantile state before they had been distinguished from one another; and may actually induce a sort of rudimentary disorder into his modes of sensation (so that the 'images' of the visualiser are transformed sounds) like those due to migraine or epilepsy or drugs like mescal. Mescal-eaters have just that impression common among readers of pure' poetry, that they are seeing very delightful but quite new colours, or knowing something which would be very important and interesting if they could make out just what it was. But how such a disturbance can be of serious importance to a reader of poetry it is not easy to see ; or how one is to be sure when it is occurring. Often it is no more than a device for insisting on ambiguities of the first type ; the main comparison is neither true nor false, and one is thrown back on a series of possible associations, as to the social setting in which these sensations would be expected, or the mood in which they would be sought out. Miss Sitwell seemed often to use the device rather as a flag of defiance, to insist that the main meaning is not what she valued, and the reader must put himself into a poetic or receptive frame of mind, (' These two things are alike in that, for quite different reasons, they harmonise with my mood.') But in a way this is only to push the notion of correspondence further back; how do these sensations come to seem proper to their social setting or their mood? Poe often seems excited about colours in a way that reminds one of people's reports from mescal, but then it is a Mexican drug and he had probably tried it; one cannot deduce anything very profound about poetry from that. And Swinburne often uses devices that seem to demand synaesthesia;

> Thy voice is an odour that fades in a flame,

and suchlike ; but that is only part of his diffused use of grammar, by which several precise conceits can be dissolved into a vague- ness; it would probably be a misreading here to confuse the modes of sensation. Nor, so far as I can see, is his use of the device at all similar to that made of it by Miss Sitwell.

Of course, when a poet is describing paintings, as Spenser does so often, the colours mentioned are supposed to act on one as they would do in a painting. Now, it is naturally harder to analyse the visual arts than poetry, because their modes of satisfaction are further removed from the verbal system on which the discursive intelligence usually supports itself. In any case, I am not competent to do such a thing and shall not attempt it here ; I mention this mysterious matter as a way in which poetry might be taking effect, but which I shall assume I can ignore. And it seems worth uttering the pious hope that such effects do not really depend on an obscure physiological perversion, which could be exploited separately, so as to 'deceive'; but that there is a field for analysis in the way the paintings admired by a particular school of poets are assumed as elements of sensibility, and referred to covertly, in their poetry.

So the discovery of the blind man may have its importance, but we must now turn to what Dionysius himself said which may be very important indeed. I mentioned a moment ago the theory that language is fundamentally a system of gestures with the tongue ; there is no doubt that, once the advocate of Pure Sound has admitted that sound has some connection with meaning. Sir Richard Paget's method of interpretation gives him a great deal of rational support. Everyone feels that, quite apart from words like 'pop,' which are like their meaning, there are words like ' wee,' which are fitted to their meaning; the Paget theory would explain this (taking only the vowel, for this brief example) by saying that while 'huge' moves the tongue back from the teeth so as to make as large a space as it can, 'wee' moves the tongue near to the teeth so as to leave as small a space as it can. In this way, not the sound itself, but our experience of the way it is produced, does, in fact, continually exhibit the idea of corporal bulk which is just what Johnson thought impossible. All the sounds may be reduced to gestures in this way, more or less fancifully; they all, then, carry some suggestion of size, or shape, or movement, or pressure, up, down, forward, or backward, and, in themselves, that is all they can convey. This theory would have a peculiar charm for the materialists who wanted to explain everything in terms of Euclid and Newton; it offers a sort of guarantee that the explanation will be a picture on the blackboard. It is rather bad luck that it should be developed so late, when the faith even of physicists in pictures on the blackboard is not what it was, but that it explains some part of the effect of language it would be hard to deny.

Evidently there is here another field for the future analysis of poetry; when it becomes possible to list the root notions that the words must by their own nature be suggesting, it will be possible and profitable to discuss in some detail how far their sound is an echo to their sense. But such a process will always be subject to curious limitations ;

> . . . owing to the comparative paucity of different mouth-gestures, each mouth-gesture — which produces its own particular sound or root word — has to stand for a considerable number of hand- (or other bodily) gestures ; to put it in another way, each root word is naturally liable to bear many different meanings. . . . One other point may be noted; the same mouth-gesture may be naturally construed in several different ways. Thus, the movement of tongue or lips may represent a pantomimic movement, symbolising a real movement, or a spatial relation of some kind, e.g, above, below, around, or it may represent a shape of some kind drawn in outline. Finally, any of these meanings may be used figuratively instead of concretely.
>
> (Sir Richard Paget, Human Speech.)

Apart, then, from the ambiguities in the fully-developed language, such as I propose to consider, one would have also to consider the ambiguities (of the same sort, but entirely different in their details) which are always latent in the fundamental symbolism of the sound.

This suggests that the process of analysing the effect of a poem, not indeed completely, but sufficiently to be any use, must be one of altogether impossible complexity; that one must instead give up all hope of doing such a thing, and fall back on a doctrinaire irrationalism. It is true that no explanation can be adequate, but, on the other hand, any one valid reason that can be found is worth giving; the more one understands one's own reactions the less one is at their mercy.

Thus it seems to be fairly true, as a matter of introspection, that one judges liie quality of a poem by something felt as ' sound' and something felt as ' rhythm,' but there are no necessary deductions from this fact, and it is liable to be misleading. One might use a spatial metaphor and a tautology to make it seem less important; 'the sound of words' does not enter that part of the mind where it is effective, except in so far as the words take effect as words.' What this 'taking effect' may be like I shall try to discuss in my last chapter.

It has been deduced from the belief in Pure Sound that the resultant meaning of the w6rds need not be known, that it is enough to know the meaning of the words in isolation and enough of their syntax to read them aloud rightly. In a degree this is often true, but it is better to regard this state of limited knowledge as a complicated state of indecision which involves much estimating of probabilities, and is less ignorance than an ordered suspension of judgment. Secondly, and more seriously, it has been deduced from this belief that you are liable to destroy the poem if its meaning is discovered, that it is important to preserve one's innocence about the meaning of verses, that one must use sensibility, and as little intelligence as possible. This, also, is often true, but I take a moral line here, and say it is true only of bad poetry. People suspect analysis, often rightly, as the refuge of the emotionally sterile, but that is only to say that analysis is often done badly. In so far as such a destruction occurs because you have used your intelligence it must be accepted, and you may reasonably expect to become interested in another poem, so that the loss is not permanent, because that is the normal process of learning to appreciate poetry.

As for the belief in Atmosphere, about which I shall now make some inadequate remarks, it may be viewed as a third deduction from the belief in Pure Sound. Critics often say or imply casually that some poetic effect conveys a direct 'physical' quality, something mysteriously intimate, something which it is strange a poet could convey, something like a sensation which is not attached to any one of the senses. This may only be a statement of how they themselves applied their conscious attention when reading the poem ; thus a musical chord is a direct sensation, but not therefore unanalysable into its separate notes even at the moment of sensing. It can be either felt or thought; the two things are similar but different; and it requires practice to do both at once. Or the statement might, one cannot deny, mean that there has been some confusion of the senses. But it may mean something more important, involving a distinction between ' sensation ' and ' feeling' ; that what the poet has conveyed is no assembly of grammatical meanings, capable of analysis, but a 'mood,' an 'atmosphere,' a 'personality,' an attitude to life, an undifferentiated mode of being.

Probably it is in this way, as a sort of taste in the head, that one remembers one's own past experiences, including the experience of reading a particular poet. Probably, again, this mode of apprehension is connected with the condition of the whole body, and is as near as one can get to an immediate self-knowledge. You may say, then, that any grammatical analysis of poetry, since it must ignore atmosphere, is trivial; that atmosphere is conveyed in some unknown and fundamental way as a by-product of meaning; that analysis cannot hope to do anything but ignore it; and that criticism can only state that it is there.

This belief may in part explain the badness of much nineteenth-century poetry, and how it came to be written by critically sensitive people. They admired the poetry of previous generations, very rightly, for the taste it left in the head, and, failing to realise that the process of putting such a taste into a reader's head involves a great deal of work which does not feel like a taste in the head while it is being done, attempting, therefore, to conceive a taste in the head and put it straight on to their paper, they produced tastes in the head which were in fact blurred, complacent, and unpleasing. But to say that the consequences of a critical formula have been unfortunate is not to say that it is untrue or even unusable; it is very necessary for a critic to remember about the atmosphere, chiefly because he must concentrate on the whole of the poem he is talking about rather than on the particular things that he can find to say.

In wishing to apply verbal analysis to poetry the position of the critic is like that of the scientist wishing to apply determinism to the world. may not be valid everywhere; though it be valid everywhere it may not explain everything; but in so far as he is to do any work he must assume it is valid where he is working, and will explain what he is trying to explain. I assume, therefore, that the 'atmosphere' is the consciousness of what is implied by the meaning, and I believe that this assumption is profitable in many more cases than one would suppose.

I shall try to recommend this opinion by giving what seems to me a striking example ; a case, that is, where an affective state is conveyed particularly vividly by devices of particular irrelevance. Macbeth, in these famous lines, may easily seem to be doing something physiological and odd, something outside the normal use of words. It is when he is spurring on his jaded hatred to the murder of Banquo and Fleance.

Come, seeling Night,

Skarfe up the tender Eye of pitiful Day

And with thy bloddie and invisible Hand

Cancel and teare to pieces that great Bond

That keepes me pale.

Light thickens, and the Crow

Makes Wing to th Rookie Wood.

Good things of Day begin to droope, and drowse,

While Night's black Agents to their Prey's doe rowse.

Thou marvell'st at my words, but hold thee still ;

Things bad begun, make strong themselves by ill :

So prythee go with me.

(ill. ii. 50.)

The condition of his skin (By the pricking of my thumbs Something wicked this way comes), the sense of being withdrawn far within his own flesh (like an old lecher, a small fire at his heart, all the rest on's body cold), the sense that the affair is prosaic, it need not be mentioned, and yet an occasional squawking of the nerves (Hobbididance croaks in Tom's belly), in short the whole frame of body, as I read the lines, is lit up and imposed upon the reader, from which Macbeth lashes his exhausted energies into a new, into the accustomed, readiness for murder.

I have tried by these almost irrelevant quotations to show much work the reader of Shakespeare is prepared to do for him, how one is helped by the rest of his work to put a great deal into any part of it, but this seems to explain very little. Various similar sound effects or associations may be noted; there is a suggestion of witches' broth, or curdling blood, about thickens, which the vowel sound of light, coming next to it, with the movement of stirring treacle, and the cluck of the k-sounds, intensify; a suggestion, too, of harsh, limpid echo, and, under careful feet of poachers, an abrupt crackling of sticks. The vowel sounds at the end make an increasing darkness as the crow goes forward. But, after all, one would be very surprised if two people got the same result from putting a sound-effect into words in this way.

It is safer to point out that rooks were, in any case, creatures of foreboding ;

Augurs, and understood Relations, have

By Magot-Pyes, and Choughes, and Rookes, brought forth

The secret'st man of Blood ;

(ill. iv. 125.)

that Macbeth looked out of the window because Banquo was to be killed soon after dusk, so he wanted to know how the tim6 was going; and that a dramatic situation is always heightened by breaking off the dialogue to look out of the window, especially if some kind of Pathetic Fallacy is to be observed outside. But to notice this particular pathetic fallacy you must withdraw yourself from the apprehension of its effect, and be ready to notice irrelevant points which may act as a clue. I believe it is that the peaceful solitary crow moving towards bed and the other crows, is made unnaturally like Macbeth and a murderer who is coming against them;

this is suggested by the next lines, which do not say whether the crow is one of the good things of day or one of nights black agents (it is, at any rate, black), by the eerie way that light itself is thickening, as a man turns against men, a crow against crows, perhaps by the portentous way a crow's voice will carry at such a time, and by the sharpness of its wings against the even glow of a sky after sundown; but mainly, I think, by the use of the two words rook and crow.

Rooks live in a crowd and are mainly vegetarian; crow may be either another name for a rook, especially when seen alone, or it may mean the solitary Carrion crow. This subdued pun is made to imply here that Macbeth, looking out of the window, is trying to see himself as a murderer, and can only see himself as in the position of the crow that his day of power, now, is closing ; that he has to distinguish himself from the other rooks by a difference of name, rook-crow, like the kingly title, only; that he is anxious, at bottom, to be at one with the other rooks, not to murder them; that he can no longer, or that he may yet, be united with the rookery; and that he is murdering Banquo in a forlorn attempt to obtain peace of mind.[4]

Interest in ' atmospheres' is a critical attitude designed for, and particularly suited to, the poets of the nineteenth century; this may tell us something about theni, and in part explain why they are so little ambiguous in the sense with which I am concerned. For a variety of reasons, they found themselves living in an intellectual framework with which it was very difficult to write poetry, in which poetry was rather improper, or was irrelevant to business, especially the business of becoming Fit to Survive, or was an indulgence of one's lower nature in beliefs the scientists knew were untrue. On the other hand, they had a large public which was as anxious to escape from this intellectual frameworK, on holiday, as they were themselves. Almost all of them, therefore, exploited a sort of tap-root into the world of their childhood, where they were able to conceive things poetically, and whatever they might be writing about they would suck up from this limited and perverted world an unvarying sap which was their poetical inspiration. Mr. Harold Nicolson has written excellently

4 It was stupid of me to present this example as a sort of test case, with a tidy solution drawn from the names of birds. Obviously the passage is still impressive if you have no opinions at all about the difference between crows and rooks. But it is at least a good example of a heavy Atmosphere, and I don't think my treatment of it was wrong as far as it went.

about Swinburne's fixation on to the excitements of his early reading and experience, and about the unique position in the life of Tennyson occupied by the moaning of cold wind round a child frightened for its identity upon the fens. Wordsworth frankly had no inspiration other than his use, when a boy, of the mountains as a totem or father-substitute, and Byron only at the end of his life, in the first cantos of Don Juan in particular, escaped from the infantile incest-fixation upon his sister which was till then all that he had got to say. As for Keats's desire for death and his mother, it has become a byword among the learned. Shelley, perhaps, does not strike one as keeping so sharp a distinction between the world he considered real and the world from which he wrote poetry, but this did not in his case improve either of them; while Browning and Meredith, who did write from the world they lived in, affect me as novel-writers of merit with no lyrical inspiration at all. Coleridge, it is true, relied on opium rather than the nursery. But of all these men an imposed excitement, a sense of uncaused warmth, achievement, gratification, a sense of hugging to oneself a private dream-world, is the main interest and material.[5]

In that age, too, began the doubt as to whether this man or that was 'grown-up,' which has ever since occupied so deeply the minds of those interested in their friends. Macaulay complains somewhere that in his day a man was sure to be accused of a childmind if no doubt could be cast 'either on the ability of his intelligence or the innocence of his character' ; now nobody seems to have said this in the eighteenth century. Before the Romantic Revival the possibilities of not growing up had never been exploited so far as to become a subject for popular anxiety.

Of course, these pat little theories are ridiculously simple; fantasy gratifications and a protective attitude towards one's inner life are in some degree essential for the production of poetry, and I have no wish to pretend the Romantics were not great poets. But I think this will be admitted, that they were making a use of language very different from that of their predecessors ; imagine Shakespeare or Pope keeping a tap-root in this way. One might expect, then, that they would not need to use ambiguities of the kind I shall consider to give vivacity to their language, or even ambiguities with which the student of language, as such, is concerned; that the mode

5 Byron I understand did not meet his half-sister at all till he was grown up. It seems no good trying to improve this paragraph, and I still think that the last sentence summing it up is sufficiently true.

of approach to them should be psychological rather than grammatical, and that their distortions of meaning will belong to darker regions of the mind.

This introduction has grown too long and too portentous ; it is time I settled down to the little I can do in this chapter, which is to list a few examples of ambiguity of the first type. Many of the preceding paragraphs are designed merely for defence ; if it is said that the verbal analyst is a crude irrelevant fellow who should be thinking about the atmosphere, the reply is that though there may be an atmosphere to which analysis is irrelevant, it is not necessarily anything very respectable.

I have already considered the comparison of two things which does not say in virtue of what they are to be compared. Of the same sort, though less common, is the ornamental use of false antithesis, which places words as if in opposition to one another without saying in virtue of what they are to be opposed. Cases in which several ways of opposing them are implied will be found in my later chapters as examples of more advanced ambiguity; but the device may be used to deny such an antithesis altogether. There is a rather trivial example of this in Peacock's War Song:

> We there, in strife be wildring.
>
> Spilt blood enough to swim in ;
>
> We orphaned many children
>
> And widowed many women.
>
> The eagles and the ravens
>
> We glutted with our foemen;
>
> The heroes and the cravens,
>
> The spearmen and the bowmen.

In the last two lines he is not concerned to be thinking, to decide something or convince somebody; he makes a cradle and rocks himself in it ; it is the tone of a man imagining himself in a mood wholly alien to him, and looking round with an amused complacent absence of reflection. The lines also give finality in that the impulse is shown to be dying away; some reflection has been implied on the difference between heroes and cravens on their equal deaths, and on the relations between eagles and heroes ravens and cravens, but the irrelevant calm of the last line says ' these distinctions may be made at other times, but they are irrelevant to our slaughter and the reaction to it of Nature,' he proceeds to another merely technical way of separating the dead into classes, and by the failure of the antithesis shows he is merely thinking of them as a huge pile.

How loved, how honoured once, avails thee not.

To whom related, or by whom begot;

A heap of dust is all remains of thee ;

'Tis all thou art, and all the proud shall be.

(Pope, Unfortunate Lady,)

The two parts of the second line make a claim to be alternatives which is not obviously justified, and this I think implies a good deal. If the antithesis is to be serious, or must mean 'one of her relations was grand but her father was humble,' or the other way about; thus one would take how to mean 'whether much or little'(it could mean 'though you were so greatly'), and the last line to contrast her with the proud, so as to imply that she is humble (it could unite her with the proud, and deduce the death of all of them from the death of one). This obscurity is part of the ' Gothic ' atmosphere that Pope wanted : ' her birth was high, but there was a mysterious stain on it ' ; or ' though you might not think it, her birth was high'; or 'her birth was high, but not higher than births to which I am accustomed.' Here, however, the false antithesis is finding another use, to convey the attitude of Pope to the subject. 'How simple, how irrelevant to the merits of the unfortunate lady, are such relationships; everybody has had both a relation and a father; how little I can admire the arrogance of great families on this point; how little, too, the snobbery of my reader, who is unlikely to belong to a great family; to how many people this subject would be extremely fruitful of antitheses ; how little fruitful of antitheses it seems to an independent soul like mine.' What is important about such devices is that they leave it to the reader vaguely to invent something, and make him leave it at the back of his mind.

Not unlike the use of a comparison which does not say in virtue of what the two things are to be compared is the use of a comparative adjective which does not say what its noun is to be compared with; since all adjectives are in a sense comparative, this source of ambiguity is a sufficiently general one. In particular, it is the chief source of euphuistic conceits and the paradoxes cultivated in the 'nineties, which give a noun two contradictory adjectives and leave it to the reader to see how the adjectives are used.[6] Examples of this sort are too well known, and are generally thought too trivial, to be worth quoting. I shall give an example from one of Mr. Waley's Chinese translations, to insist upon the profundity of feeling which such a device may enshrine.

> Swiftly the years, beyond recall.
>
> Solemn the stillness of this spring morning.

The human mind has two main scales on which to measure time. The large one takes the length of a human life as its unit, so that there is nothing to be done about life, it is of an animal dignity and simplicity, and must be regarded from a peaceable and fatalistic point of view. The small one takes as its unit the conscious moment, and it is from this that you consider the neighbouring space, an activity of the will, delicacies of social tone, and your personality. The scales are so far apart as almost to give the effect of defining two dimensions; they do not come into contact because what is too large to be conceived by the one is still too small to be conceived by the other. Thus, taking the units as a century and the quarter of a second, their ratio is ten to the tenth and their mean is the standard working day ; or taking the smaller one as five minutes, their mean is the whole of summer. The repose and self-command given by the use of the first are contrasted with the speed at which it shows the years to be passing from you, and therefore with the fear of death; the fever and multiplicity of life, as known by the use of the second, are contrasted with the calm of the external space of which it gives consciousness, with the absolute or extra-temporal value attached to the brief moments of self-knowledge with which it is concerned, and with a sense of security in that it makes death so far off.

Both these time-scales and their contrasts are included by these two lines in a single act of apprehension, because of the words swift and still. Being

---

6 Such a trick has usually one meaning which is the answer of the puzzle, but while you are puzzling the words have possible alternative meanings, and even to those who see the answers at once the alternatives are in a way present as being denied. They may appear as the views of commonplace people, who are thereby snubbed; but they can also make a real ambiguity when the denial is not felt to be complete.

contradictory as they stand, they demand to be conceived in different ways; we are enabled, therefore, to meet the open skies with an answering stability of self-knowledge ; to meet the brevity of human life with an ironical sense that it is morning and springtime, that there is a whole summer before winter, a whole day before night.

I call swift and still here ambiguous, though each is meant to be referred to one particular time-scale, because between them they put two time-scales into the reader's mind in a single act of apprehension. But these scales, being both present, are in some degree used for each adjective, so that the words are ambiguous in a more direct sense; the years of a man's life seem swift even on the small scale, like the mist from the mountains which 'gathers a moment, then scatters'; the morning seems still even on the large scale, so that this moment is apocalyptic and a type of heaven.

Lacking rhyme, metre, and any overt device such as comparison, these lines are what we should normally call poetry only by virtue of their compactness ; two statements are made as if they were connected, and the reader is forced to consider their relations for himself. The reason why these facts should have been selected for a poem is left for him to invent; he will invent a variety of reasons and order them in his own mind. This, I think, is the essential fact about the poetical use of language.

Among metaphors effective from several points of view one may include, by no great extension, those metaphors which are partly recognised as such and partly received simply as words in their acquired sense. All languages are composed of dead metaphors as the soil of corpses, but English is perhaps uniquely full 01 metaphors of this sort, which are not dead but sleeping, and, while making a direct statement, colour it with an implied comparison. The school rule against mixed metaphor, which in itself is so powerful a weapon, is largely necessary because of the presence of these sleepers, who must be treated with respect; they are harder to use than either plain word or metaphor because if you mix them you must show you are conscious of their meaning, and are not merely being insensitive to the possibilities of the language.

Beauty is but a flower

Which wrinkles will devour.

Brightness falls from the air.

Queens have died young and fair.

Dust hath closed Helen's eye.

I am sick, I must die.

Lord, have mercy upon us.

(Nash, Summer's Last Will and Testament.)

I call it a subdued metaphor here that devour should mean 'remove' or 'replace,' with no more than an overtone of cruelty and the unnatural. This may seem very different from the less evident subdued metaphor in the derivation of a word like 'apprehension,' say, but a reader may ignore the consequences even of so evident a metaphor as devour. If you go into the metaphor it may make Time the edax rerum and wrinkles only time's tooth-marks; more probably it compares long curving wrinkles on the face to rodent ulcers, caterpillars on petals, and the worms that are to gnaw it in the grave. Of these, the caterpillar (from flower) are what the comparison insists upon, but the Elizabethan imagination would let slip no chance of airing its miraculous corpse-worm.

On the other hand

Brightness falls from the air

is an example of ambiguity by vagueness, such as was used to excess by the Pre-Raphaelites. Evidently there are a variety of things the line may be about. The sun and moon pass under the earth after their period of shining, and there are stars falling at odd times ; Icarus and the prey of hawks, having soared upwards towards heaven, fall exhausted or dead ; the glittering turning things the sixteenth century put on the top of a building may have fallen too often. In another sense, hawks, lightning, and meteorites fall flashing from heaven upon their prey. Taking brightness as abstract, not as meaning something bright, it is as a benefit that light falls, diffusely reflected, from the sky. In so far as the sky is brighter than the earth (especially at twilight), brightness is natural to it; in so far as the earth may be bright when the clouds are dark, brightness falls from the sky to the earth when there is a threat of thunder. 'All is unsafe, even the heavens are not sure of their brightness,' or 'the qualities in man that deserve respect are not natural to him but brief gifts from God; they fall like manna, and melt as soon.' One may extract, too, from the oppression in the notion of thunder the idea that now, 'in time of pestilence,' the generosity of Nature is mysteriously interrupted; even at the scene of brilliant ecclesiastical festivity for which the poem was written there is a taint of darkness in the very air.

It is proper to mention a rather cynical theory that Nash wrote or meant 'hair'; still, though less imaginative, this is very adequate; oddly enough (it is electricity and the mysterious vitality of youth which have fallen from the hair) carries much the same suggestion as the other version; and gives the relief of a single direct meaning. Elizabethan pronunciation was very little troubled by snobbery, and it is conceivable that Nash meant both words to take effect in some way. Now that all this fuss has been made about aitches it is impossible to imagine what such a line would sound like.

For a final meaning of this line one must consider the line which follows it; there is another case of poetry by juxtaposition. In

> Dust hath closed Helen's eye

one must think of Helen in part as an undecaying corpse or a statue; it is dust from outside which settles on her eyelids, and shows that it is long since they have been opened; only in the background, as a truth which could not otherwise be faced, is it suggested that the dust is generated from her own corruption. As a result of this ambiguity, the line imposes on brightness a further and more terrible comparison; on the one hand, it is the bright motes dancing in sunbeams, which fall and become dust which is dirty and infectious ; on the other, the lightness, gaiety, and activity of humanity, which shall come to dust in the grave.

When a word is selected, as a 'vivid detail,' as particular for general, a reader may suspect alternative reasons why it has been selected; indeed the author might find it hard to say. When there are several such words there may be alternative ways of viewing them in order of importance.

> Pan is our All, by him we breathe, we live.
>
> We move, we are ; . . .
>
> But when he frowns, the sheep, alas.

The shepherds wither, and the grass.

(Ben Jonson, Pan's Anniversary)

Alas the word explaining which of the items in this list we are to take most seriously, belongs to the sheep by proximity and the break in the line, to the grass by rhyming with it, and to the shepherds, humble though they may be, by the processes of human judgment; so that all three are given due attention, and the balance of the verse is maintained. The Biblical suggestions of grass as symbolic of the life of man (' in the mornings it is green and growth up; in the evening it is cut down, dried up, and withered') add to the solemnity; or from another point of view make the passage absurdly blasphemous, because Pan here is James I. The grace, the pathos, the 'sheer song' of the couplet is given by an enforced subtlety of intonation, from the difficulty of saying it so as to bring out all the implications.

This last consideration is important, because it gives some hint as to why these devices belong to poetry rather than to prose, or indeed why poetry seems different from prose. A metrical scheme imposes a sort of intensity of interpretation upon the grammar, which makes it fruitful even when there is no 'song.'

I want to know a butcher paints,

A baker rhymes for his pursuit,

Candlestick-maker, much acquaints

His soul with song, or, haply mute.

Blows out his brains upon the flute.

(Browning.)

' I want to know that the whole class of butchers paints,' or ' I want to know that someone butcher paints,' or ' I want to know personally a butcher who paints'; any of these may be taken as the meaning, and their resultant is something like, 'I want to know that a member of the class of butchers is moderately likely to be a man who paints, or at any rate that he can do so if he wishes.' The demands of metre allow the poet to say something which is not normal colloquial English, so that the reader thinks of the various colloquial forms which are near to it, and puts them together; weighting their probabilities in proportion to their nearness. It is for such reasons as this that poetry can be more compact, while seeming to be less precise, than prose.

It is for these reasons, too, among others, that an insensitivity in a poet to the contemporary style of speaking, into which he has been trained to concentrate his powers of apprehension, is so disastrous, can be noticed so quickly, and produces that curious thinness or blurring of texture one finds in William Morris. And that is why the practice of putting single words into italics for emphasis (again the Victorians are guilty) is so vulgar; a well constructed sentence should be able to carry a stress on any of its words and should show in itself how these stresses are to be compounded. Both in prose and poetry, it is the impression that implications of this sort have been handled with more judgment than you yourself realise, that with this language as text innumerable further meanings, which you do not know, could be deduced, that forces you to feel respect for a style.

Also I have considered the 'implications' of sentences so far mainly as what they take for granted, as what must already be in mind if they are to be suitable. The stock example of this is, 'Have you stopped beating your wife.?', which claims to know already that it has been your habit to do so. A complementary sort of implication may be defined : what must not be in mind if the sentence is to be suitable, what it leaves vague, or is not thinking about, or does not feel. The negative here assumes you might expect this particular thing to be in mind, because otherwise you would not have thought of it as an implication. You might think it lessened the importance of a negative implication that one is only conscious of it if its assumption is unjustified; but the mind is a destroyer; any assumption may chance to be questioned ; and most people are conscious that they, therefore, can to some extent impose what they assume. In speaking of 'implications' one thinks as much of negative as of positive ones, indeed it would often be difficult to make the distinction. One would notice, to discover a negative implication, the degree to which stock phrases were used which did not fit the situation very closely, as if it did not need to be, or could not safely be, defined further, or the degree to which a form of words had been selected which only said so much and no more. For such reasons as these, private letters often seem most exquisitely adapted to their setting when written most casually; it is exactly the extent to which their language is careless, the proportion of carelessness they give to the different matters in hand, which is so precise. Similarly in conversation this more refined sort of implication is very highly developed. It is comparable to the use of facial muscles, intended for different or immensely cruder uses (such as the muscles round the eyes designed to prevent them from being gorged with blood when you scream), to convey fine shades of ' expression.' They are comparable, again, in that there are fewer verbal devices, as there are fewer ways of moving facial muscles, than there are sorts of feeling to convey by them ; this gives an inherent opportunity for ambiguity which is regularly exploited. The cult of careless ease in literature, where one is less sure of the audience, is more treacherous, but its advantages and dangers are of the same kind.

It is because of the wealth of implication which must be carried by sentences in poetry, because they must start from scratch and put the reader in possession of the entire attitude they assume, that the notion of ' sincerity ' is important, and that it is so hard to imitate a style. A poem can be cross-questioned, and one must know, to feel sure that it will survive the process with undiminished reputation, that for a wide variety of possible assumptions in the reader the assumptions of the writer will seem reasonable enough to be adopted; and further that, for a hierarchy of degrees of care in the reader, the assumptions discovered in the writer will not show themselves to be self-conflicting in a way which to such a reader will seem absurd.

The reason, then, that ambiguity is more elaborate in poetry than in prose, other than the fact that the reader is trained to expect it, seems to be that the presence of metre and rhyme, admittedly irrelevant to the straightforward process of conveying a statement, makes it seem sensible to diverge from the colloquial order of statement, and so imply several colloquial orders from which the statement has diverged. But rhythm is a powerful weapon in itself, which needs to be considered separately; I have discussed negative implications here by way of a sidelong approach to it.

Rhythm allows one, by playing off the possible prose rhythms against the super-imposed verse rhythms, to combine a variety of statements in one order. Its direct effect seems a matter for physiology ; in particular, a rhythmic beat taken faster than the pulse seems controllable, exhilarating, and not to demand intimate sympathy ; a rhythmic beat almost synchronous with the pulse seems sincere and to demand intimate sympathy; while a rhythmic beat slower than the pulse, like a funeral bell, seems portentous and uncontrollable. But even if it is a simple rhythm which is apprehended, rather than something much more complex which involves the meaning, still it is the meaning which must show at what pace the verse is to be read. And, of course, it is not one rhythmical beat, like a bell tolling, which is apprehended ; or if it is (since the ear insists on imposing rhythms, and cocaine can make one stroke into a series), then the word should be used in the plural ; the foot, the grammatical clause, the line, the sentence, the stanza or paragraph, and the whole canto or subject-heading, are all rhythmical units; the total rhythmical line which results from them must be regarded as of an immense complexity entirely defined by the meaning; and even then it is the meaning which must imply how it is to be interpreted. So that rhythm is chiefly useful as a means of insisting upon, and then limiting, the possible implications ; and though I may seem to be ignoring the rhythm through most of this book, I shall always be using it, so to speak, among the calculations on the margin, as a means of understanding the grammar.

However, one can oppose the use of rhythm to the use of ambiguity, because an interest in rhythm makes a poet longwinded, and ambiguity is a phenomenon of compression. Thus it is seldom that one finds relevant ambiguities in Spenser or Marlowe, because their method is by a variety of means to sustain a poetic effect for so long that the poetic knot can be spread out at length, and one does not see that the separate uses of a word would be a pun if they were drawn together. When Marlowe brings off his triumphs of simplicity and the delight in rhythm it is often a matter of separating the implications of a sentence and using them at different times.

Meander. Your majesty shall shortly have your wish

And ride in triumph through Persepolis.

(Exeunt all except Tamburlane and his followers.)

Tamburlane. And ride in triumph through Persepolis.

Is it not brave to be a king, Techelles,

Usumcasane and Theridamas,

Is it not passing brave to be a king,

And ride in triumph through Persepolis ?

Tamburlaine can only use the same words again and again, because his mind is glutted with astonishment at them; Marlowe's idea of the heroic soul has extreme simplicity and unbounded appetite, so that after however great an expression of his desire for glory, after one subordinate clause has opened out of another, with unalterable energy, it can still roar at the close with the same directness as in its opening line. Thus the lack of variety in his rhythm is in itself a device of some rhythmical subtlety. It is for this sort of reason that the same line is repeated here in three tones, of obsequiousness, of astonishment, and of triumph, which Shakespeare could have included in a single line.

Faustus, these books, thy wit, and our experience,

Shall make all nations to canonise us.

As Indian Moors obey their Spanish lords

So shall the spirits of every element

Be always serviceable to us three ;

Like lions shall they guard us when we please,

Like Almain rutters, with their horsemen's staves,

Or Lapland giants, trotting by our sides;

Sometimes like women, or un wedded maids.

Shadowing more beauty in their airy brows

Than have the white breasts of the Queen of Love :

From Venice shall they drag huge argosies,

And from America the golden fleece

That yearly stuffs old Philip's treasury;

If learned Faustus will be resolute.

At first sight the last line is an afterthought expressing anxiety, but when immersed in the style one accepts it as a part of the sentence always intended, that might have been put in between the second line and the third. That a conditional clause should have been held back through all these successive lightnings pf poetry, that after their achievement it should still be present with the same conviction and resolution is itself a statement of heroic character. One's total impression of the character of Valdes is obtained by combining these two interpretations. Where so much can be said by the mere order of single mighty lines there is no need for much subtlety of implication within them.

I am considering here such ambiguities of rhythm as act without implying an ambiguity of grammar, or noticeable ambiguity in the use of words. This last example in result belongs to a later chapter, because it implies two different opinions of Valdes and leaves them to be reconciled; so does the following example, because it implies two different sentiments in the author. I put them here for the slightness of the machinery; it is a machinery continually used for ambiguities of the first type, and these examples may be prominent enough to show that it is powerful.

Aye, look, high heaven and earth ail from their prime foundation.

All thoughts to rive the heart are there, and all are vain;

Horror and scorn and hate and fear and indignation ;

Oh why did I awake, when shall I sleep again ?

(A.E. Housman, Last Poems)

The main rhythm of the third line (the crest of the wave) takes hate as its chief stress, Fear gives the second emphasis, allowed by the extra foot, fear and indignation act as a unit balancing the first three, and by attraction the fear meant is seen to be of a dignified kind. But behind the energy and determination of this treatment of the line as a unit, there is a rocking, broken, agitated, and impotent grouping, which takes the first four nouns as two pairs, associates fear with hate so as to make it weak and snarling, and throws in indignation as an isolated and squeaking disapproval.

I have mentioned Spenser, whom no discussion of rhythm can ignore. To show the scale of his rhythm, it may be enough to list some of the ways in which he gave movement to the stanza of the Faerie Queene it is by the delicacy of this movement that he shows his attitude towards his sentences, rather than by devices of implication in the sentences themselves. At the same time, once such an attitude has been fixed, it is more easily described in terms of the meaning of the words than in terms of the meaning of the rhythm; in the next example, from Sidney, I shall use this other mode of approach.

Spenser concentrates the reader's attention on to the movement of his stanza : by the use of archaic words and constructions, so that one is at a safe distance from the exercise of an immediate judgment, by the steady untroubled flow of similar lines, by making no rapid change of sense or feeling, by sustained alliteration, parallel adjectives, and full statement of the accessories pf a thought, and by the dreamy repetition of the great stanza perpetually pausing at its close. Ababbcbcc is a unit which may be broken up into a variety of metrical forms, and the ways in which it is successively broken up are fitted into enormous patterns. The first quatrain usually gratifies the ear directly and without surprise, and the stanzas may then be classified by the grammatical connections of the crucial fifth line, which must give a soft bump to the dying fall of the first quatrain, keep it in the air, and prevent it from falling apart from the rest of the stanza.

It may complete the sense of the quatrain, for instance, with a couplet, and the stanza will then begin with a larger, more narrative unit, ababb, and wander garrulously down a perspective to the alexandrine. Or it may add to the quatrain as by an afterthought, as if with a childish earnestness it made sure of its point without regard to the metre, and one is relieved to find that the metre recovers itself after all. For more energetic or serious statements it will start a new quatrain at the fifth line, with a new sentence; there are then two smaller and tighter, repeatedly didactic, or logically opposed, historically or advancing, units, whose common rhyme serves to insist upon their contrast, which are summed up and reconciled in the final solemnity of the alexandrine. In times of excitement the fifth line will be connected both ways, so as to ignore the two quatrains, and, by flowing straight on down the stanza with an insistence on its unity, show the accumulated energy of some enormous climax; and again, by being connected with neither, it will make the stanza into an unstressed conversational device without overtones of rhythm, picking up stray threads of the story with almost the relief of prose. It would be interesting to take one of the vast famous passages of the work and show how these devices are fitted together into larger units of rhythm, but having said that every use of the stanza includes all these uses in the reader's apprehension of it I may have said enough to show the sort of methods Spenser had under his control ; why it was not necessary for him to concentrate on the lightning flashes of ambiguity.

The size, the possible variety, and the fixity of this unit give something of the blankness that comes from fixing your eyes on a bright spot; you have to yield yourself to it very completely to take in the variety of its movement, and, at the same time, there is no need to concentrate the elements of the situation into a judgment as if for action. As a result of this, when there are ambiguities of idea, it is whole civilisations rather than details of the moment which are their elements; he can pour into the even dreamwork of his fairyland Christian, classical, and chivalrous materials with an air, not of ignoring their differences, but of holding all their systems of values floating as if at a distance, so as not to interfere with one another, in the prolonged and diffused energies of his mind.

Nowhere in English literature can this use of diffuseness as an alternative to, or peculiar branch of, ambiguity be seen more clearly than in those lovely sestines of Sidney, which are so curiously foreign to the normal modes or later developments of the language. This time I must do some serious quotation.

Strephon. Klaius.

Strephon. You Gote-heard Gods, that love the grassie mountaines,

You nimphes that haunt the springs in pleasant vallies.

You Satyrs joyd with free and quiet forrests.

Vouchsafe your silent eares to playning musique.

Which to my woes gives still an early morning :

And draws the dolor on till wery evening.

Klaius. O Mercurie, foregoer to the evening,

O heavenlie huntresse of the savage mountaines,

O lovelie starre, entitled of the morning,

While that my voice doth fill the woeful vallies

Vouchsafe your silent eares to playning musique.

Which oft hath Echo tir'd in secrete forrests.

Strephon. I that was once free-burgess of the forrests

Where shade from Sunne, and sports I sought at evening,

1 that was once esteemed for pleasant musique,

Am banisht now amongst the monstrous mountaines

Of huge despaire, and foul afflictions vallies.

Am growne a skrich-owle to myself each morning.

Klaius. I that was once delighted every morning.

Hunting the wild inhabiters of forrests,

I that was once the musique of these vallies,

So darkened am, that all my day is evening,

Hart-broken so, that mole-hills seem high mountaines.

And fill the vales with cries instead of musique.

Strephon. Long since alas, my deadly Swannish musique

Hath made itself a crier of the morning.

And hath with wailing strength climbed highest mountaines

Long since my thoughts more desert be than forrests :

Long since I see my joyes come to their evening,

And state thro wen down to over-troden vallies.

Klaius. Long since the happie dwellers of these vallies.

Have praide me leave my strange exclaiming musique,

Which troubles their dayes worke, and joyes of evening:

Long since I hate the night, more hate the morning:

Long since my thoughts chase me like beasts in forrests,

And make me wish myself laid under mountaines.

Strephon. Me seemes I see the high and stately mountaines,

Transforme themselves to lowe dejected vallies:

Me seemes I heare in these ill-changed forrests,

The nightingales doo learne of Owles their musique :

Me seemes I feele the comfort of the morning

Turnde to the mortal serene of an evening.

Klaius. Mr seemes I see a filthie cloudie evening.

As soone as Sunne begins to climbe the mountaines :

Me seemes I feel a noisome scent, the morning

When I do si^ell the flowers of these vallies :

Me seemes I heare, when I doo heare sweet musique,

The dreadful cries of murdered men in forrests.

Strephon. I wish to fire the trees of all these forrests;

I give the Sunne a last farewell each evening ;

I curse the fiddling finders out of musique :

With envy doo I hate the lofty mountaines ;

And with despite despise the humble vallies:

I doo detest night evening, day, and morning.

Klaius. Curse to myself my prayer is, the morning:

My fire is more, than can be made with forrests;

My state more base, than are the basest vallies :

I wish no evenings more to see, each evening;

Shamed I have myself in sight of mountaines,

And stoppe mine eares, lest I go mad with musique.

Strephon. For she, whose parts maintained a perfect musique,

Whose beauty shin'de more than the blushing morning.

Who much did pass in state the stately mountaines,
In straightness past the Cedars of the forrests,
Hath cast me wretch into eternal evening.
By taking her two Sunnes from these dark vallies.
Klaius. For she, to whom compared, the Alps are vallies.
She, whose lest word brings from the spheares their musique
At whose approach the Sunne rose in the evening,
Who, where she went, bare in her forehead morning,
Is gone, is gone from these our spoiled forrests.
Turning to deserts our best pastur'de mountaines.
Strephon. These mountaines witness shall, so shall these vallies,
Klaius. These forrests eke, made wretched by our musique,
Strephon. Our morning hymn is this,
Klaius. and song at evening.
(Sidney, Arcadia)

The poem beats, however rich its orchestration, with a wailing and immovable monotony, for ever upon the same doors in vain. Mountaines vallies, forests, musique, evening, morning', it is at these words only that Klaius and Strephon pause in their cries; these words circumscribe their world; these are the bones of their situation; and in tracing their lovelorn pastoral tedium through thirteen repetitions, with something of the aimless multitudinousness of the sea on a rock, we seem to extract all the meaning possible from these notions; we are At last, therefore, in possession of all that might have been implied by them (if we had understood them) in a single sentence ; of all, in fact, that is implied by them, in the last sentence of the poem. I must glance, to show this, at the twelve other occasions on which each word is used.

Mountaines are haunts of Pan for lust and Diana for chastity, to both of these the lovers appeal; they suggest being shut in, or banishment;

impossibility and impotence, or difficulty and achievement; greatness that may be envied or may be felt as your own (so as to make you feel helpless, or feel powerful) ; they give you the peace, or the despair, of the grave ; they are the distant things behind which the sun rises and sets, the too near things which shut in your valley; deserted wastes, and the ample pastures to which you drive up the cattle for the summer.

Vallies hold nymphs to which you may appeal, and yet are the normal places where you live; are your whole world, and yet limited so that your voice can affect the whole of them; are opposed to mountaines, either as places of shelter and comfort, or as places of humility and affliction; are rich with flowers and warmth, or are dark hollows between the hills.

Forests, though valuable and accustomed, are desolate and hold danger; there are both nightingales and owls in them; their beasts, though savage, give the strong pleasures of hunting; their burning is either useful or destructive ; though wild and sterile they give freedom for contemplation, and their trunks are symbols of pride.

Music may express joy or sorrow; is at once more and less direct than talking, and so is connected with one's permanent feeling about the characters of pastoral that they are at once very rustic and rather over-civilised; it may please or distress the bystanders; and while belonging to despair and to the deaths of swans, it may share the living beauty of the lady, and be an inmate of the celestial spheres.

Morning brings hope, light and labour, evening rest, play and despair; they are the variety of Nature, or the tedious repetition of a day their patrons Venus, whom one dare not name, and Mercury, who will bring no news of her. Morning, too, has often attached to it a meaning which, by an intelligent and illuminating misprint, is inserted upon in the eleventh (and subsequent) editions;

> At whose approach the sun rose in the evening,
>
> Who where she went bore in her forehead mournings
>
> Is gone, is gone, from these our spoiled forrests,
>
> Turning to deserts our best pastor' d mountaines.

The form takes its effect by concentrating on these words and slowly building up our interest in them ; all their latent implications are brought out by the repetitions ; and each in turn is used to build up some simple conceit. So that when the static conception of the complaint has been finally brought into light (I do not mean by this to depreciate the sustained magnificence of its crescendo, but to praise the singleness of its idea), a whole succession of feelings about the local scenery, the whole way in which it is taken for granted, has been enlisted into sorrow and beats as a single passion of the mind.

I have put this poem at the end of a discussion ostensibly about rhythm, and shall mention its rhythm only to remark that it is magnificent; my point is that one can best illustrate its rhythm by showing the cumulative way it uses its words. It is seldom that the meaning of a poet's words is built up so flatly and steadily in the course of using them. And limited as this form may be, the capacity to accept a limitation so unflinchingly, the capacity even to conceive so large a form as a unit of sustained feeling, is one that has been lost since that age.

Annex on Dramatic Irony

'Effective in several ways' includes dramatic irony; I shall close this chapter with some remarks about that. An example from Macbeth has already been considered (p. i8), which imposed the pathetic fallacy on the reader by means of an ambiguity, and tricked him into an irrational or primitive mode of thought under colour of talking about the view. This is an important device, about which it is proper to elaborate the obvious; I shall consider an example from the Synge Deirdre of the Sorrows.

Deirdre, we have been told, is uniquely beautiful; she is being brought up alone in the woods to be old Conchubor's queen; troubles have been foretold; she is wilful; she has seen Naisi in the woods ; she prefers him to Conchubor. Conchubor visits her, says he will marry her in three days, and leaves her to return to his capital. She asks her nurse, who could help her against him, would the nurse herself, no, would this great man or that, possibly, more possibly, would Naisi, and there is a storm of denial :

> Lavarcham. In the end of all there is none can go against Conchubor, and it's folly that we're talking, for if any went against Conchubor it's sorrows he'd earn and the shortening of his day of life.
>
> *(She turns away and Deirdre stands up stiff with excitement and goes and looks out of the window.)*

Deirdre. Are the stepping-stones flooding, Lavarcham? Will the night be stormy in the hills ?

Lavarcham. The stepping-stones are flooding, surely, and the night will be the worst. I'm thinking, we've seen these years gone by.

Upon these words Deirdre 'tears upon the press and pulls out clothes and tapestries,' robes herself as a queen, and prepares for the coming of the young princes.

This storm is dramatically effective for various reasons. As part of the plot it makes Naisi and his brothers come for shelter when she is wanting them ; on the classical tragic model it makes the day of the action an unusual one, a day on which it seems fitting that great things should happen, and gives a sort of unity to the place by making it difficult to get there. Further, we are in doubt as to the position of Conchubor, and this allows of several implications. If we are to conceive that he has got across the stepping-stones already, then their flooding means that Deirdre's way of safety, to Conchubor and his palace and the life which is expected of her, has been cut off; that it is high time she behaved like the stepping-stones and isolated herself with Naisi ; that what in the story is done heroically by her own choice is, in dumb show, either as an encouragement or as an ironical statement of the impotence of heroic action, done by the weather; and that all these troubles which she is bringing on herself have been foretold and are beyond her control. If we are to conceive that Condiubor has not yet got across the stepping-stones, she is in danger of being condemned to his company if he turns back, as, in fact, she is in any case, since he will marry her in three days ; it is against a fatal and frankly alien heaven that she exerts her courage and her royalty; the weather is now one of the inevitable forces against which she is revolting, and is that one of those forces which makes it urgent she should revolt now. If we are to conceive that Conchubor is just getting across the steppingstones, the weather is her ally, and there is some encouragement for revolt in the thought that he may be drowned.

For the storm to mean so much it must receive particular attention, and it is assured of this by marking a change in the tone of the conversation. The preceding series of questions has received the wrong answer at its climax; Naisi is the man who can help her, and her nurse says he cannot. Since energy has accumulated towards this question, and is now dammed by the negative, it bursts out of the window into a larger world, and since we find there, instead of the indifference of external Nature, instead of the calm of accepting the statement that there is no hope, a larger release of energy and the crescendo repeated in the heavens, we compare the storm with the plot and are surprised into a Pathetic P'allacy. It is not that Nature is with her or against her, is her fate or her servant; the Fallacy here claims more generally that Nature, like the spectators, is excited into a variety of sympathies, and is all these four together. The operation is thus a complicated one, but it is normal, of course, to the crudest forms of melodrama. My point is that, for a Pathetic Fallacy to cause much emotional reverberation, it must be imposed upon the reader by an ambiguity.

Since the storm has been fixed, by all these devices, firmly in the spectator's memory, a slight reference at the other end of the tragedy can call it back to give another dramatic irony. Naisi has been killed and Conchubor left in possession.

> Deirdre. Do not raise a hand to touch me.
>
> Conchubor. There are other hands to touch you. My fighters are set in among the trees.
>
> Deirdre. Who'll fight the grave, Conchubor, and it opened on a dark night ?

The night is dark enough now, and, of course, her main meaning is that she can't be fought after she has killed herself. But she herself could not fight against the impulses of the night at the beginning of the play, when she ran off with Naisi and opened the graves which are only now being filled ; nor against the weariness which is the turning-point of the action, that sense that happiness could not last for ever which drove them back to Ireland and their enemy. This third dark night in a sense covers the other two; we are made, therefore, to feel that the unity of .time, in spite of the lovers' seven years of happiness, has somehow been preserved. The grave partly in consequence of this, is not that of Deirdre only, against which Conchubor cannot fight she is hopeless because she herself cannot fight against the grave in which Naisi is lying; and there is thus a further dramatic irony of the heroic action that defeats itself, in that it is Conchubor, as well as Deirdre, who opened a grave, whether for or for Naisi, by' his actions on either dark night that Conchubor, no more than Deirdre, can fight either of them ; that after the way Conchubor has killed Naisi, Deirdre cannot live to endure Conchubor and Conchubor cannot hold Deirdre from her grave. Lastly, there is a threat from Deirdre against Conchubor, making the grave his as well as theirs; her choice of death, or the forces he has himself loosed against her, will kill him ; as indeed he is led from the stage suddenly old and aimless and ' hard set to see the way before him.' The grave having been spread on to three persons now takes effect as a generalisation, and names the mortality of all the protagonists, incidental soldiers included; 'all life is strangely frustrated, all efforts incalculable and in vain ; we are all feeble beside the forces given to us and in the face of death all parties are on the same side.'

This implication, by the way, that all the characters are people subject to the same situation, that they all understand, though they may not take, the same attitude, is important to some types of play and often gets called their ' meaning.' However, it is less insisted upon than dramatic irony by critics because (being a less conscious form of that device) it does not need to be noticed to be appreciated, and, therefore, is at once a less likely and a less useful thing for them to notice. For the rather limited and doctrinaire pessimism exploited by Synge it is a powerful weapon ; consider this piece of dialogue, when the lovers are wondering whether to go back to Ireland, where they will find death and their proper social position :

> Naisi. If our time in this place is ended, come away without Ainnle and Ardan to the woods of the east, for it's right to be away from all people when two lovers have their love only. Come away and we'll be safe always.
>
> Deirdre. There's no safe place, Naisi, on the ridge of the world. . . . And it's in the quiet woods I've seen them digging our grave, and throwing out the clay on leaves are bright and withered.
>
> Naisi. Come away, Deirdre, and it's little we'll think of safety or the grave beyond it, and we resting in a little corner between the daytime and the long night.
>
> Deirdre. It's this hour we're between the daytime and a night where there is sleep for ever, and isn't it a better thing to be following on to a near death, than to be bending the head down, and dragging with the feet, and seeing one day a blight showing on love
>
> where it is sweet and tender ?

These may seem absurdly simple phrases for Deirdre to twist into her more gloomy meaning, but it was Naisi who first suggested the idea from which he is now trying to reassure her; it is because at the back of his mind he agrees with her that upon all phrases of comfort he can give her there lies the same shadow of the grave. You would not find this effect so naked, so much in command of the situation, in the Elizabethan playwrights, because there the forces that hold characters apart have got more kick in them; the device is always at work, I think, but the strongest example I know in Shakespeare comes from that one of his plays which has least variety of conception, which has most of this self-centred anxiety to maintain a single mood.

Sic. He's a Disease that must be cut away.

Men. Oh, he's a limb, that has but a Disease.

Mortall, to cut it off; to cure it, easye. ...

[It would be shameful ingratitude, he goes on, if they were to kill such a hero.]

Bru. . . . when he did love his country,

Men. The service of the foote

Being once gangren'd, is not then respected

For what before it was.

Bru. Wee'll hear no more :

Pursue him to his house, and pluck him thence.

Lest his infection, being of catching nature.

Spread further.

Men. One word more, one word:

This Tiger-footed rage, when it shall find

The harme of unskann'd swiftnesse, will too (late)

Tye Leaden pounds too's heeles. Proceed by Processc,

Lest parties (as he is beloved) break out,

And sacke great Rome with Romanes.

(Coriolanus iii. i. 245.)

Warburton wanted to give Sicinius the speech about gangrene, and certainly it does Coriolanus no good and is a strange speech from one of his friends. It is no ingratitude not to ' respect a foot for its service ' in a case of gangrene where it may be mortal not to cut it off. Of course, you may call it an irony to state the other side's case more strongly than they have done so far for themselves, but it springs from a clear understanding of their feelings; both sides are using the same metaphor, even if they are sure they want to draw different conclusions from it. Menenius seems hardly less conscious of his irony in his next speech, when the tiger-footed rage, the swiftness, and the act of scanning it too late may belong to the tribunes or to Coriolanus himself ; and it was precisely because they proceeded by process, instead of killing him out of hand, that Rome came so near to being sacked by a Roman before the play was done.

We are concerned here with a sort of dramatic ambiguity of judgment which does not consider the character so much as the audience ; thus Menenius seems to have been a very direct partisan of Coriolanus, but he had to agree with the tribunes to a great extent to bring out the point of the situation they were arguing about. Evidently this is an important means of handling the plot, and may be used to juggle with motivation; it is these methods which make lago so effective a villain, and such a puzzling figure if you take his character seriously. There is a simpler example in the casket scene of The Merchant of Venice. Portia is far too virtuous to attempt to evade her father's devastating scheme; she fully approves of it (' If you do love me, you will find me out'); and yet, while Bassanio is choosing, she arranges that there should be a song continually rhyming with Tead,' and ending in a conceit about coffins. The audience is not really meant to think she is telling him the answer, but it is not posed as a moral problem, and seems a natural enough thing to do ; she might quite well do it in the belief that he would not hear; the song is explaining to them the point about the lead casket, may be taken to represent the fact that Bassanio understands it, heightens the tension by repeating the problem in another form, and adds to their sense of fitness in the third man being the lucky one.

Corresponding to this doubt as to Portia's honesty is a stronger one as to Bassanio's affection; he seems superior to the other suitors only in the most incidental qualities, and is more frankly marrying for money than any of them. But Shakespeare loved his arrivistes for their success, their shamelessness and their self-deception, and Bassanio is justified by the song which leads him to choose rightly. Fancy is nothing, fancy is fleeting, and yet it is all that the dignity of poetry is based upon, and we must ring its knell as for the life of man. Lead, a fundamental mere humanity, eventual death, must be accepted, must be chosen, before one can get what one wants, and can go on with the poetry of the play; fancy can only hide lead, and lead must be enough for the maintenance of fancy.

Irony in this subdued sense, as a generous scepticism which can believe at once that people are and are not guilty, is a very normal and essential method ; Portia's song is not more inconsistent than the sorrow of Helen that she has brought death to so many brave men, and the pride with which she is first found making tapestries of them ; than the courage of Achilles, which none will question, ' in his impregnable armour with his invulnerable skin underneath it ' ; than the sleepers in Gethsemane, who, St. Luke says, were sleeping for sorrow; than the way Thesee (in Racine), by the use of a deity, at once kills and does not kill Hippolyte. This sort of contradiction is at once understood in literature, because the process of understanding one's friends must always be riddled with such indecisions and the machinery of such hypocrisy; people, often, cannot have done both of two things, but they must have been in some way prepared to have done either; whichever they did, they will have still lingering in their minds the way they would have preserved their self-respect if they had acted differently; they are only to be understood by bearing both possibilities in mind.

Dramatic irony is an interesting device for my purpose, because it gives an intelligible way in which the reader can be reminded of the rest of a play while he is reading a single part of it. Thus it gives one some means of understanding the view of a work of genius as a sort of miracle whose style carries its personality into every part of it, whose matter consists of microcosms of its form, and whose flesh has the character of the flesh of an organism. For example the messengers in hailing Macbeth Thane of Cawdor tell him that Duncan

> Andes thee in the stout Norweyan Rankes,
>
> Nothing affeard of what thyselfe didst make,
>
> Strange images of death.

This remark does not seem to belong very straightforwardly to the speech of a state messenger; it is not obvious why he expects a soldier to be frightened of his enemies only when he had made them harmless; but it is just what Macbeth was to feel about Duncan ; if the king said this he must have known a great deal about Macbeth's habits of mind. One feels the conceit must have arisen, in a mood of moral casuistry, from a sense of the oddity in that reliance on convention which gives such different reactions to killing at different times; murder as well as soldiering, therefore, were in the mind of the speaker, and are suggested to the audience. Or the negative, more simply, works backwards ; there is some question of Macbeth's being affeard of corpses; and this impression of him, given so early in the play, as a powerful and horrified figure, yielding nothing to the horror of his situation, striking out endlessly at the images of death that bank round him and shut him in, is as it were a piece of dramatic irony on its own account, gives in brief a total impression of the play, and puts no stress on the complementary part of the irony, which it assumes :

> I am afraid, to think what I have done:
>
> Looke on 't againe I dare not.

In this case, the two parts of the irony convey almost all their point separately, without your having to remember one when hearing the other. But, in many cases, Shakespeare does not help one in this way, and gives ironies for the pleasure rather of commentators than of first-night audiences. I shall close this desultory discussion with such an example. Cordelia will say nothing to show her love or gain her portion.

> Lear. Nothing will come of nothing, speak againe.

Six hundred lines later, the Fool sings some nonsense verses.

> Lear. This is nothing, foole.
>
> Fool. Then 'tis like the breath of an unfee'd Lawyer, you gave me nothing for 't. Can you make no use of nothing, nuncle ?

Lear. Why no. Boy.

Nothing can be made out of nothing.

Fool (to Kent). Prithee tell him, so much the rent of his land comes to, he will not believe a Fool.

If you fail to connect the second of these with the first, the pain of loss, and the nagging of the Fool, are almost all that the second can be taken to imply. Only if this quite distant connection is consciously achieved can you realise Lear's meaning; that he, rather than Cordelia, was the beggar for love on that occasion ; that she might well say nothings if she had known how he would act to her; that, perhaps, it was no fault of his that had spoiled Regan and Goneril, since no upbringing could have made anything of them; that these words anyway are the ripe fruit of his experience; and that there is indeed nothing that can be made out of him, now that he has become nothing by the loss of everything in his world. (He is speaking with a curiously intimate affection and disregard for dignity, as if the Fools talk was probably his own hallucination, since it gives a love that need not be paid for; and it is true that the Fool acts as a sort of divided personality externalised from the "'Ring;) Most people are so used to the text that they do not realise how much the effect depends on a verbal irony, which it would be a feat of memory to notice at the first hearing.

Possibly the richness of the deposit of cross-reference and incidental detail upon these plays may be due in some degree to the circumstances under which they were written; to the fact that Shakespeare wrote up plays already owned by his company, and in use, so that he and the actors already knew a great deal about them; to the way his version might always receive additions and alterations for a revival or a special occasion at Court; to the probability that a particular member of the company would keep to a particular part ; and to the shortness of individual runs. The last reason would keep the actors from being bored with the text; the other reasons would give them a casual but detailed knowledge (of the sort that leads to flippant quotation in the greenroom), a desire for continual additions, a capacity to see distant verbal connections, and a well-informed interest in the minor characters of the story. Shakespeare seems to assume all this in his public, and can scarcely have obtained it from anyone outside. There are some odd and pathetic relics of the state of feeling I mean in the mistakes of the folio stage directions, where Lord E and Lord G, for minor characters in All's Well, are presumably the initials of actors; French E Capt. G; faint traces of the geniality of long-past rehearsals, when they were scribbled into the prompt copy. French E and Lord G, at any rate, knew what the words were three hundred lines back; for French E and Lord G (they would be pleased to know more about their own characters), one could drop in such details as allowed Professor Bradley to treat the plays as documents from which to draw full-length biographies ; if for no other, still for an audience upon the stage, one could make those delicate cross-references that are now the discoveries of the learned.

II

There are three possible scales or dimensions, that seem of reliable importance, along which ambiguities may be spread out: the degree of logical or grammatical disorder, the degree to which the apprehension of the ambiguity must be conscious, and the degree of psychological complexity concerned. Of these, the first seems the one about which there is least danger of talking nonsense, the one it is most important to be clear about, and the one to which least critical attention has so far been paid. My seven types, so far as they are not merely a convenient framework, are intended as stages of advancing logical disorder. However, I shall continually have to be using and discussing the other two criteria, and the three are not wholly independent of one another, so that my later examples will, as a rule, appear to the casual eye 'really' more ambiguous than the earlier ones.

An example of the second type of ambiguity, in word or syntax, occurs when two or more meanings are resolved into one, There are alternatives, even in the mind of the author not only different emphasis as in the first type; but an ordinary good reading can extract one resultant from them. This is more common than any of the later types, and I shall give it most space.

The following example shows, I think, the difference between logical and psychological degrees of ambiguity; because the thought is complicated or at least doubtful, whereas the feeling is very direct.

Cupid is winged and doth range ;

Her country so my love doth change.

But change she earth, or change she sky,

Yet I will love her till I die.

(Anon., Oxford Book)

' I will love her though she moves from this part of the earth to one out of my reach; I will love her though she goes to live under different skies; I will love her though she moves from this earth and sky to another planet ; I will love her though she moves into a social or intellectual sphere where I cannot follow; I will love her though she alters the earth and sky I have got now, though she destroys the bubble of worship in which I am now living by showing herself unworthy to be its object; I will love her though, being yet worthy of it, by going away she changes my earth into desire and unrest, and my heaven into despair; I will love her even if she has both power and will to upset both the orderly ideals of men in general (heaven) and the system of society in general (earth) ; she may alter the earth and sky she has now by abandoning her faith or in just punishment becoming outcast, and still I will love her; she may change my earth by filling me, but till it comes I will go on loving.

This may look as if I was merely listing different sorts of change, which would not, of course, show direct ambiguity; but change may mean 'move to another' or 'alter the one you have got,' and earth may be the lady's private world, or the poet's, or that of mankind at large. All meanings to be extracted from these are the immediate meaning insisted upon by the words, and yet the whole charm of the poem is its extravagant, it's unreasonable simplicity.

But, in general, complexity of logical meaning ought to be based on complexity of thought, even where, as is proper to the second type of ambiguity, there is only one main meaning as a resultant. For instance, if it is an example of the first type to use a metaphor which is valid in several ways, it is an example of the second to use several different metaphors at once, as Shakespeare is doing in the following example. It is impossible to avoid Shakespeare in these matters; partly because his use of language is of unparalleled richness and partly because it has received so much attention already; so that the inquiring student has less to do, is more likely to find what he is looking for, and has evidence that he is not spinning fancies out of his own mind.

As a resounding example, then, there is Macbeth's

> If it were done, when 'tis done, then 'twere well
>
> It were done quickly ;

(double syntax since you may stop at the end of the line)

If th' Assassination

Could trammell up the Consequence, and catch

With his surcease. Success; that but . . .

words hissed in the passage where servants were passing, which must be swaddled with darkness, loaded as it were in themselves with fearful powers, and not made too naked even to his own mind. Consequence means causal result, and the things to follow, though not causally connected, and, as in 'a person of consequence,' the divinity that doth hedge a king. Trammel was a technical term used about netting birds, hobbling horses in some particular way, hooking up pots, levering, and running trolleys on rails. Surcease means completion, stopping proceedings in the middle of a lawsuit, or the overruling of a judgment; the word reminds you of ' surfeit' and ' decease,' as does assassination of hissing and ' assess ' and, as in ' supersession,' through seder e, of knocking down the mighty from their seat. His may apply to Duncan, assassination or consequence. Success means fortunate result, result whether fortunate or not, and succession to the throne. And catch, the single little flat word among these monsters, names an action ; it is a mark of human inadequacy to deal with these matters of statecraft, a child snatching at the moon as she rides thunder-clouds. The meanings cannot all be remembered at once, however often you read it; it remains the incantation of a murderer, dishevelled and fumbling among the powers of darkness.

It is clear that ambiguity, not of word, but of grammar, though common enough in poetry, cannot be brought to this pitch without chaos, and must in general be used to produce a different effect. Where there is a single main meaning (the case we are now considering) the device is used, as in the following examples from Shakespeare Sonnets, to give an interpenetrating and, as it were, fluid unity, in which phrases will go either with the sentence before or after and there is no break in the movement of the thought.

But heaven in thy creation did decree

That in thy face sweet love should ever dwell,

Whate'er thy thoughts or thy heart's workings be,

Thy looks should nothing thence, but sweetness tell.

(xciii.)

You may put a full stop either before or after the third line.

That tongue that tells the story of thy days

(Making lascivious comments on thy sport)

Cannot dispraise, but in a kind of praise,

Naming thy name, blesses an ill report.

(xcv.)

The subject of blesses is either tongue or namings but in a kind of praise qualifies either blesses or dispraise. These devices are particularly useful in managing the sonnet form because they help it to combine variety of argumentation and the close-knit rhythmical unity of a single thought.

There is in the following Sonnet one of those important and frequent subtleties of punctuation, which in general only convey rhythm, but here it amounts to a point of grammar.

If thou survive my well contented daye

When that churle death my bones with dust shall cover

And shalt by fortune once more re-survey :

These poor rude lines of thy deceased Lover :

Compare them with the bettering of the time, . . .

(xxxii.)

Line 4 is isolated between colons, carries the whole weight of the pathos, and is a pivot round which the rest of the Sonnet turns. Re-survey might conceivably be thought of as intransitive, so that line 4 could go with line 5 in apposition to them but the point is not that either line 3 or line 5 could stand without line 4, it is in fact next to both of them, and yet it stands out from either, as if the Sonnet had become more conscious of itself, or was making a quotation from a tombstone.

Thou doost love her, because thou knowest I love her.

And for my sake even so doth she abuse me,

Suffering my friend for my sake to approve her,

If I loose thee, my loss is my love's gaine.

And loosing her, my friend hath found that losse. . . .

(xiii.)

According as line 3 goes backwards or forwards, the subject of suffering is either she or 1 . The device is not here merely a rhythmic one, but it carries no great depth of meaning; the Elizabethans were trained to use lines that went both ways, for example in those chains of Sonnets, such as the Corona of Donne, in which each began with the last line of the one before.

Donne, indeed, uses these methods with vehemence; I shall break this series from the Sonnets for a moment to quote an example from the Epithalamion for Valentine's Day.

Thou mak'st a Taper see

What the sunne never saw, and what the Arke

(Which was of Soules, and beasts, the cage, and park)

Did not containe, one bed containes, through thee.

Two Phoenixes, whose joyned breasts . . .

You make a taper see what the ark did not contain. Through you one bed contains two phoenixes.' 'You make a taper see what the sun never saw. Through you one bed contains what the ark did not contain, that is, two phoenixes.' The renewal of energy gained from starting a new sentence is continually obtained here without the effect of repose given by letting a sentence stop.

Who lets so fair a house fall to decay.

Which husbandry in honour might uphold

Against the stormy gusts of winter's day

And barren rage of death's eternal cold ?

O none but unthrifts, dear my love you know.

You had a Father, let your Son say so.

(xiii.)

The phrase in italics is equally suited to the sentences before and after it ; taking it as the former, a third meaning shows itself faintly, that you know unthrifts 'the company you keep may be riotous or ascetic, but is not matrimonial.' Having quoted this for a comparatively trivial point of grammar, it seems worth pointing out that its beauty depends first on the puns, house and husbandry, and secondly on the shift of feeling from winter's day winter is short, like its days ; ' your child will grow up after you and your house will survive to see another summer,' to death's eternal cold', ' if the house does not survive this winter it falls for ever'; there is a contrast between these two opposite ideas and the two open, similarly vowel led, Mario wan lines that contain them, which claim by their structure to be merely repeating the same thought, so that the two notions are dissolved into both of them, and form a regress of echoes.

Sometimes the ambiguous phrase is a relative clause, with 'that' omitted, which is able to appear for a moment as an independent sentence on its own, before it is fitted into the grammar. '

Their images I lov'd, I view in thee,

And thou (all they) hast all the all of me.

(xxxi.)

There is some suggestion that the first clause may be wholly independent, and that I view in thee means ' I look for them in you'; but on the whole the device merely puts 'which I loved' into special prominence.

My life hath in this line some interest,

Which for memorial still with thee shall stay.

When thou reviewest this, thou dost review.

The very part was consecrate to thee,

(LXXIV)

Passing over the comma at the end of the third line, the object of review is part ; stressing the comma, it says tautologically, with the emphasis on the second thou 'it is enough immortality for me to be remembered by you,' and the fourth line becomes a separate sentence.[7]

This fluidity of grammar is partly given by rhetorical balance, because since the lines are opposed to one another in regular pairs you still get some sort of opposition by opposing the wrong pair. Sonnet LXXXI. runs this principle to death :

Or shall I live your Epitaph to make.

Or you survive when I in earth am rotten.

From hence your memory death cannot take.

Although in me each part will be forgotten.

Your name from hence immortall life shall have,

Though I (once gone) to all the world must dye.

The earth can yeeld me but a common grave.

When you entombed in men's eyes shall lye,

Your monument shall be my gentle verse,

Which eyes not yet created shall ore-read.

And toungs to be, your beeing shall rehearse.

When all the breathers of this world are dead,

You still shall live (such vertue hath my Pen)

Where breath most breathes, even in the mouths of men.

Any two consecutive lines in this, except 2-3 and lo-ii for accidental reasons, make a complete sentence when separated from their context; I do not say that this makes it a good sonnet, or that I know it ought to be read aloud.

Tongues can over-read as well as eyes and this would leave either being the subject of rehearse, or both tongues and eyes. However, tongues is particularly connected with rehearse, because the contrast of your being

7 A trivial example omitted here.

with to be ('in order to be') shows the transient tongues rehearsing your ideal being, lapping up your blood as it were, and thus implies a sort of timeless Platonic existence for Mr. W. H., informing the examples of his type, but in no way dependent on them. These shadows of his perfection were once to have been his children, but Shakespeare's partly scoptophile desire to see him settled in love has by now been with a painful irony thwarted or over-satisfied, and they are now no more than those who read his praise.

The following Sonnet is more two-faced in idea (' a complaint in the form of an assertion that he has no right to complain'), but can be put in the second type so far as concerns the ambiguity of syntax, as it reduces to a single meaning :

O let me suffer (being at your beck)

The imprisoned absence of your liberty,

And patience tame, to sufferance bide each check,

Without accusing you of injury.

Be where you list, your charter is so strong

That you yourself may privilege your time

To what you will, to you it doth belong.

Yourself to pardon of self-doing crime.

(Iviii.)

And patience tame expresses petulance by its contraction of meaning ('suffer tame patience'; 'be patience-tame,' as in iron-hard; and 'tame patience,' as in bide each check) followed by a rush of equivocal words, clinched with belong, which has for subject both your time and to pardon, and implies, still with sweetness and pathos (it is an extraordinary balance of feeling), 'that is all I could have expected of you.'

Bvt wherefore do not you a mightier waie

Make warre vppon this bloudie tirant time ?

And fortifie your selfe in your decay

With meanes more blessed than my barren

Now stand you on the top of happie houres.

And many maiden gardens yet unset.

With vertuous wish would beare your liuing flowers.

Much liker then your painted counterfeit :

So should the lines of life that life repaire

Which this (Times pencil or my pupil pen)

Neither in inward worth nor outward faire

Can make you hue your selfe in eyes of men,

To give away your selfe, keeps your selfe still.

And you must Hue drawn by your owne sweet skill.

(xvi.)

Lines of life refers to the form of a personal appearance, in the young man himself or repeated in his descendants (as one speaks of the lines of some one's figure); time's wrinkles on that face (suggested only to be feared); the young man's line or lineage — his descendants; lines drawn with a pencil — a portrait; lines drawn with a pen, in writing; the lines of a poem (the kind a Sonnet has fourteen of); and destiny, as in the life-line of palmistry — Merchant of Venice ii. ii. 163.

This variety of meaning is rooted more effectively in the context because lines of life and that life may either of them be taken as subject of repair taking the most prominent meanings, 'lineage' and 'the features of yourself and your children,' lines is subject, and this is also insisted upon by rhythm and the usual sentence order; that life means 'life such as your present one.' But that life {repair) is given a secondary claim to the position by this (. . . make), which follows, evidently in contrast, as subject in the next line. (Punctuations designed to simplify the passage all spoil the antithesis.) This has a bracket expanding its meanings : time, bringing old age that will pencil you with wrinkles, or a riper manhood that will complete your beauty; this Times pencil, firstly, the style of painting, or average level of achievement of Elizabethan portrait-painters ; secondly, the frame and 'atmosphere' given to beauty by that age of masques and gorgeous clothing and the lust of the eye (so that we must look back to the second line of the Sonnet, where the same double meaning is hinting that beautiful courtiers in the wake of Essex came to bad ends) ; my pen that describes you, pupil as immature and unskilful : as pupil of that time whose sonnet tradition I am imitating; or of Time which matures me. A natural way to take it is that life, 'your life,' and this, 'my life' (devoted to describing you), but the meaning of this opens out into all the transient effects which are contrasted with the solid eternity of reproduction, and by reflection backwards that life is made subject of its sentence, meaning ' the new way of life I propose to you,' that is, of matrimony, or of the larger extra-human life in your lineage as a whole.

Independently of whether lines of life or that life is subject and whether that life is ' your present way of life ' or ' the way of life I propose to you,' there is a double syntax for lines ii and 12. Taking them together there is a main reading, 'the age of Elizabeth is not competent to express you, either in your appearance or character' (of the two pairs one would naturally associate the artist's pencil with outward fair and the playwright's pen with inward worth but the order is the other way round, so that each works with either, or ' I try to write about your beauty, but the hand of time, graving the lines of character on your face, tries to show your inward worth'). This, the main grammar, involves a rather clumsy change from life to you in the object, and this greater directness of address, needed after the sagging of grammar in the extraordinary complexity of the intervening two lines leaves room for an alternative syntax. For, taking line ii with lo (and preferably that life as subject), it is this which is not fair either in inward or outward worth; make of the present age, which has produced out of its worthlessness such a beauty as yours, is opposed to repair of the vegetable life, capable of producing many such flowers, which I propose to you; as if the greater durability given to a type by making it repeatable, giving it to a noble house rather than a single person, was compared to making it anew, as 'risen a heavenly body,' in the next world, or to the placing of it timelessly among Platonic ideas, so that it need not be anxious about its particular patterns on earth ; live of line 12 then becomes an adjective, and the force of so many words in apposition, you live, yourself is to express wonder at the production of such a thing out of the dull world of line 1 1, and make the young man, by contrast, ideal, heavenly, or worthy of being made into a general type. Line 13, separated from lines 12 and 14 equally by commas, is as a main meaning cut off into the final couplet, ' you are not less yourself because you have had children,' but in the minor sense has for subject this your present life of pleasure and brilliance carries in it no eternity, and keeps you only to give you away.' Drawn of line 14 then may take an additional echo of meaning, as 'drawing back,' dragging yourself out of your present way of life, which your lover has not power to do for you[8].

Ambiguities of this sort may be divided into these which, once understood, remain an intelligible unit in the mind; those in which the pleasure belongs to the act of working out and understanding, which must at each reading, though with less labour, be repeated; and those in which the ambiguity works best if it is never discovered. Which class any particular poem belongs to depends in part on your own mental habits and critical opinions,

---

8 There may after all be misprints in the text. The doubt as to whether that life is subject or object, I now feel, does not add anything important to the meanings deduced. Also one should probably put a full stop at the end of the twelfth line to cut out the overrun syntax for the final couplet, which is assumed to be a final summing up. The Christian paradox of the thirteenth line could still be taken either way round.

The stops of the first edition of the Shakespeare Sonnets of course do not deserve reverence ; you sometimes even get a comma at the end of a sonnet. The claim for them is that they always deserve consideration because they seem to be an inaccurate but unedited version of what Shakespeare actually wrote.

However, I don't want this note to suggest that the Elizabethans weren't capable of making an ambiguity as to whether a noun is subject or object. One might expect the resulting muddle to be too radical to be effective, or anyway to form a habit. But it is not hard to find cases of ' lyrical ease where the problem is not felt to arise.

Sleep is a reconciling,

A rest that peace begets.

Doth not the sun rise smiling

When fair at even he sets ?

Rest you then, rest, sad eyes,

Melt not in weeping.

While she lies sleeping Softly now lies

Sleeping. (Anon. : set by Dowland.)

Whether rest begefs peace or peace rest (or peace sleep) is not a grammatical problem because each does either, just as it is the same sun which comes back after the night as before.

and I am afraid that for many readers who have the patience to follow out this last analysis, it will merely spoil what they had taken for a beautiful Sonnet by showing it to be much more muddled than they had realised. This is a pity, but however wise the view may be that poetry cannot safely be analysed, it seems to me to remain ignoble ; and in so far as people are sure that their pleasures will not bear thinking about, I am surprised that they have the patience not to submit them to so easy a destruction. The fact is, if analysis gets in your way, it is easy enough to forget it ; I do not think that all these meanings should pass through the mind in an appreciative reading of this Sonnet; what is gathered is the main sense, the main form and rhythm, and a general sense of compacted intellectual wealth, of an elaborate balance of variously associated feeling.

One is tempted to think of these effects as belonging to the later stages of Renaissance refinement, as something oversophisticated in the manner of Caroline shape-poems, and due to a peculiar clotting of the imagination. It is worthwhile then to produce examples from Troilus and Criseyde, as one of the most leisurely, simplest as to imagery, and earliest poems in English literature. In the first love scene between the two, Criseyde says petulantly she doesn't know what she's expected to say; what does he mean, now, in plain words ?

What that I mene, O swete herte dere ?

Quod Troilus. O goodly fresshe free.

That with the stremes of your eyen clere

You wolde frendly sometimes on me see ;

And then agreen that I may be he. . . .

(iii. 128.)

and so on for three verses, an enthusiastic and moving statement of the chivalric evasion of the point at issue. Stremes has the straightforward meaning of 'beams of light' (Compleynte unto Pite line 94). The N.E.D. does not give this meaning, but shows stremes as already a hyperbolical commonplace use for blood and tears, or ' beams of sweet influence,' like those of the Pleiades. Thus after fresh and free, there is some implication of a stream (Naiads) that he can drink of and wash in, cleansing and refreshing, so that one glance of her eyes recovers him as by crossing a stream you break the spells of black magic, or the scent by which the hounds of your enemies are tracking you down ; and the ready tears of her sympathy are implied faintly, as in the background.

At the climax of the great scene in the second book, when Pandarus has got his ward alone to talk to her about her money affairs, mysteriously congratulated her on her good luck, and gradually led her through the merits of Troilus to an appeal to her pity for his unhappiness, Cressida seems suddenly to guess his meaning and makes a great display of outraged virtue. One must not suppose, of course, because Chaucer shows us her machinery – 'I shal fele what he meneth, I-wis' – 'It nedeth me ful sleyly for to pleye ' – that we are not to believe in the reality of the virtue, or that it is not the modest and proper machinery.

What ? Is this al the joye and al the feste ?

Is this your reed, is this my blisful cas?

Is this the verray mede of your biheste ?

Is al this pcynted proces seyd, alas.

Right for this fyn ?

(ii. 421.)

The last three lines, I submit, are extremely Shakespearean ; they have all the concentrated imagery, the bright central metaphor steeped and thickened in irrelevant incidental metaphors, of his mature style. I thought at first the meanings might have been quite simple in Chaucer's English, and have acquired a patina of subtlety in the course of time ; it would have been fun to maintain that Shakespeare learnt his style from a misunderstanding of Chaucer; but the N.E.D. leaves no doubt that (whether Shakespeare was influenced by it or not) time has faded rather than enriched the original ambiguity.

Reed of course, is advice; he had told her her cas was blissful, to have caught the eye of the prince; mede meant at that time wages, a bribe, merit, a meadow and a drink made with honey; biheste meant a vow, a promise, and a command ; proces meant a series of actions, the course of a narrative, proceedings in an action at law, and a procession; and fyn meant generally 'end,' with accepted derivatives like the object of an action, death, and a contract; by itself it would not suggest a money penalty before 1500, but it might suggest 'money offered in the hope of exemption.' Thus the materials are ample enough, but this is not to say they were all used.

I shall pause to illustrate the force of beheste and the harangue of Pandarus that has gone before :

> Now understand, that I yow nought requere
>
> To binde ye to him thorough no beheste,
>
> But only that yew make him bettre chere,
>
> Than ye had don er this, and more feste.
>
> So that his life be saved, at the leste.

Either ' I do not ask it, as a command from your guardian, that you should bind yourself to him (permanently or sinfully),' or 'I do not ask you to bind yourself to him with anything so definite as a vow.'

> Think eke, how elde wasteth every houre
>
> In eche of yow a party of beautee ;
>
> And therefore, er that age thee devoure,
>
> Go love, for olde, ther wol no wight of thee.
>
> Lat ihis proverbe a lore unto yow be ;
>
> ' To late y-war, quod Beautee, whan it paste';
>
> And elde daunteth daunger at the laste.

It is not at first plain why there is so much power of song in the poetical commonplace of the first four lines; why its plainest statement seems to imply a lyric ; so that the modern reader feels the pre-Raphaelites in it, and Chaucer felt in it his Italians {Filostrato, ii. 54). A statement of the limitations of human life is a sort of recipe for producing humility, concentration, and sincerity in the reader; it soothes, for instance, jealousy, makes the labours of the practical world less pressing because less likely to make any real difference (games have the same mode of approach); sets the mind free, therefore, to be operated on by the beauty of the verse without distraction; and makes you willing to adopt, perhaps to some slight extent permanently, the point of view of the poet or of the character described, because, having viewed your limits, marked your boat's position with regard to distant objects on the shore, you are able without losing your bearings to be turned round or moved to another part of the bay.

Further, to think of human life in terms of its lowest factors, considered as in themselves dignified, has a curious effect in dignifying the individual concerned; makes him a type, and so something larger and more significant than before; makes his dignity feel safer, since he is sure he has at least these qualifications for it ; makes him feel accepted and approved of by his herd, in that he is being humble and understanding their situation (poor creatures) ; makes it seem likely, since he understands their situation, because he feels it in himself, that they will return to him also this reserved and detached sympathy; makes him, indeed, feel grander than the rest of his herd, for a new series of reasons; because by thinking of them he has got outside them; because by forming a concept of them he has made them seem limited ; because he has thereby come to seem less subject to the melancholy truths he is recognising; because to recognise melancholy truths is itself, if you can be protected somehow, an invigorating activity; and (so that we complete the circle back to humility) because to think about these common factors has a certain solidity and safety in that it is itself, after all, one of the relevant common factors of the human mind.

However, it is the mode of action of the last two lines which is my immediate business. Y-war may mean prudent or experienced too late, ' Then first when too late/ or ' going on until too late 'First prudent when too late' — I have found that one should be careful to avoid risks, perhaps such as that of never getting a lover, but, more strongly, such as are involved in unlawful satisfactions. 'First conscious when too late" — I have found too late that one should be determined to obtain satisfaction. ' Having been prudent until too late — I have found that one can wait too long for the safest moment for one's pleasures, 'Having been conscious till too late ' — I have found that one can seek one's pleasure once too often. Pandarus, of course, only meant the second and third ; Chaucer (it is shown not as irony but as a grand overtone of melancholy) meant all four. (This, by the way, is the fourth type of ambiguity, but I am taking the whole passage together[9].)

And elde daunteth daunger at the last.

Daunt means subdue or frighten; daunger at this time had a wealth of meaning that it has since lost, such as disdain, imperiousness, liability, miserliness, and power. 'Old age will break your pride, will make you afraid of the independence you are now prizing; the coming of old age is stronger than the greatness of kings, stronger than all the brutal powers that you are now afraid of, stronger even than the stubborn passion of misers that defeat it for so long; you must act now because when you are old you will be afraid to take risks, and you may take heart because, however badly you are caught, it will be all the same after another century; even in your own lifetime, by the time you are an old woman you will have lived down scandal. Or taking elde as an old woman, not as the age that defeats her, the phrase interacts with the passing of beauty, whether after a life of sin or of seclusion (there appear to have been no alternatives) in the preceding line, and the old hag is finally so ugly that all the powers in daunger shrink away from the gloom of her grandeur, are either lost to her or subdued to her, and the amorous risks and adventures will be at last afraid to come near.

The line is straightforward ambiguity of the second type, and I hope the reader will not object that I have been making up a poem of my own. Mr. Eliot somewhere says that is always done by bad critics who have failed to be poets ; this is a valuable weapon but a dangerously superficial maxim, because it obscures the main crux about poetry, that being an essentially suggestive act it can only take effect if the impulses (and to some extent the experiences) are already there to be called forth; that the process of getting to understand a poet is precisely that of constructing his poems in one's own mind. Of course, it is wrong to construct the wrong poem, and I have no doubt Mr. Eliot was right in his particular accusations.

Is this the verray mede of youre beheste ?

Is this your reed, is this my blisful cas?

replies Cressida, to these ambiguities of Pandarus : ' Is this the wage

9 A dramatic irony as such need not be called fourth-type, but this one, I think, marks a complexity of feeling in Chaucer (that is, he half agreed with Pandarus and half not). I don't think there are other examples in this chapter which properly belong in later chapters.

that is offered to me in return for obeying your commands ? Is this my inducement to be a good ward, that I must continually have the trouble, and pain to think you so wicked, of repelling solicitations ? Is this what your advice is worth ? Is this what your promise to look after me is worth ? ' The honest meaning (wage) carries contempt; the dishonest meaning (bribe) an accusation. ' Is this why the prince has been so friendly with you.' Is this what you stand to make out of being my guardian ? ' And if mede carries any echo of meaning (it is impossible at this distance of time to say) from the natural freedom of the open meadow, or the simple delightfulness of that form of beer, we have, ' Is this the meadow, or the beer, you had promised me, or proposed for yourself? Is this my blissful case you have described ? ' It is the two meanings of beheste which give her so powerful a weapon against Pandarus, in his double position of guardian and go-between.

Is al this peynted proces seyd, alas,

Right for this fyn ?

These two lines have a lesser but a more beautiful complexity; Pandarus' great harangue is seen, by using the puns on fyn and process, as a brightly coloured procession (peynted would suggest frescoes in churches) moving on, leading her on, to dusty death and the everlasting bonfire ; and behind this simple framework, that gives the movement, the immediate point, of the phrase, process hints at a parallel with legal proceedings, ending where none of the parties wanted, when at last the lawyers, like Pandarus, stop talking and demand to be paid; and rising behind that again, heard in the indignation of the phrase, is a threat that she may expose him, and peyntd and fyn suggest legal pains and penalties.

'To whom do they suggest these things?' the reader may ask; and there is no obvious reply. It depends how carefully the passage is supposed to be read; in a long narrative poem the stress on particular phrases must be slight, most of the lines do ncft expect more attention than you would give to phrases of a novel when reading it aloud ; you would not look for the same concentration of imagery as in a lyric. On the other hand, a long poem accumulates imagery; I am dealing with a particularly dramatic point where the meaning needs to be concentrated ; and Chaucer had abandoned his original for a moment to write on his own.

It is a more crucial question how far peynted, in a proper setting, can suggest ' pains ' ; how far we ought to leave the comparatively safe ground of ambiguity to examine latent puns. The mle in general, I believe, is that a mere similarity of sound will not take effect unless it is consciously noticed, and will then give an impression of oddity. For it is the essential discipline of language that our elaborate reactions to a word are called out only by the word itself, or what is guessed to be the word itself; they are trained to be very completely inhibited by anything near the word but not quite right. It is only when a word has been passed in, accepted as sensible, that it is allowed to echo about in the mind. On the other hand, this very inhibition (the effort of distinction, in cases where it would have been natural to have taken the other word) may call forth effects of its own; that, for instance, is why puns are funny; may make one, perhaps, more ready, or for all I know rhythmically more and less ready, to react to the word when it comes. I have sometimes wondered whether Swinburne's Dolores gets any of its energy from the way the word Spain, suggested by the title and by various things in the course of the poem, although one is forced to wonder what the next rhyme is going to be, never appears among the dozen that are paired off with Our Lady of Pain. But so little is known about these matters that it is rather unwise to talk about them; one goes off into Pure Sound and entirely private associations; for instance, I want to back up my ' pains ' from peynted by calling in 'weighted' and 'fainted,' and the suggestion of labour in all that painted. The study of subdued bad puns may be very important, but it is less hopeful than the study of more rational ambiguities, because you can rely on most word associations being called out (if one's mind does not in some way run through the various meanings of a word, how can it arrive at the right one ?), whereas the puns, in a sense, ought not to be there at all.

A good illustration of this point, not that most people will require to be convinced of it, is given by the words 'rows' and 'rose.' 'Rows' suggests regimentation, order, a card index system, and the sciences; 'rose' suggests a sort of grandeur in the state of culture, something with all the definiteness and independence of Nature that has been produced within the systems of mankind (giving a sort of proof of our stability), some of the overtones of richness, delicacy, and power of varying such as are carried by 'wine'; various sexual associations from its appearance and the Romaunt of the Roos; and notions of race, dignity, and fine clothes as if from the Wars of the Roses. These two words never get in each other's way; it is hard to believe they are pronounced the same. Homonyms with less powerful systems of association, like the verb 'rows' and the 'roes' of fishes, lend themselves easily to puns and seem in some degree attracted towards the two more powerful systems; but to insist that the first two are the same sound, to pass suddenly from one to the other, destroys both of them, and leaves a sort of bewilderment in the mind[10].

On the other hand, there was a poem about strawberries in Punch a year or two ago, which I caught myself liking because of a subdued pun ; here what was suggested was a powerful word, what was meant was a mere grammatical convenience :

> Queenlily June with a rose in her hair
>
> Moves to her prime with a langorous air.
>
> What in her kingdom's most comely ?
>
> By far Strawberries, strawberries, strawberries are.

I was puzzled to know why the first line seemed beautiful till I found I was reading Queenlily as ' Queen Lily,' which in a child's poetry-book style is charming; 'the lily with a rose in her hair,' used of a ripening virgin and hence of early summer, in which the absolute banality of roses and lilies is employed as it were heraldically, as a symbol intended not to be visualised but at once interpreted, is a fine Gongorism, and the alternative adverb sets the whole thing in motion by its insistence on the verb. It is curious how if you think of the word only as an adverb all this playful dignity, indeed the whole rhythm of the line, ebbs away into complacence and monotony.

It is a little unfair, perhaps, to use Chaucer for my purpose; I have used him because it is important if true that these effects are somehow part of the character of the language, since they were so much in evidence so early, and in a writer apparently so derivative from the French and Italian literatures, which don't seem ambiguous in the same way. I admit it is much easier to muddle one's readers when using the unfamiliar stresses

---

10 What you normally get from a likeness of sound is an added force to the Paget effect (p. 14) in cases where there is a clear group of words with similar sound and meaning {e.g. skate, skid, sky, scrape). But this makes you feel the meaning of the one word more vividly, not confuse it with the meanings of the others. On the other hand, it might be that a controlled partial confusion of this sort is the only real point of using alliteration and rhyme.

of fourteenth-century speech, and when dealing with unfamiliar uses of words. This, for instance, I thought at first was an ambiguity, when Troilus' sickness, caused by love of Criseyde, and used to arrange a meeting with her, is announced to the assembled company :

Compleyned eke Eleyne of his sycknesse

So feithfully, that pitee was to here,

And every wight gan waxen for accesse

A leech anon, and seyde, ' in this manere

Men curen folk; this charm I wol yow lere

But there sat oon, al list hir nought to teche.

That thoughte, beste coude I yet been his leche.

(ii. 1576.)

Access in the fourteenth century meant some kind of feverish attack, and I believe is not used in any other sense by Chaucer; but it was used by Wyclif to mean the act of coming near, or the right of coming here, and acquired later the meaning of accession to an office of dignity. So that it might mean that everybody said they knew how to cure fevers so as to seem dignified at the party, so as to put themselves forward, and perhaps so as to be allowed to visit the prince on his sick-bed. The break of the line which separates access from leech and connects it with gan helps this overtone of ironical meaning, which is just what the social comedy of the passage requires; and if you wish to stress the influence of Chaucer as a stylist, it is these later meanings, and not the medical meaning, which were most prominent by the sixteenth century; this, for instance, is just the suggestive way Shakespeare would use a Latinised word. But to Chaucer at any rate, I believe, the joke was strong enough to stand by itself, and too pointed to call up overtones ; I have put it in to show a case where a plausible ambiguity may be unprofitable, and the sort of reasons that may make one refuse to accept it.

Rather a pretty example turns up when Criseyde is reflecting it would be unwise to fall in love (ii. 752). I am, she says,

Right yong, and stand unteyed in lusty lese

Withouten jalousye or swich debaat.

Lese, among the absurd variety of its meaning, includes lies, a snare for rabbits, a quantity of thread, a net, a noose, a whip-lash, and the thong holding hunting dogs; one would take with these lusty in the sense of amorous. Or lese may mean a contract giving lands or tenements for life, a term of years, or at will (hence guaranteed permanence and safety), open pasture-land (as in leas), picking fruit, the act of coursing (she is her own mistress), or a set of three (the symbol of companionship as opposed to passion) ; one would take with these lusty in the sense of hearty and delightful, its more usual meaning at the time. Thus, while the intended meaning is not in doubt, to be in lusty lese may be part of the condition of being unteyed or of being teyed. I have put down most of the meanings for fun ; the only ones I feel sure of are : 'lam not entangled in the net of desire,' and ' I am disentangled like a colt in a meadow'; these are quite enough for the ambiguity of syntax.

You may say that these meanings should be permuted to convey doubt : ' I am sprawling without foothold in the net of desire and ' I have not been turned out to grass in the wide meadow of freedom/ But in paraphrasing these meanings I have had to look for an idiom that will hide the main fact of the situation, that she is unteyed. Or you might say that stand attracts in so that lese must be taken only with unteyed. But withouten suggests a parallel with unteyed, which would make lese go with teyed. It would have been consistent enough with Criseyde's character to have been expressing doubt, but about this line, whatever its meaning, there is a sort of complacency and decision which convince me it is only of the second type.

At the same time, I admit that this is a monstrously clotted piece of language; not at all, for instance, a thing it would be wise to imitate, and it would be unfair to leave Chaucer without reminding the reader of something more beautiful. It is during the scene, then, leading to the actual seduction of Criseyde, when she has no doubt what she wants but is determined to behave like a lady, when Troilus is swooning about the place, always in despair, and Pandarus sees no immediate prospect of pushing them into bed together, that this sheer song of ironical happiness pours forth from the lips of their creator.

> But now pray God to quenchen al this sorwe.
>
> So hope I that he shall, for he best may.

For I have seen of a full misty morwe

Folwe ful ofte a merie somer's day.

And after winter folweth grene May.

Men sen alday, and reden eke in stories.

That after sharpe shoures ben victories.

It is the open and easy grandeur, moving with the whole earth, of the middle lines, that made me quote them; my immediate point is shoures. It meant charge, or onslaught of battle, or pang, such as Troilus' fainting-fits, or the pains of childbirth; if you take it as showers of rain (i. iv. 251), the two metaphors, from man and the sky, melt into each other ; there is another connection with warriors, in that the word is used for showers of arrows ; there is another connection with lovers in that it is used for showers of tears.

I hope I have made out a fair case for a poetical use of ambiguity, in one form or another, as already in full swing in the English of Chaucer; so that it has some claim to be considered native to the language. I really do not know what importance it has in other European languages; the practice of looking for it rapidly leads to hallucinations, as you can train yourself always to hear a clock ticking : and my impression is that while it is frequent in French and Italian, the subsidiary meanings are nearly always bad idiom, so that the inhabitants of those countries would have too much conscience to attend to them. At any rate it is not true, obviously enough, that Chaucer's ambiguities are copied from Boccaccio; I found it very exciting to go through my list in a parallel text and see how, even where great sections of the stuff were being translated directly, there would be a small patch of invention at the point I had marked down.[11]

I shall now stop beating about the Chaucerian bushes, and pursue my thesis into the very sanctuary of rationality. During the eighteenth century English poets were trying to be honest, straightforward, sensible, grammatical and plain ; thus it is now my business to outwit these poor wretches, and to applaud them for qualities in their writings which they would have been horrified to discover. It is not surprising that this should

11 I do not know that any critic has either refuted or defended this treatment of Chaucer. I still believe in it myself.

be possible ; 'what oft was thought' has a merely delusive simplicity, and 'what were ne'er so well expressed' as in a compact antithesis are these shifts and blurred aggregates of thought by which men come to a practical decision. Sometimes they would have called what I call an ambiguity a grace, sometimes a generalisation. How far their ambiguities are typical of their age and method, how fundamental for understanding their verse, it would be more difficult to decide.

What murdered Wentworth, and what exiled Hyde,

By kings protected, and to kings allied?

What but their wish indulged in courts to shine.

And power too great to keep, or to resign ?

(Johnson, The Vanity of Human Wishes,)

Allied may mean 'connected with by marriage,' or 'of a similar species to,' so that they were royal, or ' allied by treaty to' in their intrigues. Wentworth and Hyde may have wished merely to shine to shine in courts to shine indulged by king and courtiers, or to shine indulged by king and courtiers in courts; or they may have indulged their own wish to shine, or to shine in courts ; or there may be a separate general reflection, putting commas after wish and courts that

the wish to shine is after all usually indulged in courts, usually, that is, thought a harmless absurdity and perhaps helped out by one's neighbours, or (a very different idea) usually recklessly indulged in by oneself. Not all these give very different senses, but they are all different ways of reading the line aloud, and the two meanings of indulged carry some wealth of reflection and variety of feeling, in particular scorn, sympathy, respect, and a sort of naturalist's sense that it was all predetermined.

In the fourth line power may be parallel to wish, or one of its objects; their downfall may have been caused by power of a certain kind, or a wish of a certain kind for power. Power, in the first case, which people felt was too great for a single favourite, so that it aroused resentment, or was too difficult, as a matter of calculation, to use rightly; and which could not be resigned because it was too tempting to keep it, or because the king would not let them go, or because, though they might try not to be involved in intrigues, they found themselves so important that any action, however apparently negative, became a hint and was construed as intriguing, or because, even if they resigned their power with the king, they would still have power through what had now become a false reputation of influence, or simply because they would now feel too responsible, when something was going on, not to take a hand. Their wish, in the second case (which respects them less and makes them less aware of their difficulties) was to get so much, power that it was too great, for reasons such as those listed above; or to get power so great that they could resign (wish ... to resign . . . power) with plenty of money, or a sense of security, or a sense that vanity was now satisfied, and power having been now gained and displayed need not further be used ; or simply, taking the last clause as a separate case, their fall came when they became afraid of their power and wanted to get rid of it, and made efforts to resign which, entangled as they were, could only excite suspicion. However little these later meanings are intended to be considered by the reader, the line, I think, conveys by its knotted complexity, by the sense that there are grammatical depths the casual reader has not plumbed, some such ideas of fatal involution as these I have been elaborating.

These couplets are a triumph for Johnson, but they are the by-product of a failure to achieve, rather than the reward for achieving, the compactness and polish he desired. The slighter ambiguity which is normal to the heroic couplet is of a different sort, and we must dip back into the first type to fish it up.

It is odd to consider that what is a double meaning[12] in one language is often only a compactness of phrasing in another; that in the sophisticated tongues of many savage tribes you cannot say : ' Bring me my gun, the dogs, and three beaters ' — using the same verb, and the same inflexion of it, for three such different actions — without being laughed at as a man who has made a bad pun. It is the part of a civilised language to be simplified in structure and generalised in its notions; of a civilised people to keep their linguistic rules and know what they are about; but this must not blind us to the nature of such phrases as

12 In the first edition I put ' ambiguity ' not double meaning, but this no doubt extends the term ambiguity confusingly. Effect worth calling ambiguous occur when the possible alternative meanings of word or grammar are used to give alternative meanings to the sentence.

There thou, great Anna, whom three realms obey.

Dost sometimes council take, and sometimes tea.

(Pope, Rape of the Lock,)

where the effect of limited comprehensiveness, of a unity in variety mirrored from the real world, is obtained by putting together two of the innumerable meanings of the word take.

To rest, the cushion and soft dean invite,

Who never mentions hell to ears polite,

(Pope, Moral Essays, iv.)

depends on an even slighter, but still genuine enough, ambiguity of the verb.

This way of suggesting grasp of mind, ingenuity, and control over things, this use of a word with several extended meanings so as to contract several sentences into one, is the fundamental device of the Augustan style. The word is usually a verb precisely because the process is conceived as an activity, as a work of the digesting and controlling mind. The Decline and Fall of the Roman Empire for instance, is one enormous panorama of these little witticisms.

Of course, the zeugma is not an eighteenth-century invention, but it was not handled before then with such neatness and consciousness, and had not the same air of being the normal process of thought.

As such a starre, the Magi led to view

The manger cradled infant, God below ;

By vertue's beams by fame derived from you

May apt soules, and the worst may, vertue know.

The first may means ' may be expected to,' the second ' can if they choose.' This is the sort of construction Pope would have handled well; Donne does it very clumsily. Notice, however, that the second by may either be parallel to the first, so that the beams of virtue are its fame, or may be subordinate to it so as to show how the beams of virtue came to be distributed. This, and the two uses of vertue, corresponding to the two conceptions of it as an attribute of, or personified in, the Countess of Huntingdon, give some weight of thought to an otherwise clumsy construction.

Your (or you) vertue two vast uses serves,

It ransomes one sex, and one Court preserves.

'Your virtue serves two uses'; or 'you, being virtue itself, serve two uses' ; or ' you serve (the cause of) virtue two uses.' Donne's unfortunate address to the Countess of Bedford may serve to remind us that the eighteenth-century ambiguity was essentially easy and colloquial; it was concerned to exploit, as from a rational and sensible mental state, the normal resources of the spoken language.

Its possible grace and slightness may be shown by a fine detail from the Rape of the Lock. When Belinda wins at cards

The nymph, exulting, fills with shouts the sky;

The walks, the woods, and long canals reply.

Oh thoughtless mortals, ever blind to fate,

Too soon dejected, and too soon elate,

Sudden these honours shall be snatched away.

And cursed for ever this victorious day.

Reply may be transitive or intransitive. It is the poet who makes these classical reflections, but, as far as the grammar is concerned, the speaker may as well be the environs of Hampton Court, accustomed as they are to the fall of favourites and the brevity of human glory.

Such a use of the verb may be insisted upon by prepositions or adverbs placed where the different meanings are wanted; this needs no illustration, and my example is intended chiefly to show in how small a compass these typical devices may be employed.

Oh, if to dance all night, and dress all day,

Charmed the small pox, or chased old age away.

Who would not scorn what housewives cares produce,

Or who would learn one earthly thing of use

(Essay on Women,)

Here charmed at first means 'fascinated,' so as to make it sit still and do no harm, as one would do to snakes or one's husband; and then, because chased insists on the activity of this process, and because away is in a prominent position at the end of the line, charmed takes on a new meaning as charmed away 'removed entirely even when it had already arrived,' no doubt by some apparently unreasonable incantation, as one does warts. It is these slight variations of suggestion, I think, that give vivacity to the line.

In the same way, the lyrical outburst of good sense that follows on from this plays continually on the border-line between the first and second types of ambiguity.

But, since, alas, frail beauty must decay.

This insists it is reasonable by being a tautology : ' in so far as beauty is frail it is exposed to decay'; hut frail from its setting also carries a suggestion of moral as well as physical fragility, which continues to haunt the verses.

Curled, or uncurled, since locks will turn to grey.

Locks may have been curled by art (or uncurled for that matter), or have been, to start with, (naturally) curled; so that we have now three ways of dividing up women – chaste-susceptible, from the first line ; beautiful-ugly, if uncurled hair is out of fashion, and artificial-natural, from the second. Will turn to grey is in part a simple and inexorable future tense, the statement of Nature or the poet, and in part the metre makes it a statement of the lady; 'It will turn to grey, the nasty stuff, I can't stop it.'

Since, painted, or not painted, all shall fade.

Artificial-natural, with its associate susceptible-chaste, is now strengthened against beautiful-ugly as the distinction in question, but not left in possession of the field ; painted might be applied to 'meads' in Pope's dialect, and had not quite lost the sense of 'coloured from whatever cause.'

The verb is now only future, as the place of the ambiguous will at the place of emphasis has been taken by all Both these changes help the crescendo.

And she who scorns a man must die a maid.

The wave as it breaks returns to tautology, from which the original beautiful-ugly criterion seems to have faded out. It may combine artificial-natural with wanton-chaste; 'modesty and virtue are no security, because if you don't make the most of yourself you won't get a husband'; or may oppose them to one another; 'artificiality and virtue are no security, because if you think yourself too fine for any of the available men you won't get a husband either.' The tautology chiefly breaks down in its tenses, and thus implies that ' you may not want a husband now, whether because you are too humble or too fanciful, too chaste or too gay, but in the end, every woman must admit it was what she needed.' In this roundabout way, by not defining the relation between two criteria and leaving a loophole in a tautology. Pope arrives, as did Chaucer in flat sentences, at what may indeed be the fundamental commonplace of poetry, a statement of the limitations of the human situation. 'Seeing then the inherent crudity of all possible earthly happiness, considering the humility of those demands which can alone hope to be satisfied . . .'

What then remains, but well our power to use.

And keep good humour still, whate'er we lose ?

Well may mean 'thoroughly' or 'with moderation,' and thus implies a sort gf humility and good humour in deciding which of them is best in any particular situation. Still may mean that we must always keep our balance, always be prepared to laugh at the absurdity of our world and our own nature, or keep it still may mean that we must be careful not to laugh too publicly, to give ourselves away by not insisting on our dignity or our rights[13]. Reviewing, finally, the three sets of opposites, we may lose beauty, refinement, or virginity, the lover we had desired, the privacy we had built up, or the husband it would have been wise to obtain.

It is interesting to find Dryden using the sort of ambiguity of syntax we have considered in the Shakespeare Sonnets, which, on the whole, is not encouraged by the couplet :

---

13 The idea that the rival idiom 'keep still' pokes up, I now«think, was a folly on my part. It would suggest ' Keep good humour ^from acting,' and Pope would not intend to contradict himself flatly in a moral sentiment. But still (' even then ') does, I think, enrich itself a little with the idea ' calm.'

And what to Guiscard is already done.

Or to be done, is doom'd by thy Decree,

That if not executed first by thee,

Shall on my Person be perform'd by me.

Or to he done conveys 'is to be done to Guiscard,' or 'is doomed to be done by thy decree,' going with the phrase before or after; Sigismond's broken tones of horror are not unheard, though subdued to the firm coherence of her language, and though actually conveyed by its unusually intense logical interconnection. All the Chaucer ambiguities I have used, by the way, were composed by that poet in the intervals while he was writing out of his own head, and had abandoned Boccaccio for the moment, so this is our first opportunity of comparing a translator's ambiguity with the original :

Per do che io t'accerto che quello che di Guiscardo fatto avrai o farai, se di me non fai il simigliante, le mie mani medesime il faranno.

No one, of course, would expect the ambiguity to be in the Boccaccio, but it is worth quoting to show that Dryden was following it as closely as he could, so that perhaps his effect was forced upon him by the genius or the weakness of English, and you may say that he would have been at pains to alter it if it had been pointed out to him. This may be true, but I am sure he would have felt it was a pity.

And again :

Sometimes tis grateful to the rich, to try

A short vicissitude, and fit of Poverty:

A savoury dish, a homely treat,

Where all is plain, where all is neat,

Without the stately spacious Room,

The Persian Carpet, or the Tyrian Loom,

Clear up the cloudy foreheads of the Great.

The third line either goes backwards, as 'what the rich try,' or forwards, as 'what clears up their foreheads.' The fifth line either goes backwards, as ' outside,' so that the man is remembering his Room which is quite near, and has just come outside for a picnic, or as ' without assistance from ' so that only the reader is thinking of it ; or goes forwards, as ' at a time when they cannot clear up,' or 'even admitting that these stronger things cannot clear up.' If both lines three and five go backwards, 'which' must be understood before clear up. All this gives the last line at once an extra emphasis and a curiously accidental air, and gives one a vague impression that it is an Alexandrine[14].

Again, this is a translation; it seems likely that Dryden in his original writing was anxious to keep English syntax out of its natural condition of ambiguity and squalor, but when he was translating there were too many other things to think of, and he slipped back into the loose forms of syntax to which his instrument was accustomed. I shall quote the lines from which these are expanded ; perhaps some ambiguity arises from the effort to put as much stress on the final verb as possible, in imitation of the original:

Plerumque gratae divitibus vices

Mundaeque parvo sub lare pauperum

Cenae, sine aulaeis et ostro,

Sollicitam explicuere frontem.

(Horace, Odes iii. 29.)

The heroic couplet is rich in a peculiar ambiguity of syntax of the second type, which gives fluidity of thought and several superimposed rhythms, and may partly explain why this metre is not as monotonous as it has so often been said to be. For instance, at the climax of Absalom and Achitophel, David breaks silence with

Thus long have I by Native Mercy sway'd,

My Wrongs dissembl'd, my Revenge delay'd ;

14 This interpretation does not work for the printed text, because the punctuation gives one clear syntax. But it would be hard to read the verse aloud so that a listener was not tempted into the other syntax.

So willing to forgive th' Offending Age ;

So much the Father did the King assuage.

Sway'd dissembled delay'd may each be either verb or participle independently. Granting that at least one must be a verb, there are seven rhythms in all, seven sets of evidence for deciding exactly how strongly David is feeling, how harshly he is likely to punish. Sway'd if verb, gives, 'I have ruled the country by merciful means'; if participle, 'my natural mercy has induced me either to delay or to dissemble, or both.' You notice the two following lines, by making a sentence and a clause parallel to one another, increase the plausibility of mixing up the two grammatical forms; the use of this in the third and fourth lines themselves is to give finality to the fourth, while yet making it parallel to the third. For the variety of possible feeling in the first two lines (this method of making overtones cancel is here being used to give a judicial, non-partisan air to the speaker without detracting from his majesty), consider first swayed as the only main verb so that the second line is merely jaunty, and then delay'd as the only main verb so that the couplet advances with a terrible continence to its revenge.

The heroic couplet in any case depends very much on participles for its compactness, so that an opportunity for this device often turns up. It is most often used in a subdued form, as in the following example, where the second half of the antithesis is given finality by a faint ambiguity of sense, and this is supported by an ambiguous participle.

> But true Nobility is of the Mind ;
> Not given by Chance, and not to Chance resigned.
> (Dryden.)

Resigned may convey 'not given back when adverse chance demands it,' or in a wider sense which really includes both halves of the line, so as to sum it up, 'kept back from the control of chance; upheld by absolute and extra-temporal sources of strength; not dependent on chance as its fundamental cause.

'It did not resign itself to chance taking the participle as active past tense, gives a sort of resonance to this second meaning, as if the thing had been settled once and for all, was a plain matter of previous contract, was a privilege left to us at the Fall of Man.

And in Gray's Cat (of so much variety is a linguistic device capable) the ambiguous participle shows us the creature, in a thoughtful, complacent mood, folding her paws :

Demurest of the tabby kind

The pensive Selina reclined.

Gazed on the lake below.

Reclined is either participle, heraldically, as in 'couchant,' or verb so as to give a dumpy repose to the verb with the same subject immediately after.

Mr. T. S. Eliot provides a grand example of this trick.

The Chair she sat in, like a burnished throne.

Glowed on the marble, where the glass

Held up by standards wrought with fruited vines

From which a golden Cupidon peeped out

(Another hid his eyes behind his wing)

Doubled the flames of seven-branched candelabra

Reflecting light upon the table as

The glitter of her jewels rose to meet it.

From satin cases poured in rich profusion;

In vials of ivory and coloured glass

Unstoppered, lurked her strange synthetic perfumes.

Unguent, powdered, or liquid – troubled, confused

And drowned the sense in odours ; stirred by the air

That freshened from the window, these ascended

In fattening the prolonged candleflames.

Flung their smoke into the laquearia.

Stirring the pattern on the coffered ceiling.

What is poured may be cases jewels glitter or light and profusion,

enriching its modern meaning with its derivation, is shared, with a dazzled luxury, between them; so that while some of the jewels are pouring out light from their cases others are poured about, as are their cases on the dressing-table. If referring to glitter poured may, in any case, be a main verb as well as a participle. There is a more trivial point of the same kind in the next line, where glass may stand alone for a glass bottle or may be paired with ivory ('vials of glass'); and unstoppered may refer only to glass or to vials of glass and of ivory ; till lurked which' is for a moment taken as the same grammatical form, attracts it towards perfumes. It is because of this blurring of the grammar into luxury that the scientific word synthetic is able to stand out so sharply as a dramatic and lyrical high light.

The ambiguity of syntax in poured is repeated on a grander scale by

Unguent, powdered, or liquid – troubled, confused.

And drowned the sense in odours ; stirred by the air ...

where, after powdered and the two similar words have acted as adjectives, it gives a sense of swooning or squinting, or the stirring of things seen through heat convection currents, to think of troubled and confused as verbs. They may, indeed, be kept as participles belonging to perfumes to suggest the mingling of vapours against the disorder of the bedroom ; for it is only with the culminating drowned that we are forced either to accept the perfumes as subject of a new sentence, or the sense as an isolated word, perhaps with 'was' understood, and qualified by three participles. For stirred after all this, we are in a position to imagine three subjects as intended by these perfumes sense and odours (from which it could follow on without a stop); there is a curious heightening of the sense of texture from all this dalliance ; a suspension of all need for active decision ; thus ascended is held back in the same way as either verb or participle in order that no climax, none of the relief of certainty, may be lacking to the last and indubitable verb flung.

It may be noted that the verse has no variation of sense throughout these ambiguities, and very little of rhythm ; it loses nothing in definiteness from being the poetry of the English past participle.

Webster was much possessed by death

And saw the skull beneath the skin ;

And breastless creatures underground

Leaned backward with a lipless grin.

(T. S. Eliot, Poems.)

Leaned again, may be verb or participle; either 'Webster saw the skull under the skin and the skeletons under «the ground, which were leaning backwards' (leaned may be verb with 'that' understood, as so often in English, but it is hard to distinguish this case from the participle), or, stressing the semi-colon, 'Webster saw the skull under the skin, but meanwhile, independently of him, and whether seen or no, the creatures underground leaned backward,' both in order to have their laugh out, and to look upward at the object of their laughter. The verse, whose point is the knowledge of what is beyond knowledge, is made much more eerie by this slight doubt.

Donne, I suppose, was such another,

Who found no substitute for sense ;

To seize and clutch and penetrate,

Expert beyond experience.

He knew the anguish of the marrow

The ague of the skeleton;

No torments possible to flesh

Allayed the fever of the bone.

According as lines 3 and 4 go forwards or backwards, there are two versions of the syntax, corresponding to the two elements of the paradox in line 4. ' Donne found no substitute for desire and the world of obvious reality known through the senses, as a means of investigation, because the habits of the body, or its apprehension of reality, have always information still reserved from one who is experienced in them, and are more profound than any individual who lives by them is aware.' This is the meaning if the first verse is a self-contained unit, whether expert refers to sense or Donne, and line 3 to substitute or expert. Or, taking lines 3 and 4 with the next verse, ' Donne, who was expert beyond the experience of sense at penetrating, who could form ideas which sense could not have suggested, knew also those isolated and fundamental pains, the anguish of the marrow and the ague of the skeleton, which sense could not have known, and could not allay.' ' Value and a priori knowledge are not known through sense ; and yet there is no other mode of knowledge. No human contact is possible to our isolation, and yet human contacts are known to be of absolute value.' This I take to be the point of the poem, and it is conveyed by the contradictory ways of taking the grammar. Of course, you may say the lines are carefully punctuated, so that the grammar can only be taken one way, but in each case it is the less obvious grammar which is insisted on by the punctuation.

However, in finding reasons to admire such effects, one must remember that' the English language makes them difficult to avoid; here is Andrew Marvell playing exactly the same tricks without any excuse that I can see.

See how the Orient Dew,

Shed from the bosom of the Morn

Into the blowing Roses

Yet careless of its Mansion new;

For the clear Region where 'twas born

Round in itself encloses :

And in its little Globes Extent,

Frames as it can its native Element.

(On a Drop of Dew.)

Shed is active verb in the perfect tense, or past participle ; careless may or may not understand 'is'; or, etc., conveys 'for the sake of the upper region where it was born, and to keep up its tradition, it encloses round in itself,' or ' being careless, because the upper region where it was born is still enclosing it round,' whether because the drop cannot conceive of being enclosed by anything else, or because its clear region does in fact enclose the whole earth; and in the last line but one may be taken as applying either to the subordinate clause or to the complete sentence that follow;

and frames, in the closing line, is the only word that is undoubtedly a main verb following how.

Marvell's own Latin version of this, by the way, begins

> Cemis ut Eoi descendat Gemmula Rons

with a complete sentence right away. I don't suppose he was very proud of the delicious weakness and prolonged hesitation of his English syntax; but you may say it conveys the delicacy of the dewdrop, and how sickeningly likely it was to roll off the petal.

I shall now return to Shakespeare and allow myself a couple of digressions; about the emendations of his text and his use of a particular grammatical form.

Some readers of this chapter, I should like to believe, will have shared the excitement witlx which it was written, will have felt that it casts a new light on the very nature of languages, and must either be all nonsense or very startling and new. A glance at an annotated edition of Shakespeare, however, will be enough to dispel this generous illusion; most of what I find to say about Shakespeare has been copied out of the Arden text. I believe, indeed, that I am using in a different way the material that three centuries of scholars and critics have collected; without such a claim it is impertinent to add to the vast library about Shakespeare; but the difference here is merely one of interpretation.

The conservative attitude to ambiguity is curious and no doubt wise ; it allows a structure of associated meanings to be shown in a note, but not to be admitted; the reader is encouraged to swallow the thing by a decent reserve; it is thought best not to let him know that he is thinking in such a complicated medium. So it is assumed, except when a double meaning is very conscious and almost a joke, that Shakespeare can only have meant one thing, but that the reader must hold in mind a variety of things he may have meant, and weight them, in appreciating the poetry, according to their probabilities. Here as in recent atomic physics there is a shift in progress, which tends to attach the notion of a probability to the natural object rather than to the fallibility of the human mind.

Very likely the editors do not seriously believe their assumption; indeed I have myself usually said 'either ... or' when meaning 'both . . , and.' But the tone of the convention is well shown by the following note on a passage I have already considered (p. 1 8). It is with a pretty turn of grammar, such as might have been included in my seventh type among perversions of the negative, that the Arden editor insists on the variety of associations the word rooky had for an Elizabethan audience.

> This somewhat obscure epithet, however spelt (and it should be spelt rouky) does not mean 'murky' or 'dusky' (Roderick, quoted by Edward's Canons of Criticism 1765); nor 'damp,' 'misty,' 'steamy with exhalations' (Steevens, also Craig); nor 'misty,' 'gloomy' (Clar. Edd.); nor 'where its fellows are already assembled (Mitford), and has nothing to do with the dialectic word 'roke' meaning 'mist,' 'steam,' etc. . . . the meaning here ... I THINK, is simply the 'rouking' or perching wood, 1. ., where the rook (or crow) perches for the night.

Now, of course, the reason an honest editor puts down the other possibilities, as well as the one he is tentatively in favour of himself, is simply that these meanings had seemed plausible to scholars before; might, for all we know, therefore, have seemed plausible to anybody in the first-night audience ; might have seemed plausible to Shakespeare himself, since he was no less sensitive to words than they. There is no doubt how such a note acts; it makes you bear in mind all the meanings it puts forward. I cannot now make the imaginative effort of separating the straightforward meaning of the line from this note; I feel as if one was told elsewhere in the text, perhaps by the word thickens or by the queer hollow vowels of rooky wood that the wood was dark and misty; but rooky by attraction from crow and ignoring the rest of the note, merely suggests ' built over by rooks; where other rooks are; where this rook will perch.' Since this is the normal experience of readers, we must conclude either that a great deal has been added to Shakespeare by the mere concentration upon him of wrong-headed literary attention, or that his original meaning was of a complexity to which we must work our way back, and which we may as well acknowledge without attempting to drape ourselves in a transparent chain of negatives.

Thus, I believe the nineteenth-century editor secretly believed in a great many of his alternatives at once, and there is no need for exhortation in the matter. The eighteenth-century editor had none of this indifferentism; his object was to unmix the metaphors as quickly as possible, and generally restore the text to a rational and shipshape condition. We have no longer enough faith to attempt such a method,^ but its achievements must be regarded with respect, both because it has practically invented some of Shakespeare's most famous passages and because, in its more naive forms, it may often show how the word it supplants came into Shakespeare's mind.

Thus, to take one of the famous cruces in Macbeth

> My way of life
>
> Is falne into the Seare, the yellow Leafe,

is an achievement we must allow no emendation to remove; but Johnson's May of life seems to me a valuable piece of retrospective analysis, because it shows how the poetry was constructed ; first, there would be an orderly framework of metaphor, then any enrichment of the notion which kept to the same verbal framework and was suggested easily by similarity of sound. Indeed, considering Shakespeare's known sensibility for puns, I think Pope's gibe was a sort of opposite of the truth :

> There hapless Shakespeare, yet of Tibbald sore.
>
> Wished he had blotted for himself before ;
>
> (Dunciad,)

he had blotted for himself, and Tibbald was bringing back the first draft.

It requires a stronger faith to apply this method to the words immediately preceding :

> I am sick at heart . . . this push
>
> Will cheere me ever, or dis-eate me now.

Emendations are chair and cheer (then pronounced the same); disseat, disease disseizes and defeat. Cheer suggests the plaudits of a victorious army and recovery from melancholia; eate suggests the hostile army, regarded as an ogre that would eat him up, and the remorse that was gnawing at his entrails.

Now, it seems most unlikely that Shakespeare was less conscious of these alternatives than his commentators, and most unlikely that he would be satisfied by dis-eate considered as a word on its own, and intended to mean the opposite of eating. You may say, then, in defiance of Heminge and Condell, that the present text shows the printer baffled by successive corrections, from one to another of the emendations you fancy ; or you may say that Shakespeare actually intended, by putting down something a little removed from any of the approximate homonyms, to set the reader groping about their network. One must consider, before dismissing this second idea as absurd, that the Elizabethans minded very little about spelling and punctuation; that this must have given them an attitude to the written page entirely different from ours (the reader must continually have been left to grope for the right word) ; that from the comparative slowness, of reading as of speaking, that this entailed, he was prepared to assimilate words with a completeness which is now lost; that only our snobbish oddity of spelling imposes on us the notion that one mechanical word, to be snapped up by the eye, must have be^#n intended; and that it is Shakespeare's normal method to use a newish, apparently irrelevant word, which spreads the attention thus attracted over a wide map of the ways in which it may be justified. Or, thirdly, if we must not suppose the Child of Nature ever blotted, in the course of pouring immortality in a cramped, trying script on to the page, you may say that he knew better than to pause and allow his mind to be clotted with emendations; that he put down diseate because it was the first word he could drag out by the heels out of an intense and elaborate speech-situation that included all the puns editors have yet devised for it; that this had at all costs to be swept out of Ris way to make room for the May of life and its galaxy of puns (which were evidently going to produce something better) ; and that it was only by being as ruthless as this that he could bear in mind the soliloquy as a whole. I am sorry to appear so fantastic, but I can form no other working notion of what this unique mind must have been like when in action; and to propose emendations without having any such notion to correct them by is merely to hack out of the quarry a small poem of one's own[15].

Of the simpler thesis, more capable of being tested, that one main type of emendation goes back to the poet's (probably mental) rough draft, the best example I know comes in Measure for Measure i. iii. 19:

Duke. We have strict Statutes, and most biting Laws,

(The needful bits and curbes to headstrong weeds)

---

15 Of course, if this is true, the Bard is not to be praised' for the result in the present case, and the actor ought to choose some intelligible emendation.

Which for these fourteen years, we have let slip,

Even like an o'ergrowne Lyon in a Cave

That goes not out to prey.

' Tibbald ' emended weeds to ' steeds,' also slip to ' sleep.' Here, if anywhere, one would think, an emendation is justifiable; if you fix 'steeds' firmly in your head the other becomes nonsense. But it is curious, now that we have a simple straightforward line and one tidy metaphor, how the rhythm has become a plain didactic sing-song, how it might all have come out of Promos and Cassandra the original version of the story. And what does come out of Promos and Cassandra on the same theme, is

Promos. So that the way is by severity

Such wicked weedes even by the rootes to teare.

Thus Shakespeare is likely to have had the image from weeds lying about in his mind; and if you wish to expiress contempt of Lucio, it is certainly better done by calling him a 'fat weed that roots itself at ease on Lethe wharf' than by invoking the energy and beauty, the martial and aristocratic associations, of a stallion. You may say that Shakespeare, though not the Duke, had both attitudes towards the wicked in mind, and would have been prepared to call them 'steeds.' But this element in his judgment is sufficiently expressed by calling them headstrong it is Measure for Measure to move

from one attitude to the other; and it is in keeping with the tone of this period of his development that he should start with 'steeds' and then change, with a twinge of disgust, to weeds. Bitingy it is pleasant to see, besides making a sort of pun with bits, expresses

the effect of a curb on a 'steed' and the effect of a scythe on a weed. Or, for that matter, of a 'steed' on a weed the Duke will not mind seeing himself under this character, and there is usually a certain amount of interaction between such rival ideas.

The issue between slip and 'sleep' is less sharp; but not different; 'sleep' will apply to bits which are not being used for curbing 'steeds,' and it might suggest the transition to weeds, but when 'steeds' has been changed to weeds, slip is better, because it applies both to ' letting the growing weeds escape one's notice ' (which would have been covered by 'sleep') and to 'letting the weeds slip out of the closing jaws of the shears ' ; further, in so far as it concerns bits (which unlike 'steeds' are retained in the final version) it will cover 'leaving the reins slack so that the horse can get the bit between his teeth.' It seems very likely, then, that Theobald was quite right, though not in the way he meant; that Shakespeare first thought of some prosy remarks for the poor Duke in the style of the text he was working from, and then, feeling this was rather thin, and being reminded of another image in the text which he had himself used elsewhere, dragged that in as well by two small emendations, and felt he had cheered the thing up as much as possible. I don't say the result is uniquely good poetry, but when Shakespeare's mind is working at high pressure we have not the same chance of seeing what it is doing.

Another example of this that deserves mention occurs in a Sonnet I have already discussed (p. 54):

Be where you list, your charter is so strong

That you yourself may privilege your time

To what you will, to you it doth belong

Yourself to pardon of self-doing crime.

Do what you will is the emendation, making a parallel with Be where you list, and giving the lines the sing-song, chivalrous, and detached air of a Sonnet by Sir Philip Sidney. So that this is very like the preceding example; Sidney had set the fashion Shakespeare was writing in; he would naturally conceive the lines as directly rhythmical, after his model, and then improve them into the larger, more revealing, and grammatically more fertile scheme which has come down to us.

It is amusing to see that in taking this view of eighteenth century emendation I am forestalled by Pope :

Wondering he gazed : when lo a Sage appears,

By his broad shoulders known, and length of ears.

(Dunciad, iii. 27.)

Pope supplies for this a tremendous piece of textual criticism in the notes, 'partly by Mr. Theobald,' which moves ears back to 'years,' plumes itself very much on its sagacity, misses the point about donkeys altogether, and explains ' That Mr. Settle was old is most certain, but he was (happily) a stranger to the Pillory.' (Which in any case would only have made his ears shorter.) ' It is, therefore, amazing that Mr. Curll himself should overlook it.' But evidently this process is more valuable than Pope thought ; the emendation would throw a great deal of light on his line, if any were needed, by insisting on the subdued pun which gives it its point, its innocent and colloquial ease.

This example may make plain, too, that I do not think Shakespeare necessarily wrote down the emendations I have been applauding, any more than Pope wrote 'years'; in either case the simpler version was at the back of the author's mind, and made part of his reason for finding the line satisfactory.

In talking about Chaucer (p. 63), I said that, in general, puns and verbal connections of sound were unimportant and not to be sought out; and now, you will say, I have been using them to explain cruces in Shakespeare. Alas, you have touched on a sore point; this is one of the less reputable aspects of our national poet.

> A quibble is to Shakespeare [Johnson could not but confess] what luminous vapours are to the traveller ; he follows it at all adventures ; it is sure to lead him out of his way and sure to engulf him in the mire. It has some malignant power over his blind. ... A quibble was for him the fatal Cleopatra for whom he lost the world, and was content to lose it.

Nor can I hold out against the Doctor, beyond saying that life very high in those days, and that he does not seem to have lost the world so completely after all. It shows lack of decision and will-power, a feminine pleasure in yielding to the mesmerism of language, in getting one's way, if at all, by deceit and flattery, for a poet to be so fearfully susceptible to puns. Many of us could wish the Bard had been more manly in his literary habits, and I am afraid the Sitwells are just as bad[16].

It might, I think, be possible to relate a poet's attitude to life with his

16 All this may seem tediously facetious, but the subject of subdued puns is, I think, puzzling and hard to approach directly.

attitude to words, as apart from what he said with them, but there would be many other things to be decided first. To relate a taste for puns with the author's sexual constitution, one would have to consider what a variety of notions of manliness have held sway; that curious controversy in which the Lords Tennyson and Lytton, each with conviction and upon clear grounds, denied one another's virility; the tears and swooning's through which that of Troilus was asserted; the later Puritan notion that it is manly to be indifferent to sexuality ; the vital and virile rhythm of American music which springs from a hypnotised abandonment of self to the exact rhythms of machinery; the precisely similar extravagant gestures with which the Ganymede's and the Titans of Michael Angelo express respectively their yielding and their power.

But, perhaps, to say that an interest in puns is not virile is a divergence from the Doctor's opinion; the eighteenth-century use of ' quibble ' seems to mean that a pun cannot carry much feeling, and is a petty (rather than a womanish) pleasure. Some of the early comedies may justify this, but on the whole it is due to lack of historical sense ; Johnson had been bored by charades recited in coffee-houses, and thought the Elizabethan pun was the same. But Shakespeare's interest in the sound relationships between words was in no degree detached from his interest in their total meaning; however he arrived at a word he apprehended it, and the grasp of his imagination was such that, having arrived at a term by a subsidiary quibble, while his attention was yet giving sufficient weight to the matter mainly in hand, he could work the elaboration due to the quibble into the total order. When I said that subdued puns were not the most important objects of analysis, I meant that very few poets are so sensitive to the sounds of language, that very few poets can afford so to exploit their sensitivity to the sounds of language, and that perhaps no other poet has been able to concentrate, on to the creative act of a moment, such a range of intellectual power.

I shall now mount the second of the hobby-horses with which I am ending off this chapter, and examine the way Shakespeare uses a combination of 'and' and 'of.'

In so far as it is valuable for a poet to include several rhythms, grammatical forms, or shades of meaning in a single phrase, those linguistic forms are likely to be most convenient which insist on no definite form of connection between words and allow you simply to pass on from one to the other.

Thus the word ' and ' will be convenient if you are bringing forward two elements of a situation, conceived as of the same logical type; consider the word ' and ' in my last sentence ; it could have been ' so that they ' or 'but.' The word 'of' will be convenient if the two elements are related to the situation differently, and stand in some asymmetrical relation to one another. A mild form of this vague use of 'of' may be shown in a very normal and grammatical passage by Mr. Eliot:

I can sometimes hear

Behind a public bar in Lower Thames Street

The pleasant whining of a mandoline.

(The Waste Land)

Taking the last line as unit, whining is the main noun, and the other words are draped about it, but reading the whole sentence with the slight emphasis necessary on the ends of lines, the grammatical skeleton becomes ' I . . . heard ... a mandoline,' and whining is almost an adjective like pleasant. If I may destroy Mr. Eliot's poetry for a moment, and read ' The pleasant, whining sort of mandoline,' it is evident that mandoline becomes the real object of hear, Elizabethan verse continually does this; it combines pomp of syntax with immediacy of statement :

What means (the warning of) this trumpet's sound ?

Till, swollen with (cunning of) a self-conceit . . .

(Spanish Trag. l. ii. 192, Faust, Prol)

King Lear is more desperate in his variety of uses for the genitive :

Blasts and fogs upon thee.

The untented woundings of a father's curse

Pierce every sense about thee.

(Lear i, iv. 320.)

The wounds may be cause or effect of the curse uttered by a father independently of this, they may reside in the father or his child. The curse, indeed, might be uttered against the father by the child, and certainly the king would have meant this if he had thought of it. All the meanings arrived at by permuting these versions make up one single-minded curse; any pains Lear has felt or is still to feel, any pains Cordelia has felt or is still to feel, as an effect or cause whether of this curse on Goneril or of his previous curse on Cordelia, or of Goneril's implied curses on him, all these give him good reason for cursing Goneril with the same pains in return; and if any pains in Goneril are to be cause or effect of any of these cursing, so much the better, let them pierce her. These pains are already all that he can foresee from the cursing of fathers; they, therefore, mean also 'all the curses that a father can impose on his child.[17]'

The uses of 'and,' though no less various, are less distinct. The reader may be forced to give it an extended meaning when it connects two words which are mutually exclusive unless applied in different ways. For example, Othello speaks of

> the flinty and Steele Cooch of Warre.
>
> (i. iii. 231).

A soldier's couch is flinty in that he lies on pebbles, steel in that his weapons are beside him. This satisfies the suggestion that the adjectives apply in different ways, which is conveyed by their different forms and by the fact that one of them has a capital ; both suggest the hardness both of external circumstance and of the inner man that confronts it (so that the first ' both ' mirrors the second); and, taking them together as a unit, they are the flint and steel with which you fire your gun. I hope the reader will agree with me that the word 'and' here is standing for three different ways of fitting words into a structure.

I propose to consider a linguistic form common in Shakespeare's verse, and typical of his method; 'the (noun) and (noun) of (noun)'; in which two, often apparently quite different, words are flung together, followed by a word which seems to be intended to qualify both of them. This implies that they are both early attempts (the result of two casual shots) at saying the same thing; in fact, the whole unit often takes a singular verb; and hence

17 Critics have objected that verbal ingenuity here is very irrelevant to the feelings of Lear. Anyway all Shakespearean heroes must be supposed superhumanly articulate ; but Lear in particular, I think, did enjoy the wealth and force of Ais language ; it was all he had left, and he felt it had magical power. However, I have cut a sentence which claimed double meanings in undented ; as the word is put next to wounds it is probably limited to the medical sense.

their main meaning, it is implied, is a sort of highest common factor of the two of them. This implies, again, a statement that they are not prime to one another; thus,

were 't to renounce his Baptisme,

All Seales, and Symbols of redeemed sin :

(Othello II. iii. 356.)

is a reflection about the character of a symbol that it depends on the fixture or sealing down of an association, and is thus analogous to an act of faith. Similarly,

All bond and privilege of Nature breake

(Cor., v. iii. 25.)

states the two opposite ends of the idea of contract, which is not such a trivial intellectual feat as it may appear. It is in part this sort of subsidiary meaning that critics are bearing in mind when they praise the comprehensiveness of Shakespeare's outlook upon the world. Bond and privilege here is in effect a single word which combines two opposite notions; I must refer the reader to my seventh chapter for a discussion of such words and their importance to poetry.

And since this form demands that the reader should find a highest common factor of its first two nouns, it implies that he must open his mind to all their associations, so that the common factor may be as high as possible. That is, it is a powerful means of forcing him to adopt a poetical attitude to words.

but 'tis not so above ;

There, is no shuffling, there the Action lyes

In his true Nature, and we ourselves compell'd

Even to the teeth and forehead of our faults

To give in evidence.

(Hamlet, iii. hi. 63.)

You put your hand down the hole, feel at the rat's head and face [forehead] in an attempt to drag it out, and then [teeth] it bites back at you[18]. ' God will force us to bring our faults out into the open, however much we struggle.' A forehead, besides being a target for blows, is used both for blushing and frowning. ' We will be ashamed and a little indignant at having to confess such things.' Teeth, besides being a weapon of offence, are used in making confessions, and it is a mark of contempt, I suppose for your weakness, even where you might seem most dangerous, that you are struck there. 'We must confess all in plain words, or God will give us the lie in our teeth.' Perhaps, too, the forehead covers the brain where the fault is planned, while the teeth are used (whether for talking or biting) in carrying it out, so that they stand for the will to sin and the act of sin respectively. Or, making a fair attempt to give its grammatical meaning, so that the teeth and forehead are not ours but our faults ' ; ' We shall have to start giving evidence at the very bottom of our faults, and go right on up to the top where they are at their most striking and important.' Teeth are a naked part of the skeleton and the foreheads bone is near the surface; 'The Last Judgment will give little or no margin to the flesh; we shall have to go right down to bedrock in turning up our faults.'

This is all very fanciful and irrelevant, the reader may think. But what is relevant to these notes of the material for rhetoric, this poetry by physiological shorthand ? All we are given is two parts of the body and the Day of Judgment; these have got to be associated by the imagination of the reader. There is no immediate meaning, and in spite of this there is an impression of urgency and practicality, and being in the clutches of an omnipotent ferret. Such an effect must rely, not perhaps on flashes of fancy in the directions I have indicated; I doubt if such occur in the normal reader; but on a sense that the words themselves, in such a context, include, as part of the way in which they are apprehended, the possibility of flashes of fancy in the directions I have indicated. The words are intended for the stage; they certainly convey something to an audience ; and there is no time for them to convey anything more definite than this before the soliloquy has swept on to another effect of the same kind.

---

18 Miss M. C. Bradbrook pointed out that forehead chiefly meant impertinence to Shakespeare ; and teeth no doubt would chiefly suggest the ' lie in your teeth' situation of challenge. But after this simplification you have still to interpret the phrase as a syntactical unit ; and it has much the same effect, I think, whether you put these ideas in or leave them out.

In this last example the genitive may be said to have been used normally, if our faults have been personified so as not to be very distinguishable from ourselves; at least, it has the same sense for each of the first two nouns. The following case, though the sense is plain enough, is more complex. 'The new deputy is very strict '.

Whether it be the fault and glimpse of newness

(Measure for Measure i. ii. 59.)

'or because he thinks it best to show his strength at once, and make sure of his prestige.' The fault of newness would be simple, and have for grammar, 'this mistake isn't the deputy's fault, it's Newness's fault.' The glimpse of newness would be fairly simple ;

' He is dazzled with the brightness of his position, and still self-conscious, with a suggestion of peeping, because of its novelty.' The first 'of' would thus mean 'belonging to,' the second, 'caused by.' But to impose one on top of the other puts the reader at some distance from either meaning; makes fault convey a meaning of 'discontinuity' (the sense 'gap' which led to the geological use) so as to be more like glimpse, glimpse suggest 'spying' and a wilful blindness so as to be more like fault, and leaves various ways of making them both grammar floating about in one's mind; 'this isn't the deputy's fault, it' of his glimpse of newness'; or separating 'the' fault from the rest of the phrase, ' This is original sin coming out, as it often does when a man changes his circumstances.

Shakespeare is fond of this double use of a preposition, which a reader is not supposed to be sufficiently conscious of to think witty or precise :

To keep her constancy in plight and youth

Outliving beauty's outward . . .

(Troilus and Cressida, ill. ii. 173.)

Do, with like timorous accent and dire yell

As when, by night and negligence, the fire

Is spied in populous cities.

(Othello i. i. 76.)

' Her constancy to the thing she has plighted in its original state of vigour'; 'caused by negligence during the night-time. But I think there is more in it than this; if the prepositions were being used in quite distinct senses, one for each word, the effect would be a conscious one, and irrelevant to the dramatic moments concerned. Her constancy may be thought of as in a state of being continually plighted (kept in a pickle of virtue) so long as she is in a state of mind to keep the original plighting) so that the alternative meaning of in does something rather like transforming a surface integral to a volume integral, and insists on the spirit rather than the letter. Similarly, in the other example, the fire may have spread 'by reason' of night as well as of negligence. because the fire occurred at night, there was nobody about to see it beginning; or, attaching the two to spied the fire might be found because it showed up in the dark, and because there were then idlers about in the streets to notice it. The most prominent thing about the line is the gusto and Miltonism with which lago now releases his accumulated excitement into an act; the ambiguity gives scale to his rhythms. I know of no case where Shakespeare has made a flat pun out of a preposition, one meaning to each noun ; I believe that (if done at all seriously) to be a unique property of the Augustans.

In Shakespeare's great parades of associations the attendants are continually quarrelling among themselves, on the pattern of

Glend. When I was born . . .

The heavens were all on fire, the earth did tremble.

Hotspur. O' then the earth shook to see the heavens on fire

And not in fear of your nativity.

(i Henry IV, ill. i. 24.)

Consider with this in mind :

That I did love the Moore, to live with him,

My downeright violence, and storme of Fortunes,

May trumpet to the world.

(Othello i. iii. 249.)

It is after the pattern we have considered, except that the adjective throws a new term into the calculation; it qualifies either violence or violence and storme, and tends to detach violence from fortunes. On the normal pattern of qualifies both nouns, but it was Desdemona who was violent, after all (she does not become young and helpless till she is married), precisely because she stood up to, answered back, and in part created her Fortune which was stormy. The Folio's comma, which heightens the civil war in the line by dividing it in two, is usually omitted by editors, I think wrongly; both rhythm and grammar should be rocking and tempestuous, in a precise echo to the meaning.

The normal form I am considering, then, is liable to break up at the join between the first two nouns, which I had claimed would carry so many implications. But this reaction seldom goes the whole way ; the form itself is so strong that its elements hold together. It is strongest, evidently, when the two first nouns are almost synonyms, and in this form, partly because it is such a satisfactory form of padding, partly because it appeals to the dictionary interest in words that was so strong in the Elizabethans, Shakespeare uses it very often ; it has been drummed, therefore, into the ears of his readers till they take it for granted.

> Within the book and volume of my brain.
>
> Upon the heat and flame of thy distemper.
>
> The flash and outbreak of a fiery mind.
>
> The pales and forts of reason.
>
> The slings and arrows of outrageous fortune.
>
> The whips and scorns of time.
>
> The natural gates and alleys of the body.

In these random cases either word gives the sense alone. This shows a pride in the possession of language such as appears in people talking to a specialist on some subject of which they have a little knowledge ; they make haste to use all the technical terms they can remember. Such examples as I have noted in Shakespeare's predecessors are of this form :

She sent him letters, which myself perus'd,

Full-fraught with lines and arguments of love.

Preferring him before Don Balthazar.

(The Spanish Tragedy ii. i. 86.)

Fa. Tell me what is that Lucifer thy lord?

Me. Archregent and commander of all spirits.

(Faustus I. iii.)

I cut my arm, and with my proper blood

Assure my soul to be great Lucifer's,

Chief lord and regent of perpetual night.

(I v.)

But the form is rare before Shakespeare, and even in Shakespeare before Hamlet it is not likely to be sought for by an author unless he wants to hold a thought in the reader's mind while he plays round its implications, unless, in fact, he feels it is likely to be useful in the way I am describing. Consider

But we are old, and on our quickest decrees

Th' inaudible, and noiseless foot of time

Steals, ere we can affect them.

(All's Well, V. iii. 40.)

These two adjectives might seem to be used as synonyms, from a dictionary interest only, with no stress on their difference. The first is from Latin (external and generalised), the second, native (with immediate gusto and a sense of textures) ; in English this difference is often fruitful ; but here it is overshadowed by negation and they take effect as the same sort of word.

And yet, rather as two forces almost in the same line may have a small resultant in quite another direction, so the slight difference between the meanings of inaudible and noiseless points towards curious places, and is accepted as evidence of the fantastic broodings of melancholy. ' Not only can nobody hear the foot of time, but it actually never makes a sound; even when safely alone, like a clock in an empty room, even at its headquarters, it is silent; you might be hearing in a different way sounds outside the human range, and yet this all-important reality, this devouring giant, would make no sound.' Certainly this implication is very far in the background, but I think it was because Shakespeare was ready to use such differences that he was ready to use two contiguous synonyms. The earlier, more naive dictionary interest (Hear, oh ye kings; give ear, oh ye princes) has a different purpose; it does not repeat the two words together, it uses them as an excuse to repeat the rhythm of a whole phrase[19].

Shakespeare's fondness for such pairs of words is fundamental to his method, and in particular is the cause of the form I am considering. It is because he so often put down two almost synonymous nouns that it became natural to add a qualifying noun so as to connect them; it is because, when he used this form, he so often made the first two nouns act as synonyms, that it comes by habit to be so strong a unit in his reader's mind. Since, however, the two words are here adjectives and not nouns, this example serves another purpose ; it shows the normal form grown so strong as to be able to tear two synonyms apart and make them different parts of speech. For the Folio's comma makes the inaudible in some degree a noun, as a Miltonism for destiny, and the part of Saxon to its Latin is then played by foot or time.

Apart from making the two first words synonyms, the strongest way to hold them together would be to make them an oxymoron, with the first acting as adjective to the second.

> In the dead wast and middle of the night.
>
> (Hamlet i. ii. 198.)

Wast seems to be a pun on ' waste,' ' waist,' and ' vast ' ; if ' waist,' it has a strong common factor with middle if 'vast,' the connection could be that the night seems longest when you are in the middle of it; if 'waste,' the connection is that people are about at the two ends of a night but

19 I should have mentioned the legal habit of putting synonyms one after another in a document in case the other man claims a difference later. The historical reason why these stock pairs are so often Norman and Saxon is not because it's pretty but to make sure that both groups understood. I have an idea that Mr. George Rylands was the first to point this out fin Words and Poetry),

the middle is a desolate region put to no good. If I say that any of these connections in itself constitutes an oxymoron, I am making philosophical assumptions such as I would wish to avoid, but they are easily treated as such in paraphrasing — 'in the dead and wasted middle of the night.' Or one may make 'dead' a noun like the other two ('in the dead of night), or the idea may be 'during one of those periods of the night which seem vast and yet are only a small part of the middle of it,'so that 'dead waste' or 'dead vast 'can be separated from night and made to stand alone. The pun on 'waist' is not so much a meaning as a force holding together wast and middle it may perhaps personify the night as one of the terrible women of destiny. The difference between Shakespeare's and Milton's use of a phrase like 'the dead vast' is simply that Shakespeare always gave it an alternative, more usual construction to fall back on.

As a rule, these two forces of oxymoron and tautology are both operative in attaching the first norm to the second and the third; but they do not attach it as closely to either as the second is attached to the third, and it has some life on its own. I shall list a few examples showing the action of the resulting ambiguity.

Hor. In what particular thought to work, I know not:

But in the grosse and scope of my Opinion,

This boades some strange erruption to our State.

(Hamlet I. i. 68.)

'Taking it as a whole' (in the gross 'judging from the whole unanalysed lump in my mind, as fully as my coarse powers allow' (in the gross of my opinion) and 'expressing only a personal and limited view;' (in the scope of my opinion).

Hamlet does the same in prose :

... to hold, as 'twere, the mirror up to nature, to show the

very age and body of the time his form and pressure.

(Hamlet in. ii. 26.)

The age is apparently the same as the body of the time but the normal form pairs it with body so as to carry a sense of ' condition of body,' for instance, how old it is. I quote this mainly to show the group being referred to in the singular.

The two nouns may achieve their variety in unity by giving two different metaphors for the same idea. Thus, ' If we put all our eggs in one basket . . .

. . . therein should we read

The very Bottome, and the soule of Hope,

The very list, the very utmost Bound

Of all our fortunes.

(i Henry IV,, iv. i. 50.)

This is obviously a case of dictionary interest, which uses the display of synonyms as an excuse for repeating the rhythm of a whole phrase. This fact, and the capitals, tend to make Bottome separate from soule of Hope but, on the other hand, the fact that very is only left out before soul makes the line seem one phrase. Soule here may be a pun on 'sole,' 'our one hope is being risked,' or it may mean ' the very essence of hope,' or, stressing the verb, 'we would be looking into the eyes of Hope, having its true character brought home to us'; whereas Bottome either means 'the nadir of our fortunes,' taking it as apart from Hope or just 'all the hope we have in stock'; we see the bottom of the tub of Hope, as if it was so much treacle.

Doubt as to the interpretation of a metaphor may be common to both words, without sharing its alternatives between them, and still will attach itself to this ambiguity of the normal form :

Tell her my love, more noble than the world

Prizes not quantitie of dirtie lands.

The parts that fortune hath bestowed on her :

Tell her, I hold as giddily as Fortune :

But 'tis that miracle, and Queen of lems

That nature pranks her in, attracts my soule,

(Twelfth Night, ii. iv. 8o.)

Fortune might be said to have bestowed on her looks as well as her estate, so it is not clear whether the miracle is her soule or her body. It is true that the Folio punctuation, by firmly connecting parts with lands, makes parts unlikely to include beauty, and so gem unlikely to mean soule but arguments from punctuation are doubtful, and the final phrase attracts my soule gives the nineteenth-century editors some excuse for their more spiritual interpretation. The Duke's rather dismally self-centred condition gives no help either; he is in the mood to make a high toned remark about admiring the soul, and also in the mood to say it is essential for his soul to have things about it that it likes the look of; or (putting it more generously) he is including her character and her looks in a single act of admiration. Thus he is a fair case for ambiguity.

There is also the doubt normal to this form as 1:o whether nature pranks her in a miracle or in a miracle of gem , and whether either of these is the same as a queen of gems. These independent doubts are easily connected. To take miracle alone is more like a catalogue of compliments, to take miracle with queen is more cumbrous and excited; has to be said with a hushed and naive air because the two words are so much heavier and stronger than the word gems which is to connect them. Thus, the first shows detachment and admiration, the second, reverence and humility; a distinction which is perhaps the meaning of, rather than similar to, that between beauty and character. Or you can make miracle and miracle of gems correspond to her beauty, queen of gems to her character.

The ambiguities of this form may convey a variety of feelings on the subject in hand. Poor Bertram, in this example, has been beaten down into civility and a readiness to marry when he is told:

> When I consider
>
> What great creation, and what dole of honour
>
> Flies where you bid it . . .
>
> (All's Well ii. iii. 170.)

What creation of honour is courtly and reserved, but standing alone, as the intervening what may suggest, creation becomes more abject, and means 'you make and break people according to your liking.' On the other hand, taking great creation and dole together, and feeling for a connection, one passes from the idea of 'doling out' to the idea of 'doleful'; 'how terribly the sort of honour you give people weighs them down ' ; he is overheard, as it were, muttering under his breath.

Or the subsidiary meaning may act as pure dramatic irony, without the knowledge of the speaker.

Or that perswasion could but this convince me.

That my integritie and truth to you,

Might be affronted with the match and waight

Of such a winnowed purity in love :

(Troilus and Cressida, iii. ii. 176.)

Affronted may mean 'confronted' (it never does elsewhere); match may refer to pairing things and seeing that they are equal ; waight may convey equal strength, adequate solidity, and perhaps capacity for waiting. Or affronted may mean 'offended,' with a suggestion of battles; match may refer to single combats and to the matches which convey flames (the word, of course, is older than Lucifer matches, and applied in particular to touching off guns); waight may remember his long waiting for her in Chaucer's version ; and his love is to be winnowed by adversity. It is not quite true to say this is meant as unconscious; as the combatants in this play use sexual metaphors for fighting, so the lovers (more naturally) use terms of war; of this, no doubt, they are aware, but there is a painful irony as to the interpretation :

Tro. I am as true as truth's simplicity

And simpler than the infancy of truth.

'In that I'll war with you,' replies Cressida; and, indeed, she defeats him.

The (noun) and (noun) of (noun)' has kept its head above water in a variety of difficult circumstances ; we may take a last look at it being submerged by collision with a stronger form.

My vouch against you, and my place I' th' state

Will so your accusation overweigh,

That you shall stifle in your own report.

And smell of calumnie.

(Measure for Measure ii. iv. 155.)

Report and smell of calumny is the familiar form; the first two nouns Latin and Saxon respectively; of with a fair variety of meaning. 'You will stifle in the calumnious report you have yourself set about, in the social situation of accusation and self-righteousness you have yourself caused.' But this model collides, owing to the short half-line, with another model that makes smell a verb ; here is no great difference of meaning, except that the new version is rather less rude to her; to 'smell of calumny' might happen to anyone, and does not seem so deserved a fate as that of stifling in one's own smell.

Praise of the victorious model will add dignity to the old one. This short half-line is used to repeat briefly, with a calming or clinching effect, what has been said elaborately in several lines before. 'While determined, I do not wish to nag; I will stop talking now on the understanding that I have made my point sufficiently clear.' It should use less abstract and elaborate, more earthly and immediate terms, with an air of comradely appeal to the good sense of the person addressed. ' I suppose I an come down to your level now that I have asserted myself ;f what I mean is quite simple really, I can say it in four words.' There should be an implication that he has poured out into language the energy of his judgment, and can now put it finally (having found out in the course of talking just what it implies) on the last wave of his desire for expression. 'In short . .

But cruel are the Times, when we are Traitors

And do not know ourselves ; when we hold Rumour

From what we feare, yet know not what we feare,

But float upon a wilde and violent Sea

Each way, and move.

(Macbeth, tv, ii. i8.)

It is as a variety of this model that the last word (which so many commentators have wished to alter) may be justified. He has described, as one living through such a time, its blind agitation and disorder, and then, calmed by the effort of description, gazes out over the Sea with a hushed and equable understanding; so that the whole description is called back into the mind, remembered as in stillness or as from a distance, by the last word. And here is being used, as so often, to connect two different ways of saying, two different attempts at saying, the same thing; but in this case one way takes over four lines of packed intensity and elaborate suggestion; the other takes one word, perhaps the flattest, most general, and least coloured in the English language. I am glad to close this chapter with so rich an example of an imposed wealth of meaning.

III

An ambiguity of the third type, considered as a verbal matter, occurs when two ideas, which are connected only by being both relevant in the context, can be given in one word simultaneously. This is often done by reference to derivation; thus Delilah is

That specious monster, my accomplished snare.

The notes say: Specious, 'beautiful and deceitful'; monster ' something unnatural and something striking shown as a sign of disaster'; accomplished, 'skilled in the arts of blandishment and successful in undoing her husband.' The point here is the sharpness of distinction between the two meanings, of which the reader is forced to be aware ; they are two pieces of information, two parts of the narrative ; if ingenuity had not used an accident, they would have required two words.

The meanings of a pun of the third type may, of course, be 'connected' in this sense, that their being put into one word produces an additional effect ; thus here they are used to concentrate feeling upon the single line in the speech, focussed in this way to hold all Samson's hatred, when he expresses his grievances against her. Indeed, if the pun is producing no additional effect it has no function and is of no interest ; and you may say that, in so far as an ambiguity is justified, it is moved upwards or downwards on my scale out of the third type. If this were true, the type would gain in theoretical importance but contain no examples of interest to the reader of poetry. But I think it is not true, because the matter is complicated by questions of consciousness, of the direction of the reader's attention, of the interaction between separated parts of his mind, and of the means by which a pun can be justified to him. To begin with, I should call it an ambiguity of this type when one is mainly conscious of the pun, not of its consequences. There may be an additional meaning, given because two meanings have been fitted into one word, which takes effect only when the reader is attending, not to it, but to the fact that they have been fitted into one word, so that one could call it a deduction from the fact that they have been fitted into one word.

> Ye, who appointed stand,
>
> Do as you have in charge, and briefly touch
>
> What we propound, and loud that all may hear.
>
> (Paradise Lost, vi. 565.)

It is a bitter and controlled mood of irony in which Satan gives this address to his gunners; so much above mere ingenuity that the puns seem almost like a generalisation. But here, as for ironical puns in general, to be put into the state of mind intended you must concentrate your attention on the ingenuity; on the way the words are being interpreted both by the gunners themselves and by the angels who have not yet heard of artillery; on the fact that they are puns. I want to insist that the question is not here of ' consciousness ' of a device as a whole, but of consciousness of a particular part of it; for one must continually feel doubtful about antitheses involving the idea of 'unconscious,' which, like the infinities of mathematics, may be a convenient fiction or a product of definition. In literary matters it covers a variety of antitheses, as between taste and analysis, and seeing or not seeing the consequences of a proposition ; here I mean by the conscious part of the effect the most interesting part, the part to which it is most natural to direct your attention. In this sense, clear or wide distinction between the two meanings concerned is likely to place the ambiguity at the focus of consciousness; threaten to use it as a showpiece to which poetry and relevance may be sacrificed; make it more obvious to the reader, more dependent on being overtly observed, and less intimately an expression of sensibility. Thus its most definite examples are likely to be found, in increasing order of self-consciousness, among the seventeenth-century mystics who stress the conscious will, the eighteenth-century stylists who stress rationality, clarity, and satire, and the harmless nineteenth-century punsters who stress decent above-board fun.

A pun may be justified to the reader, so long as its two parts have not strong associations of their own and do not suggest different modes of judgment, by saying two things, both of which were relevant and expected, or by saying what is expected in two ways which, though different, are seen at once to come to the same thing. In such cases the pun requires no extraneous apology and will receive no particular attention. Or it may name two very different things, two ways of judging a situation, for instance, which the reader has already been brought to see are relevant, has already been prepared to hold together in his mind; their clash in a single word will mirror the tension of the whole situation. The pun may then be noticed as a crucial point, but it will not separate itself from its setting, and will be justified by that. The puns I am considering now, indeed most puns that are ordinarily recognised as such, fall between these two classes, they demand an attention which is not absorbed into the attention demanded by the rest of the poem, and are a separate ornament on their own. If, then, the reader is not to think them irrelevant and therefore trivial, they require some kind of justification.

The most obvious way to justify them is by derivation, with an air of learning and command of language. The puns from Milton I have just quoted acquire their dignity in this way ; when a reader can see no similarity between the notions concerned, such as a derivation is likely to imply, the pun seems more trivial and to proceed from a less serious apprehension of the word's meaning. The stock case is Milton's line about Elijah's ravens:

Though ravenous, taught to abstain from what they brought.

(Paradise Regained ii. 269.)

This is ridiculous, but if it had been justified by derivation, as perhaps it claims to be, it would have been all right; the meaning would be 'though, as everyone admits, so that their name itself implies it, this required a serious miracle.' And as a development from this, a pun may be all right if one is induced to give a pseudo-belief, like that in personification, to the derivation ; as in Marvell's delightful line about the tawny mowers. ' And now when the work is done . . .'

And now the careless victors play

Dancing the triumphs of the hay.

(Upon Appleton House)

The ornamental comparison with an army, and the anthropological forces (John Barleycorn and so forth) from which the comparison draws its strength, make one delighted with hay and therefore willing to justify it by a belief that the dance and the crop are connected by derivation; a belief which may have been shared by Marvell, but which the New English Dictionary does not encourage.

If a pun is too completely justified by its derivation, however, it ceases to be an example of the third type, at any rate from the point of view of verbal ingenuity. One must distinguish between puns which draw some excuse from their derivation and the use of technical words outside their own field.

When thou, poor Excommunicate

From all the joys of love, shalt see

The full reward and glorious fate

Which my strong faith shall purchase me,

Then curse thine own inconstancy.

(Carew, To his Inconstant Mistress.)

Excommunicate is on the verge of being a pun, but all that is done is to use its actual meaning so as to bring in other modes of judgment; if it conveys an ambiguity of the third type, it is not by a pun but by an ornamental comparison such as I shall consider in a moment. This use of technical words was one of the central devices of seventeenth-century poetry; it is usually a matter of generalising the idea, or, contrariwise, of taking an unusual particular case. Thus the process is much the same as that which developed the two meanings of a word from its derivation : but in the case of the puns from Milton, for instance, the intervening steps have been lost; the two meanings are not thought of as proceeding from a single sense; one's knowledge that they have the same origin is a secondary matter; and in the English language they are puns.

Or a pun may not need to be justified by derivation because the word itself suggests the connection by which it is justified. Thus, in Marvell's Dialogue between the Resolved Soul and Created Pleasure the Soul says to Music

Had I but any time to lose

On thee I would it all dispose.

Cease Tempter ! None can chain a mind

Whom this sweet Chordage cannot bind.

It is exquisitely pointed, especially in that most cords are weaker than chains so that the statement is paradox, and these chords are impalpable, so that it is hyperbole. But it is not a pure pun (it is, by the way, justified by derivation) because the mind has not to jump the intervening distance; there is a conceit, implied by the word itself, upon the strings of musical instruments, which keeps one from any just irritation (in that ' this is the wrong way for a poet to be thinking about words') at having to jump at random and too far.

It is partly this tact which makes Marvell's puns charming and not detached from his poetry; partly something more impalpable, that he manages to feel Elizabethan about them, to imply that it was quite easy to produce puns and one need not worry about one's dignity in the matter. It became harder as the language was tidied up, and one's dignity was more seriously engaged. For the Elizabethans were quite prepared, for instance, to make a pun by a mispronunciation, would treat puns as mere casual bricks, requiring no great refinement, of which any number could easily be collected for a flirtation or indignant harangue. By the time English had become anxious to be 'correct' the great thing about a pun was that it was not a Bad Pun, that it satisfied the Unities and what not; it could stand alone and would expect admiration, and was a much more elegant affair.

The change, however, was not sharp; I must include, to contradict what I have just said, a curious ambiguity from Dryden, which seems to show quite the Shakespearean innocence as to the means by which a total effect is being obtained. From the Death of Amyntas :

but soon he found

The Welkin pitched with sullen Clouds around,

An Eastern Wind, and Dew upon the ground.

In the resounding intensity of Dryden's brief and clear statements of detail, in this Roman use of language, one would not look for a sensuous richness of meaning. But pitched means both 'blackened as with pitch by the thunderclouds' and 'pitched like a tent,' so that the Welkin seems at once muffled and to have come lower; perhaps even the two meanings act upon one another, and the material of the tent has been tarred and blackened in a forlorn attempt to keep out the rain. The effect is not 'rich,' because even here, where the word has two meanings, Dryden is using both with a sort of starkness, and they are both drawn sharply from the practical world. But it seems to me a remarkable case, because it is a full-blown pun, such as the Restoration poets would normally have been aware of, and made, if they had used it, into an ambiguity frankly of the third type, and yet the reader seems meant to absorb it without realising it is there. Dryden uses the same turn of phrase elsewhere, and again it is a pun:

> O call that Night again ;
>
> Pitch her with all her Darkness round ; then set me
>
> In some far Desert, hemm'd with Mountain Wolves
>
> To howl about me :
>
> (Rival Ladies, ii. i.)

(She's is the Night). He thought, I suppose, of the phrase 'pitch round,' meaning 'plant round and blacken,' not as a pun, nor as intended to be analysed, but as an ' idiom,' like the French idioms involving words like 'jeu.' The attempt then in progress to make English 'regular,' like French, gives Dryden, I think, other puzzling ambiguities of this sort. He seems to claim only to be saying one thing, even when one does not know which of two things he is saying. Polyphemus thinks Galatea

> More turbulent than is the rising flood.
>
> And the praised peacock is not half so proud.

'The peacock which is commonly praised for its dignity,' or 'the peacock when it has just been praised'? It is merely a direct translation of laudato pavone superhior but the doubt feels larger in English than in Latin.

I shall now list four eighteenth-century puns, in order of increasing self-consciousness.

Let such raise palaces, and manors buy.

Collect a tax, or farm a lottery ;

With warbling eunuchs fill a licensed stage.

And lull to servitude a thoughtless age,

(Johnson, London.)

Licensed refers, I understand, to the passing of the Licensing Act, and adds with a peculiarly energetic sneer that they had all kinds of goings-on. This, I take it, is a joke, one would say it with an accent on licensed and look knowingly at the listener to make sure he saw the point. You may say this is only the use of a technical word in a generalised sense, but it is not a metaphor; the two meanings are different and he means to say both of them.

Most manfully besiege the patron's gate,

And, oft repulsed, as oft attack the great.

With painful art, and application warm.

And take at last some little place by storm.

(Young, Love of Fame, Satire iii.)

Place is hardly more than an ambiguity by vagueness ; it is only because the ornamental comparison is between such different activities (one 'poetical,' the other prosaic and considered sordid) that the political and military meanings of the word seem different enough to be funny.

The watchful guests still hint the last offence.

The daughter's petulance, the son's expense;

Improve his heady rage with treacherous skill.

And mould his passions till they make his will.

(Johnson, The Vanity of Human Wishes.)

This is a careful, very conscious pun, which had to be dovetailed into its setting ; but still it does not stand out from its setting and seem the point of it ; the pun is thought of as of the same kind as the other devices employed. Consider the word heady, which means both that he was head of the family and that his passions soon came to a head ; it is the same sort of pun as the conscious one about the will, and yet one can absorb it without recognising it at all.

Where Bentley late tempestuous wont to sport

In troubled waters, but now sleeps in port.

(Pope, Dunciad, iv.)

The pun is sustained into an allegory by the rest of the couplet; tempestuous and sport are satirical in much the same way as the last word. But here, I grant, we have a simply funny pun; its parts are united by derivation indeed, but too accidentally to give dignity; it jumps out of its setting, yapping, and bites the Master in the ankles.

The eighteenth-century use of a pun is always worldly; to join together so smartly a business and a philosophical notion, a nautical and a gastronomical notion, with an air of having them in watertight compartments in your own mind (each such subject has its rules which save a man from making himself ridiculous, md you have learnt them), so that it seems to you very odd and to have jumped from one to the other – all this belongs to the light-weight tattling figure (it is odd it should have been Doctor Johnson's), very ready to form a group and laugh at a man in the street, or to 'smoke' Sir Roger de Coverley in the theatre ; the man quick to catch the tone of his company, who knows the talk of the town. In each case, too, the pun is used as the climax of a comparison between the subject of the poem, something worldly, and a stock poetical subject with which :he writer is less intimately acquainted, which excites feelings simpler and more universal. Wit is employed because the poet is faced with a subject which it is difficult to conceive poetically.

The nineteenth-century punster is quite another thing; to begin with he is not rude ; I suppose he came in with the Christmas Annuals, and supplied something which could be shown to ill the daughters of the house, which all the daughters of the louse could see (at a glance, without further information) was very whimsical and clever. Apart from this it is difficult to see[20] why a man like Hood, who wrote with energy when he was roused, should have produced so much verse of a trivial and directed verbal ingenuity; trivial, not because fitting together phrases wholly separate, drawn from everyday life, or lacking in heir own emotional content, but because, so far from 'being interested in mere words,' he uses puns to back away from the echoes and implications of words, to distract your attention by insisting on his ingenuity so that you can escape from sinking into he meaning. It is partly, perhaps, a result of the eighteenth century contempt for ' quibbles ' (so that the verbal acrobat must)e desperately unassuming) and partly a result of profound changes in the attitude to life of the Duke of Wellington's England; of a nervous Puritanism which had had quite enough of in rest and the Romantic Revival, and felt, if the girls must read verse, let us see they get something that cannot possibly go to their heads.

Not a trout can I see in the place,

Not a grayling or rud worth the mention,

And though at my hook With attention I look

I can ne'er see a hook with a tench on.

At a brandling once gudgeon would gape,

But they seem upon different terms now ;

Have they taken advice Of the Council of Nice

And rejected their Diet of Worms now ?

For an eel I have learnt how to try

By a method of Walton's own showing,

But a fisherman feels

Little prospect of eels

On a path that's devoted to towing.

Such virtuosity cannot be despised ; I have warmed to admiration in copying it out. But the nervous jumping of the style, the air of feeling that

20 Mr. Edmund Blunden rebuked me by pointing out that Hood had to :rind away at the stuff to make a living; so the only problem is why his public wanted it.

all feeling (ahem) is a little better avoided, gives a sort of airlessness to the humour. One feels a sort of sympathetic embarrassment about the relation it implies to his public ; there may, at any moment, be an anxious hush because just for once dear Mr. Hood is not, perhaps, in perfect taste, and at the end there must be a sigh of relief because he has avoided the pitfalls of his subject very skilfully. A verse of his 'serious' poetry seems symptomatic :

And blessed will the lover be

That walks beneath their light,

And breathes the love against thy cheek

I dare not even write.

But such puns are a sound poetical training; given a subject so accepted that even the punster can afford to show feeling, given an occasion where he can indulge at once his reader, s' snobbery and his own humanity, how delicately the instrument can be used.

How frail is our uncertain breath !

The laundress seems full hale, but death

Shall her ' last linen' bring ;

The groom will die, like all his kind ;

And even the stable-boy will find

This life no stable thing.

Cook, butler, Susan, Jonathan,

The girl that scours the pot and pan,

And those that tend the steeds.

All, all shall have another sort

Of service after this — in short

The one the parson reads.

One or, perhaps, two puns are sufficient for a verse ; notice the fourth line, from which Shakespeare would have extracted a pun on 'kine,' but which here mentions the groom merely to lead up to the stable-boy. Each verse moves about its pun as an axis, and yet the result is so lyrical and strong that one wonders if it can really be a matter of punning; whether the same effect could not be conveyed without an overt pun at all.

Thou needst not, mistress cook, be told

The meat to-morrow will be cold

That now is fresh and hot :

Ev'n thus our flesh will, by and by.

Be cold as stone; Cook, thou must die.

There's death within the pot.

I don't know what his readers thought of this brave piece of writing; I wish only to point out that, though of the same form as the verses that moved round puns, it has not got any; the two associations of flesh take their place. Associations of this kind, used in the same way as puns are used, are an important extension of the third type, and occur more often than puns themselves. I must now consider their action.

An ambiguity of the third type, then, as a matter concerning whole states of mind, occurs when what is said is valid in, refers to, several different topics, several universes of discourse, several modes of judgment or of feeling. One might call this a general ambiguity of the third type; it includes, for instance, the eighteenth-century puns I have just considered. Now, there are two main ways of constructing such an ambiguity. It may make a single statement and imply various situations to which it is relevant; thus I should call it an ambiguity of this type when an allegory is felt to have many levels of interpretation; or it may describe two situations and leave the reader to infer various things which can be said about both of them; thus I should call it an ambiguity of this type when an ornamental comparison is not merely using one thing to illustrate another, but is interested in two things at once, and is making them illustrate one another mutually.

There is a variety of the 'conflict' theory of poetry which says that a poet must always be concerned with some difference of opinion or habit between different parts of his community; different social classes, ways of life, or modes of thought; that he must be several sorts of men at once, and reconcile his tribe in his own person. It is especially to generalised ambiguity of the third type that this rather limited formula will apply.

In the following full-blown ornamental comparison men and bees are the two social types, with each of which the poet must be in sympathy.

for so work the honey-bees . . .

They have a king, and officers of sorts ; . . .

Others, like soldiers, armed in their stings,

Make boot upon the summer's velvet buds ;

Which pillage they with merry march bring home,

To the tent-royal of their emperor;

Who, busied in his majesty, surveys

The singing masons building roofs of gold;

The civil citizens kneading up the honey ;

(Henry F., l. ii. 320.)

and so forth. The commentators have no grounds for deciding from this passage, of course, whether Shakespeare knew much or little about bees : we can only see what effects he was producing by a distorted account of their habits. It is a vision of civil order conceived as natural, made at once charming and convincing by its expression in terms of creatures so petty and apparently so irrelevant. The parallel passage in Vergil uses the same methods ; it pokes fun at bees and their pretensions to humanity, and so, with a sad and tender generosity, elevates both parties in the mind of the reader by making a comparison between them. For matters are so arranged that the only things the reader thinks of as in common between men and bees are the more tolerable things about either of them, and since, by the compactness of the act of comparison, a wide variety of things in which bees and men are alike have appeared in his mind, he has a vague idea that both creatures have been adequately described. Both, therefore, are given something of the charm, the suppression of unpleasing detail, and the cosiness (how snug they all are down there !) of a bird's-eye view.

I shall only consider the line about masons[21], Bees are not forced by law or immediate hunger to act as masons ; ' it all comes naturally to them'; as in the Golden Age they sing with plenty and the apparent freedom of their social structure. On the other harid, bees only sing (indeed, can only sing) through the noise produced by their working ; though happy they are not idle ; and the human opposition between the pain of work and the waste of play has been resolved by the hive into a higher unity, as in Heaven. Milton's 'the busy hum of men' makes work seem agreeable by the same comparison in a less overt form.

Roofs are what they are building; the culmination of successful work, the most airy and striking parts of it; also the Gothic tradition gave a peculiar exaltation to roofs for instance, those magnificent hammer-beam affairs which had angels with bee like wings on the hammers, as if they were helping in the singing from a heavenly choir; and to have masons, building a stone roof, with mortar instead of nails, is at once particularly like the methods of bees and the most solid and wealthy form of construction. But bees build downwards from the roof, so that they are always still building the roof, in a sense ; the phrase is thus particularly applicable to them, and the comparison with men makes this a reckless or impossible feat, arguing an ideal security. In the same way, both parties are given wealth and delicacy because the yellow of wax is no surface gilding, not even such as in the temple of Solomon (built without sound of hammer, in the best bee tradition, though it was) shone thickly coated upon ivory, but all throughout, as the very substance of their labours, is its own pale ethereal and delicious gold.

It is sometimes hard to distinguish these ambiguities from the corresponding cones of the first type; to distinguish allegories which are felt to have many levels of interpretation, or comparisons of which both parties are the subject, from similes which are effective from various points of view.[22] (It may, indeed, be too hard ever to be worthwhile, but

---

21 G. K. Chesterton had praised this line, I think in one of his detective stories. He had'*great powers as a verbal critic, shown mainly by incidental remarks, and 1 ought to have acknowledged how much I was using them.

22 What I was puzzling over here was a more general version of the objection raised by critics, that a pun is not in itself an ambiguity.

it would still be useful to know that the distinction existed.) Perhaps it is enough to say that they are more complicated, or have to be thought of as if they were. The mind has compartments holding opinions and modes of judgment which conflict when they come together; that, in fact, is why they are separated; compartments, therefore, which require attention, and one is particularly conscious of anything that mixes them up. If the two spheres of action of a generalisation, or the two halves of an ornamental comparison, involve two such compartments which must be thought of in two ways, we have the conditions for a general ambiguity of the third type.

It is this (in some sense conscious) clash between different modes of feeling which is the normal source of pleasure in pastoral; or, at any rate, in so far as pastorals fail to produce it, one may agree with Johnson and call them a bore.

Thou shalt eat crudded cream

All the year lasting.

And drink the crystal stream

Pleasant in tasting ;

Whig and whey whilst thou lust

And brambleberries.

Pie-lids and pastry-crust,

Pears, plums, and cherries.

(Anon., Oxford Book)

The delicacy of versification here (alliteration, balance of rhythm, and so forth) suggests both the scholar's trained apprehension and the courtier's experience of luxury; but it is of the *brambleberry* that he is an epicure; the subject forces into contact with these the direct gusto of a 'swain.' That all these good qualities should be brought together is a normal part of a good poem; indeed, it is a main part of the value of a poem, because they are so hard to bring together in life. But such a case as this is peculiar, because one is made to think of the different people separately ; one cannot pretend to oneself that the author is the rustic he is impersonating; there is an element of wit in the first conception of the style. It is a faint and subtle example of the mutual comparison which elevates both parties.

Or the different modes of feeling may simply be laid side by side so as to produce ' poetry by juxtaposition ' ; the last verse of a poem by Nash (discussed on p. 25) gives a very grand and dramatic example of this :

Haste therefore each degree

To welcome destiny;

Heaven is our heritage,

Earth but a player's stage.

Mount we unto the sky ;

I am sick, I must die –

Lord, have mercy upon us.

(Summer' s Last Will and Testament,)

The first line of the last three gives the arrogant exaltation of the mystic; it has so total and naive a belief in the Christian dogma of immortality (a belief, too, in the righteousness of the assembled company, or the ease with which such righteousness may be attained) as to convey a sort of pagan hubris and triumph ; one remembers that it was written for a scene of at once worldly and ecclesiastical pomp. The second, sweeping this mood aside, gives the mere terror of the natural man at the weakness of the body and the approach of death. The third gives the specifically Christian fusion of these two elements into a humility so profound as to make the hope of personal immortality hardly more than incidental to a consciousness of the love of God.

You may say that this is not in any direct sense ambiguous, because the elements are isolated statements which succeed one another flatly; I should reply that it becomes ambiguous by making the reader assume that the elements are similar and may be read consecutively, by the way one must attempt to reconcile them or find each in the other, by the way the successive ideas act in the mind. Or you may say that the experience they convey is too strong to be conceived as a series of contrasts ; that one is able to reconcile the different elements; that one is not conscious of their difference but only of the grandeur of the imagination which brought them together. In so far as this is true, the example belongs to my fourth chapter. Or, indeed, you may say that two opposites – the fear of death and the hope of glory — are here stated together so as to produce a sort of contradiction ; and that the humility of the last line then acts as evasion of the contradiction, which moves it out of the conscious mind into a region of the judgment which can accept it without reconciling it. In so far as this is true, the example belongs to my seventh chapter. But I find myself that I cannot forget the difference, that I read it aloud 'dramatically,' as a dialogue between three moods. For this is a very dramatic device indeed, it is a form of dramatic irony. I should say that the most exciting and painful example of its use by Shakespeare (in so crude a form) is that scene at the end of I Henry IV,, where Falstaff, Harry Percy, and Prince Henry (natural gusto, chivalric idealism, and the successful politician), in a series of lightning changes, force upon the audience in succession their mutually incompatible views of the world.

I am not sure, then, that this last example is in the right chapter; it may be enjoyed, as it could be read aloud, in various ways. The following more limited example is, I think, strictly of the type in question ; it is the sort of mutual comparison which affects one as a pun. Sacred and profane love (in a devotional setting which would consider them very different) are seen as one for their generosity, just as men and bees have been seen as one for their orderliness.

Lord what is man ? that thou hast overbought

So much a thing of nought

Love is too kind, I see; and can

Make but a simple merchant man.

Twas for such sorry merchandise

Bold painters have put out his eyes.

(Crashaw, Caritas Nimia.)

In this case, though not always in Crashaw, it seems a matter of conscious ingenuity and artifice that Cupid and the love of Christ should so firmly be used to interpret one another; he is well enough aware that they belong to different worlds, but in the generosity of his heart it seems very gay and conveys a sort of reliance on the good-humour of Jesus to treat them as the same, or to explain one by the other.

The following example may serve to show that Mutual Comparison can degrade instead of elevating both parties. It is not an example of Pope's more poetical satire. The mood is simple, and though the mock-heroic scheme as a whole has a rich imaginative background the pleasure intended here seems only that due to the strength and ingenuity of the attack.

High on a gorgeous seat that far outshone

Henley's gilt tub, or Fleckno's Irish throne,

Or that where on her Curlls the Public pours

All-bounteous, fragrant grains, and golden showers.

Great Tibbald sat.

(Dunciad ii.)

Various different situations of mean, vain, and trivial absurdity are being concentrated on the hero by comparison. Now, comparison has two uses, one to show that one thing has more or less of some quality than another, the other to show that the two things are comparable in regard to that quality; an ornamental comparison concentrates on the second of these, and it is the second of these that Pope is exploiting. It may be worth quoting the original Milton :

High on a Throne of Royal State, which far

Outshon the wealth of Ormus and of Ind

Or where the gorgeous East with richest hand

Showers on her Kings Barbaric Pearl and Gold,

Satan exalted sat.

(Paradise Lost ii.)

The comparison with Milton puts Theobald on a ' bad eminence ' to start with, and then makes him petty and ridiculous because the eminence is too great. His seat is then said to outshine, and be similar to, the pillory in which Curll stood, high and lifted up, and glittering with bad eggs. The word grains is chosen to match pearl and mean rotten food in general ; golden showers may mean that people emptied chamber-pots at him from neighbouring windows. But another world of pettiness and vanity is piled on to these two ; curl may be a pun meaning one's wig, or the great structures worn by ladies, since the public is female : and then the other throne, than which the hero's was far more squalid, would be the powdering-tub, showers would be hair-oil and grains powder. Perhaps one is more conscious here of the difference between the two sorts of Curl than of the difference between the powdering-tub and the pillory; I might, therefore, have used this example among the puns, and it may help to show the connection between what I have called the special and general varieties of the same type.

The point of the joke here is the contrast between the different sorts of throne or rather between the attitudes to life, the social settings, represented by them. But in these last two examples the meanings of the symbols are in some degree connected together; their difference is included within a single act of worship or of satire.

That they may have almost no inherent connection is clear in the following small example by Scott, which merely happens not to be a pun.

> Stop thine ear against the singer ;
>
> From the red gold keep thy finger ;
>
> Vacant heart and hand and eye
>
> Easy live and quiet die.

Marriage and commerce, avarice and desire, with pert decision, are fitted by Sir Walter into a single image.[23]

The following complete poem by George Herbert keeps the symbols apart with the full breadth of the technique of allegory ; though the contrast in question is the same as that of the Crashaw example.

> I gave to Hope a watch of mine : but he
>
> An anchor gave to me.

---

23 Perhaps the charm of the song comes from a more real Ambiguity ; that the ' moral' is so much opposed to his temperament and even to his style.

Then an old prayer-book I did present :

And he an optick sent.

With that I gave a viall full of tears :

But he a few green eares :

Ah, Loyterer! Fie no more, no more I'll bring.

I did expect a ring.

(Herbert, The Temple.)

One can accept the poem without plunging deeply into its meaning, because of the bump with which the short lines, giving the flat, poor, surprising answer of reality, break the momentum of the long hopeful lines in which a new effort has been made; the movement is so impeccable as to be almost independent of the meaning of the symbols.

And, indeed, the symbols themselves seem almost to be used in a way familiar to the mathematician; as when a set of letters may stand for any numbers of a certain sort, and you are not curious to know which numbers are meant because you are only interested in the relations between them. One would think that an indefiniteness of this sort in poetry must, if it is tolerable, be of the first type, and unlikely to repay study; but George Herbert, here and elsewhere, has put to extraordinary uses these dry and detached symbols.

To begin with, there is an irony in that he treats only with Hope, not with the person or thing hoped for; he has no real contact with his ideal but only with its porter. This bitterness is common to any interpretation of the symbols.

You may regard the poem as chiefly about the soul's irritation and despondency at the slowness with which it can achieve perfect union with God ; so that the watch is the brevity of human life, and the length of time already spent in waiting (since it means both these, a symbol of time, not of time considered either as long or short, was wanted) ; the anchor either the certain hope of resurrection, or an acquired power of endurance, of holding on to the little that has already been gained; tint prayer-book prayer and an ordered rule of life ; the optick faith that can look up to the sky, or the mystical event of a faint illumination (granted to encourage the mystic) and distant view of Heaven ; the viall a mark of repentance, or of the pains of desiring perfect union with God, or the pains of desiring what has been renounced for him; the green eares faint signs of spiritual growth or mystical achievement, which carry a distant promise of something better; and the ring Omega, the perfect figure of Heaven or of eternity, marriage with God, or a halo[24]. But, even then, this single meaning or subject for the poem contains metaphors, hardly less important than itself, either from the earthly state of courtship, taking the prayer-book as containing the marriage service and the ring as a sexual symbol, perhaps only as employed in that ceremony; or from the life of secular ambition, since the notion of exchanging presents suggests Court ceremonial and modes of obtaining preferment, and the ring might be a mark of office.

I am not sure why the prayer-book was old; it was a traditional and venerable thing, he had himself lived according to its rule, or wanted to use it in marriage, for a long time; and there may be a hint at the religious controversies with which the life of secular ambition was then so closely concerned. But it is also used to give a sort of humility and reality, something of the conviction of steady prose, to this flat and as it were pastoral exchange of gifts. I have already considered the means by which Shakespeare makes one accept words imaginatively; the means by which Herbert makes one accept them soberly, as things rich in their interpretation rather than in their meaning, is harder to explain in terms of syntax.

The symbols, then, apply to three different situations, and from this point of view the poem belongs to my third type. But of an ambiguity of the

24 Herbert would not have meant that he himself expected the halo of a saint, and would have thought it very bad taste in an interpreter to say that he did. I remember how cross I was when a reviewer of my own verse used a poem in which I had addressed myself as a twister. He said that this was a surprising confession and exactly what was the matter with me. I thought that this showed an almost imbecile incompetence on the part of the critic. The reason for the clumsiness here is that (as in several other cases) I was listing beside the possible primary meanings the suggestions at the back of the mind which would reinforce them. The group of ideas about the marriage ring and the circle of eternity is strengthened by the idea of the halo ; the halo is therefore worth listing, though not as a candidate for the primary meaning. It would seem pedantic to distinguish the two things all the time, but failure tp do so sometimes makes the analyses look wilder than I intended. And yet after all, though I want to give full weight to this point of view, I am not sure th^ Herbert did not mean the poem dramatically as said by a foolish character, so that the halo could poke up its head quite prominently.

third type, whether special or general, the reader needs to be conscious, and it seems possible to read this poem more simply. It may be read so as to convey, apparently in terms of the imagined movements of muscles, a statement of the stages of, a mode of feeling about, any prolonged endeavour; so that the reader is made to accept them all as alike in these particulars, and draw for his sympathy on any experience of the kind he may have had. In so far as the lines really act like this, by the way, they are much more ' like ' music than are the releasing effects of open vowels which are usually given that praise. Now, it is an absurd stretching of the idea of ambiguity to call a generalisation ambiguous because it has several particular cases, and in so far as the poem is read in this way its ambiguity, at any rate, lies deep within the obscurity of the first type.

That two such different classes should tumble on top of one another may seem an important failure of my system; but, as a matter of fact, all generalisations act like this. In absorbing them, one usually thinks of several particular cases and sees if they are true ; this is so both for deep thoughts about life and for the propositions of science and mathematics. In so far as a generalisation is thought of as the aggregate of the particular cases which have been chosen to test it, it may be called an ambiguity; in so far as, accepting it, you regard the taking of particular cases as a use of it rather than as an unpacking of its meaning, it becomes a single proposition. The difficulty arises because I am not using the word 'ambiguity' in a logical, but in a psychological sense; the notion of relevance is necessary to pick out cases of it, and it is conceived as always conscious in one mode or another. But in this particular case one may fall back on a logical distinction, between a class defined by numeration (' courting the favour of God, of a mistress, and of the King') and a class defined by a property (' any course of action which involves prolonged endeavour'); a statement about the first class may be called an ambiguity, a statement about the second a generalisation. From a statement about the first, which appears complex, one infers a statement about the second, which appears simple. One may say, then, that in ordinary careful reading this poem is of the third type, but when you know it sufficiently well, and have accepted it, it becomes an ambiguity of the first or (since it is verbally ingenious) of the second type.

It is usual, of course, for a poet to feel his subject is a good one because it throws light on matters of another sort, because it illustrates life, or what not ; such an unexpressed ambiguity is a very normal feature of good poetry. Often what on a first reading seems faulty or irrelevant has been put in to insist on this feeling; that is not to say it is not genuinely faulty, because unnecessary. Dr. Johnson's objections to Gray's Cat can, I think, only be answered in this way.

> Selina, the cat, is called a nymph, with some violence both to language and sense; but there is good use made of it when it is done ; for of the two lines —
>
> What female heart can gold despise ?
>
> What cat's averse to fish
>
> the first refers merely to the nymph, and the second only to the cat.

The Doctor complains here that the separation is too neat, which is true enough; but since cat and nymph have been confused in the first part of the verse, it is a relief to the reason (such as he would have been the first to admit into poetry) that they should be separated at the end of it. As to the violence done to language, it is justified by a sort of honesty, because we are meant to be so conscious of it; that we are asked to make that collocation is the point of the poem; and Johnson's pretty distinction between merely and only is unfair, because both nymph and cat are the main subject.

> If what glistered had been gold, the cat would not have gone into the water, and, if she had, would not less have been drowned.

Here he complains that they are not sufficiently separated, or not connected sufficiently verbally. Two logical statements conveying the two morals could easily have been constructed, but to put them logically into one, as a generalisation, would require a sort of wit different from the sort Gray is using. Certainly it gives pleasure when there is a sentence applying to two things separately, by a sort of pun ; but then it gives pleasure in another way when one has to see that a nonsensical sentence (Johnson rightly insists that it is nonsense) is conveying a double meaning. For, of course, the clash is not only between nymph and cat but between two metaphorical nymphs; between snatching at a pleasure, real but dangerous (the cat and the less spiritual nymphs), and mistaking a false love for a true one (the more spiritual nymphs) believing that happiness to be permanent which will, in fact, be fleeting. Thus, by the last line of the poem, gold, which in the earlier line quoted means chiefly 'money' ('women are avaricious'), has come to mean 'of genuine value' ('what will pay in the long run').

This ambiguity enables him to give advice about the pursuit of happiness with the sort of reality and good sense which belongs to advice about the pursuit of pleasure ; he assumes a charming humility in the more spiritual nymphs, and implies that the happiness which they seek is a genuine one. I am not sure that pleasure and happiness give the right antithesis, but after all he was a Christian trained in Pagan literature; he is playing off against one another two different notions of love, two different standards of morality, and it is precisely the achievement of this which produces the nonsense of which Johnson complains.

Johnson's good sense (a quality urgent for literary critics) was, I think, too harsh in this way only, that he would not allow such implied comparisons as require to be observed. A comparison, in his view, must either be overt or such as could be ignored without making nonsense; this is unreasonable, because it ignores the way people's minds in fact work; and as long as the Romantics stuck to this issue they could score points off him.

Allegory, which leads you to think of several particular interpretations, is nowadays rare and unpopular; but one must remember that, in a form rather different from that of my last example, it is among the roots of Elizabethan literature, must have come very easily to the readers of that age, and, however it may have been abandoned later, was one of their chief impulses towards greater subtlety of language.

> Her Majesty fell upon the Reign of Richard II. saying am Richard the second, know ye not that?' – 'Such a wicked imagination was determined and attempted by a most unkind Gent., the most adorned creature that ever your majesty made.' – 'He that will forget God will also forget his benefactors ; this tragedy was played forty times in open streets and houses.

There was always this simple political interest, connecting Hamlet with James from their treatment of their mothers, for instance, which must have been a continual danger and annoyance to Shakespeare ; he seems to have evaded its consequences himself, but he had to pay fines for the mistakes of others, and was acting in the production of Sejanus at Court after which Jonson was arrested for Popery and treason. This, though historically important, seems poetically rather trivial, but the book which may be said to have been the origin of Elizabethan literature has a more complex and more certainly intended ambiguity. In the Shepheard's Calendar the same shepherds appear in precisely the three capacities that are treated of in Herbert's poem, as lovers, as courtiers, and as divines. And in the Faerie Queene, by the process I have just considered, this variety of meaning has been blurred into generalisation, and you can read all kinds of political and religious interpretations, indeed any interpretations that come naturally to you, into a story offered as interesting in itself, and as giving an abstracted vision of all the conflicts of humanity.

You might think that almost any seventeenth-century conceit could now be included in the third type; they all play off one subject against another, and use arguments that do not work because they are ' on another plane.' But Donne, and the secular love-poets who follow him, are much too interested in one of the two worlds contrasted to use the other as more than a weapon.

> Alas, alas, who's injured by my love?
>
> What sailor's ships have my sighs drowned ?
>
> Who says my tears have overflowed his ground ?
>
> When did the heats that my veins fill
>
> Add one more to the plaguey Bill ?
>
> Soldiers find wars, and lawyers find out still
>
> Litigious men, that quarrels move,
>
> Though she and I do love.
>
> (The Canonization.)

The other ways of viewing the world, in such a case, are brought in not as things that are also true, but as things once valuable which no longer seem important; they show him feeding the fire with all the furniture in the room. This advocate's mood is not an ambiguous one. Herbert and the devotional poets, on the other hand, use a conceit to diffuse the interest back on to a whole body of experience, whose parts are supposed eventually reconcilable with one another; and the reader must pause after each display of wit to allow the various moods in which it could be read, the various situations to which it could refer, to sink into his mind. There is a curious contrast between the momentum obtained by secular, and the stasis obtained by devotional, metaphysical poets, from the same sort of conceits ; I should explain this by calling only the second way of using them an ambiguity of the third type.

But this form of ambiguity, though it was prominent in early Elizabethan writings, was soon felt as a triviality and abandoned by the dramatic writers. For if you are thinking about several situations at once you are detached from all of them, and are not observing any with an immediate intensity. I do not say this is impossible, only unlikely ; indeed, it is the contrast between this sort of abstraction and the intensity he is conveying in other ways (the fact that he has overcome this difficulty) which makes the poetry of George Herbert seem the product of an inner life so fully unified and of a belief so permanently held.

So far I have dealt with the ambiguity of this type which talks about several things at once; there is also the ambiguity which talks about one thing and implies several ways of judging or feeling about it. This tends to be less rational and self-conscious, therefore less strictly fitted to the third type ; it is more dramatic and more aware of the complexities of human judgment. Pope continually makes use of it; partly because, though himself a furious partisan (or rather because of it, so as to pretend he is being fair), he externalises his remarks very completely into statements of fact such as must always admit of two judgments; partly because his statements are so compact, and his rhythmic unit so brief, that he has not always room for an unequivocal expression of feeling. The word ' equivocal ' is a good one here ; much of the force of his satire comes from its pretence of equity. He stimulates the reader's judgment by leaving an apparently unresolved duality in his own – 'this is the truth about my poor friend, and you may laugh if you will.' The now fashionable attitude to the eighteenth century rather tends to obscure this point; it is true the humour of the period is often savage, but that does not show that the judgments with which it is concerned are crude.

Is Pope sneering or justifying, for instance, in one of the best known of these spare but widely buttressed constructions ? –

who, high in Drury Lane,

Lulled by soft zephyrs through the broken pane,

Rhymes e'er he wakes, and prints before term ends.

Obliged by hunger, and request of friends.

(Epistle to Arbuthnot.)

No one can deny that these words ridicule, but: obliged by hunger: I am not sure that they titter; it is only after you have been faced with the dignity of human need that you are moved on to see the grandeur of human vanity. Much recent apologetic for Pope has contented itself with saying how clever it was of the little fellow to be so rude ; but to suppose this line means merely ' the man must have been a fool as well as a bore, since he was hungry,' is not merely an injustice to Pope's humanity, it is a failure to understand the tone he adopts towards his readers.

Soft were my numbers, who could take offence

When pure description held the place of sense? . . .

Yet then did Gildon draw his venal quill.

1 wished the man a dinner, and sat still.

(Epistle to Arbuthnot.)

Good, sympathetic Mr. Pope, one is to think; he has a profound knowledge of human nature. The situation in these two examples is the same; the first stresses his contempt, the second his magnanimity ; but in neither can one be sure what proportions are intended. A more verbal expression for this doubt is given in the line about the Goddess of Dulness :

Where, in nice balance, truth with gold she weighs,

And solid pudding against empty praise.

(Dunciad 152.)

Neither truth nor gold neither praise nor pudding, are to be despised, and the pairs may be connected in various ways. A poet is praised by posterity for attending to what Pope called truth; whereas gold and pudding are to be gained by flattery. Gold may be the weights of the balance with which truth is weighed, so that the poet will tell any lie that he decides will pay; or all four things may be alike and equally desirable, so that, though the author is hungry and sensible, he is also truthful and anxious for his reputation ; his proportion of praise and pudding has to be worked out with honest care. This spectacle, in its humble way, is taken to be charming; so that this version is contemptuous but without the bitterness of the first one. For these versions, praise is that of good critics, and it is empty beside pudding in a sense that would sympathise with the poet's hunger, or as an imagined quotation from him so as to bring him into contempt. But it might be empty as unjustified, as being the praise of (that is, from or to) the rich patrons who had bought the compliments; gold then takes on the suggestion of contempt, never far from it in Pope's mind, and means 'shoddy poetical ornament'; pudding is paired with truth, in the natural order of the antitheses, and means either the cheap food which is all he would be able to buy, or the solid reality of his dull but worthy writings. At any rate, the epithets solid and empty contradict the antithesis 'venal' and 'genuine'; it is gay and generous of Pope to have so much sympathy with pudding and it is this detachment from either judgment in the matter (the truth such men could tell, the praise they could win, is nothing for Pope to be excited about) which makes the act of weighing them seem so absurd.

This process of interpretation may evidently be applied to the feelings a reader imposes on the material; there may be an interest due to the contrast between the stock response and the response demanded by the author. I think myself, in the following border-line case, that I am describing the attitude of Pope, but such an analysis would have achieved its object if it described the attitude only of the majority of his readers. It is that description of a great eighteenth-century mansion in which Pope is apparently concerned only to make its grandeur seem vulgar and stupid.

his building is a town,
His pond an ocean, his parterre a down.
Who but must laugh, the master when he sees,
A puny insect, shuddering at a breeze.
My lord advances, with majestic mien,
Smit with the mighty pleasure to be seen.
But hark, the chiming clocks to dinner call ;

A hundred footsteps scrape the marble hall :

Is this a dinner ? this a genial room ?

No, 'tis a temple, and a hecatomb.

(Moral Essays iv.)

All this is great fun; but before concluding that Pope's better judgment really disapproved of the splendour that he evidently envied, one must remember the saying that as Augustus found Rome, so Dryden found English ' brick, and left it marble ; that the Augustans minded about architecture and what Augustus did ; that great part of the assurance and solidity of their attitude to life depended on solid contemporary evidences of national glory. When Pope prophesies the destruction of the building his language takes on a grandeur which reflects back and transfigures it:

Another age shall see the golden ear

Embrown the slope, and nod on the parterre,

Deep harvest bury all his pride has planned,

And laughing Ceres reassume the land.

These lines seem to me to convey what is called an intuitive intimacy with nature ; one is made to see a cornfield as something superb and as old as humanity, and breaking down dykes irresistibly, like the sea. But, of course, it embrowns as with further, more universal, gildings and nods on the parterre like a duchess; common things are made dignified by a mutual comparison which entirely depends on the dignity of Canons. The glory is a national rather than a personal one; democracy will bury the oligarch; but the national glory is now centred in the oligarch; and if the whole people has been made great, it is through the greatness of the Duke of Chandos.

This seems to me rather a curious example of the mutual comparison which elevates both parties ; in this case, it is the admiration latent in a sneer which becomes available as a source of energy for these subsidiary uses : and also an example of how the Wordsworthian feeling for nature can be called forth not by an isolated and moping interest in nature on her own account, but by a conception of nature in terms of human politics. I hope, at any rate, you agree with me that the lines convey this sort of sympathy intensely; that there is some sense of the immensity of harvest through a whole country ; that the relief with which the cripple for a moment identifies himself with something so strong and generous gives these two couplets an extraordinary scale.

It is not, of course, the normal use of allegory to make a statement which is intended to have several interpretations. The normal use is to tell a homely story and make clear that it means something else, something, for instance, religious or political, but not both ; so that there is only one real meaning, which the first meaning is frankly a device to convey.[25] The reader does not think of it as ambiguous, but as pretending to be ambiguous, perhaps to evade some censorship ; and the critic must consider the consequences of the device before saying whether it is ambiguous or not. In devotional verse it is often used, like poetry itself, to impose calm on the writer and allow him to evade his own habits of reticence; almost all sexual language, too, as in Gray's Cat, is a hierarchy of devices of this kind. It may be ambiguous in this sense, that two modes of feeling are implied about the one matter in hand ; but, for this, allegory is only of incidental convenience. As an example of its incidental convenience, I shall consider a verse of that curious and superb Pilgrimage of Herbert, which so closely anticipates the Pilgrim's Progress, and contains both special and general ambiguity of the third type, both pun, allegory, and variety of feeling.

That led me to the wild of Passion, which

Some call the wold :

A wasted place, but sometimes rich.

Here I was robbed of all my gold.

Save one good Angel, which a friend had tied

Close to my side.

Angel, of course, is a pun on the name of a coin ; wild and wold seem, as Herbert pronounced them, to have been puns on ' willed ' and ' would.' The most striking thing about the verse is its tone, prosaic, arid, without momentum, whose contrast with the feeling and experience

25 Whether allegory is to be called ambiguous or not, the allegorical method has to be considered because it can be used for effects which are undoubtedly ambiguous ; thus the problem of definition is again secondary.

conveyed gives a prophetic importance to this flat writing; there is the same even-voiced understatement in the language of the Gospels. This is made possible because, in the apparent story, he adopts the manner of a traveller, long afterwards, mentioning where he has been and what happened to him, as if only to pass the time. Several pretty devices carry this out, particularly in the word good, by which the traveller means, as in 'my good sword,' 'a thoroughly useful piece of gold,' while the mystic, actually meaning ' holy,' uses it as a distinguishing mark : ' I mean the good angel, not the bad one, of the two that accompany a man.[26] Passion, in the apparent story a proper name which insists on the allegory, has a wide range of meanings, such as an irritated lack of patience, the loves of the flesh, and the ambitions at Court which he had abandoned; nor is it easy to map out its underground connections, by opposites, with the Passion of the Christ. (I am speaking, of course, of its poetical meaning; its prosaic meaning is not in doubt. 'He was not exempt from passion and choler,' said his brother, 'being infirmities to which all our race is subject, but that excepted, without reproach in his actions.')

One must bear these meanings in mind when considering the third line, which seems to me exceedingly beautiful. It' fits precisely into the apparent story; the traveller lets drop a comment on the general appearance of the place before going on to the incident which made it worth mentioning; and yet in wondering what the occasional riches of a wold can be like you find yourself (after reviewing deserts and oases, Spain's vineyards and barren rock, and Horace Walpole's remark about Blenheim, that it was like the castle of an ogre who had desolated the surrounding country) in the knightly fairyland of Spenser, among vast and inhuman wildernesses, and the portentous luxury of enchanted castles. As a statement about Herbert's own life, it sums up with a pathetic generosity his long and painful process of judgment on the matter, with an air of saying as much as reticence allowed ; reading the poem is thus made into a social situation calling for some tact and delicacy; his readers are agog to see how much they can deduce from what he lets drop.

I am including this example in the third type, because its methods, allegory and the overt pun, are the most conscious of all devices to produce ambiguity, and because the mood of the apparent is so effectively in

26 Critics are accustomed to say that the angel was his wife ; this seems to me a secondary meaning, but it ought to be listed.

contrast with the mood of the intended story. But this particular pair is one so normal in ordinary life, the situation itself is so 'strong,' that the various meanings are felt as a coherent unit, and the verse might reasonably have been placed in the fourth type. Notice, in particular, the reverse reaction, as the chemists say, obtained by taking Passion in the liturgical sense, so that the verse is now about the life of renunciation instead of about the life of ambition. It is still true that the place was mountainous (full of difficulties), wasted (both in the sense of 'having wasted its own strength' and 'laid waste by monsters'), that it was sometimes rewarding, and that going to it lost him all his gold (no longer in the allegorical sense) except for one good Angel. That there should be a hint of this alternative reading gives an impression, not of doubt, but of pathos and humility, in that after all his struggles he is only leading one of the possible good lives. I do not know whether this device is best produced or appreciated by holding it in the focus of consciousness ; it is too deeply rooted an ambiguity to be fitted into the third type.

We have thus practically arrived already at the fourth type, in which the ambiguity is less conscious, because more completely accepted, or fitted into a larger unit. I shall close this chapter with some remarks about the transition.

It is in the third type of ambiguity, when the two notions of the ambiguity are most sharply and consciously detached from one another, that one finds oneself forced to question its value. It must seem trivial to use one word with an effort when there is time enough to say two more simply; even if time is short it seems only twice as useful, in a sort of numerical way. And the value of the general variety of ambiguity of the third type is no more obvious; you remember how Proust, at the end of that great novel, having convinced the reader with the full sophistication of his genius that he is going to produce an apocalypse, brings out with pathetic faith, as a fact of absolute value, that sometimes when you are living in one place you are reminded of living in another place, and this, since you are now apparently living in two places, means that you are outside time, in the only state of beatitude he can imagine. In any one place (atmosphere, mental climate) life is intolerable; in any two it is an ecstasy. Is it the number two, one is forced to speculate, which is of this encouraging character ? Is to live in 1 places necessarily more valuable than to live in tz ? When there is no connection between the two halves of an ornamental comparison, the two meanings of a pun, except that they are both relevant to the matter in hand, one would think that the comparison can only give trivial pleasure and the pun not be particularly funny. Thus we return to the notion I put at the beginning of the chapter, that in so far as an ambiguity is valuable, it cannot be purely of the third type.

I consider that I have shown by examples how an ambiguity can approach the third-type definition, which is perhaps rather like a limit, and yet remain valuable; I might say, too, that there is a sort of formal satisfaction in such a connection between two ideas, even which they are merely both relevant and need not have been particularly connected. For one is accustomed to such devices being used to connect things in an illuminating way, and there is at least the pleasure of expectation in seeing the shell even when it is empty. Much of the cult of ' style ' is a sort of practising in this way. But, indeed, one can say more boldly that Proust's belief, as a matter of novel-writing, is very convincing; that the pleasure in style is continually to be explained by just such a releasing and knotted duality, where those who have been wedded in the argument are bedded together in the phrase ; that one must assume that n+i is more valuable than n for any but the most evasively mystical theory of value. Those who adopt this view are taking refuge in the mysterious idea of an organism, of all things working together for good ; we shall expect, from this point of view, to find more important cases of ambiguity when several ambiguities are put together, when they belong to my next chapter, and represent a state of mind.

IV

An ambiguity of the fourth type occurs when two or more meanings of a statement do not agree among themselves, but combine to make clear a more complicated state of mind in the author. Evidently this is a vague enough definition which would cover much of the third type, and almost everything in the types which follow; I shall only consider here its difference from the third type.

One is conscious of the most important aspect of a thing, not the most complicated; the subsidiary complexities, once they have been understood, merely leave an impression in the mind that they were to such-and-such an effect and they are within reach if you wish to examine them. I put into the third type cases where one was intended to be mainly conscious of a verbal subtlety; in the fourth type the subtlety may be as great, the pun as distinct, the mixture of modes of judgment as puzzling, but they are not in the main focus of consciousness because the stress of the situation absorbs them, and they are felt to be natural under the circumstances. Of course, different readers apply their consciousness in different ways, and a line which taken alone would be of the third type may become of the fourth type in its setting; but the distinction, I think, is usually clear.

I never saw that you did painting need.

And therefore to your fair no painting set,

I found (or thought I found) you did exceed.

The barren tender of a Poet's debt :

And therefore have I slept in your report,

That you yourself being extant well might show.

How far a modern quill doth come too short,

Speaking of worth, what worth in you doth grow.

This silence for my sin you did impute,

Which shall be most my glory being dumb,

For I impair not beauty being mute,

When others would give life, and bring a tomb.

There lives more life in one of your fair eyes,

Than both your Poets can in praise devise.

(Sonnets Ixxxiii.)

Shakespeare is the writer upon whom ingenuity has most often been misapplied ; and if his syntax appears ambiguous, it may be because the Elizabethan rules of punctuation trusted to the reader's intelligence and were more interested in rhetoric than in grammar. One must pause before shadowing with irony this noble compound of eulogy and apology. But one may notice its position in the sequence (Shakespeare seems to have been taunted for his inferiority, and is being abandoned for the rival poet) ; the mixture of extraordinary claims and bitter humility with which it is surrounded; and that the two adjacent Sonnets say: 'Thou truly fair wert truly sympathised In true plain words by' thy truth-telling friend,' and 'You to your beauteous blessings add a curse. Being fond on praise, which makes your praises worse.' It is not true that the feeling must be simple because it is deep; irony is similar to this kind of lyrical self-abandonment, or they relieve similar situations; by the energy with which such an adoration springs forward one can measure the objections which it is overriding, by the sharpness of what is treated as an ecstasy one may guess that it would otherwise have been pain.

Line 2, then, goes both with line i and line 3. Taking it with line I, Shakespeare was only concerned for the young man's best interests : ' I did not praise you in verse because I could not see that your reputation could be set any higher by my praise.' Even for this, the primary, meaning there are two implications ; either never ' until you told me to praise you,' an order accepted humbly but with some echo of being fond on praise, or never 'until I found you out ' ; ' At one time I had not yet discovered that your cheeks needed rouge, and your character whitewash'; 'When I first loved you I did not realise that you had this simple and touching desire for flattery.'

The first line may also stand alone, as an introduction, with these meanings, so that line 2 goes with line 3 ; for this version one would put a comma after therefore', ' And so, when no painting had been set to your fairness ' (paint to your cheeks or to a portrait, praise to your beauty or to your virtue, apology to your vices), ' I found that you exceeded ' (in beauty, in virtue, or in wildness of life) ; ' And so, judging you simply, not foreseeing the defences I should have to build up against feeling harshly of you, it came to me as a shock to know you as you are.' The first version is much the stronger, both because I found is parallel to I never saw and because exceed wants to pass over the comma and take the fourth line as its object; indeed, I put the second version down less from conviction than because I cannot now read the line without thinking of it[27].

For the various senses of line 4 we must first consider the meaning of tender which is almost wholly limited into its legal sense by debt ; ' offered payment of what is due.' This is coloured, however, by 'tender regard' (I Henry IV., v. iv. 49); also the meaning 'person who looks after' may be fancied in the background. Taking the word as object of exceed, we have : ' I found you were worth more than the normal compliments due from a poet hired to write eulogies of you,' ' I found that you exceeded what I could express of beauty in verse,' ' I found your tenderness towards me exceeded the barren tenderness I owed you as your tame poet,' ' I found that you were more to me than the person who would see to it that the hired poet wrote adequate praises.' These assume the poets debt is a debt owed by a poet. Taking it as owed to a poet, we have : ' I found that you gave me more than you need have done,' ' I found that you treated me more as a friend than as a hired poet,' and ' I found you felt for me more generously than I felt for you, when I merely looked after my job and wrote eulogies of you.' I am being verbose here to show the complexity of the material ; the resultant ideas from all these permutations are only two: 'You were treating me as a friend, not as a poet,' and ' You were more than I could describe.' Here tender is the object of exceed, but, stressing the comma after exceed, tender may be either, as a mere echo, a second object

27 One must, I think, either say that the comma after exceed is a misprint or that it is intended to attract attention to the word and suggest that W. H. exceeded in more ways than one. But the complexity of feeling is still there if it is a misprint.

of found, 'I found only the barren tender,' 'You did not treat me more as a friend than as a poet, so I stopped writing' (or thought I found is now a more generous doubt), or may be a comment in apposition to the whole first three lines : ' This was merely my business ; I thought your beauty and virtue so excessive because that was the proper thing ; to be expected from a poet in love ; to be expected from a professional poet trying to win favour at Court.' Most people in reading the line only recognise the meaning, 'You were more than I could describe,' but they are made to feel also in the word barren a more dreary and more petty way of feeling about the matter, they know there is some bitterness which this way of generosity has submerged.

Therefore in line 5 seems parallel to therefore in line 2, so that it could refer to found or saw. Or with a larger rhythm, the fifth line refers to the whole first quatrain and starts a new one. Alternatively, therefore may refer forward to line 6 : 'for this reason ... in order that.' Report is either what people in general say or what Shakespeare says, or what Shakespeare writes, about him ; thus I have slept in your report means either 'I have stopped writing about you,' or ' I have stopped contradicting rumours about you,' or ' I have bolstered up my faith in you by accepting the public's good opinion of you. ' That means ' in order that ' (you might show well), ' the fact that ' (I have slept, which your being extant well shows), or 'for fear that' (your being extant might show how far a modern quill comes too short). Extant means visible, or successful and respected, or the subject of scandal. How and what follow show and speaking respectively, but for variations of grammar which leave them detached they may be regarded as introducing an exclamation and a question. The last line of the quatrain evidently refers backwards as its main meaning: 'A modern quill comes too short when attempting to write of as much worth as is in you ' ; it can also refer forwards, but in trying to regard it in this way one is bothered by a modern usage which could take it alone; 'and, talking of worth, are you worth anything, now, frankly ? ' This is not an Elizabethan idiom and was certainly not intended, but its coarseness is hard to keep out of one's mind, because the version which takes line 8 with line 9 is very similar to it : 'I was describing all the worth I could find in you without the effort of flattery, and this amounted to the silences of which you, being fond on praise, have been complaining.' If you like you may call this version ridiculous, and hurriedly place a colon at the end of the second quatrain; but please notice that the line may still be read as: 'I was afraid that a modern quill might come short of a high standard of worth in describing all the worth that it can find in you.'

This seems to me a good illustration of the difference between the third type of ambiguity and the fourth. Shakespeare was exquisitely conscious of such subsidiary uses of grammar and the jokes that could be made out of bad stops (if example is needed, consider Quince in Act v., scene i. of the Dream); but I do not think he was conscious of these alternatives (certainly I do not think that the reader who is apprehending the result as poetry should be conscious of these alternatives) in a clear-cut way as if they were jokes. They do not need to be separated out to give their curious and harrowing overtone to the quatrain; and once they have been separated out, they can only be connected with the mood of the poem if you hold clearly in mind the third quatrain which is their reconciliation. I might first paraphrase the second. ' I have not written or talked about you fully, as the absence, or the particular kind, or the excess of scandal about you shows; either because your reality was already a sufficient expression of your beauty and virtue, or in order that you might still make a good show in the eyes of the world, as you might not if I were to describe you as I now know you, or for fear that the contrast between you and your description might be bad for the literary reputation of the Elizabethans, or for fear that the contrast between what this time and previous times could produce in the way of beauty and virtue might be bad for the Elizabethan reputation as a whole.'

It would be possible to regard line 12, which clinches the third quatrain, as an antithesis: 'When others would bring life, I in fact bring a tomb.' This might be Shakespeare's tomb; 'I do not flatter you but I bring you the devotion of a lifetime.' More probably it is W. H.'s; 'I do not attempt to flatter you at the moment; I bring you the sad and reserved gift of an eternal praise.' We may extract from this some such meaning as : 'I do not describe your beauty or your faithlessness, but my love for you.' However, there are two other ways of taking the syntax which destroy this antithesis: 'When others would bring life, I, if I wrote about you, would bring a tomb,' and 'When others would try to write about you, would try to give you life, and thereby bring you a tomb ' ; for both these the tomb must imply some action which would impair beauty. The normal meaning is given by Sonnet xvii. :

Who will believe my verse in time to come

If it were fild with your most high deserts ?

Though yet Heaven knowes it is but as a tombe

Which hides your life, and shows not halfe your parts.

This first use of the word has no doubt that it is eulogy; the Sonnet is glowing and dancing with his certitude. But when the metaphor is repeated, this time without being explained, it has grown dark with an incipient double meaning; ' I should fail you, now that you have behaved so badly to me, if I tried to express you in poetry; I should give you myself, and draw from my readers, a cold and limited judgment, praise you without sincerity, or blame you without thinking of the living man.' (' Simply the thing I am Shall make me live'; Shakespeare continually draws on a generosity of this kind. It is not 'tout comprendre,' in his view, it is merely to feel how a man comes to be a working system, which necessarily excites a degree of sympathy.)[28]

A literary conundrum is tedious, and these meanings are only worth detaching in so far as they are dissolved into the single mood of the poem. Many people would say that they cannot all be dissolved, that an evidently delicate and slender Sonnet ought not to take so much explaining, whatever its wealth of reference and feeling, that Shakespeare, if all this is true, wrote without properly clarifying his mind. One might protest via the epithet 'natural,' which has stuck to Shakespeare through so many literary fashions ; that he had a wide rather than a sharp focus to his mind ; that he snatched ideas almost at random from its balanced but multitudinous activity; that this is likely to be more so rather than less in his personal poetry ; and that in short (as Macaulay said in a very different connection) the reader must take such grammar as he can get and be thankful. One might apologise by saying that people have always read obscure meanings

---

28 The tomb is formal praise such as would be written on a tombstone, whereas the real merits of the man are closely connected with his faults, which can't be mentioned in a formal style of praise. I am not now sure that the ambiguities of word and syntax add a great deal to what is clear enough as the theme. That the feeling behind the poem is ambivalent would not, I suppose, be denied.

Maybe I should explain that I put another complete analysis 'of a Shakespeare Sonnet (xvi.) in the second chapter (p. 54) on the ground that it has much less background of rudeness to W. H, than this later one.

into Shakespeare, secure in the feeling, ' If it means less, why is it so beautiful ? ' and that this analysis can only be offered as another mode of approaching so mysterious a totality, another glance at the effects of language. Or it may boldly be said that the composition of feeling, which never falls apart among these ambiguities (it is, on any interpretation, pained, bitter, tender and admiring; Shakespeare is being abandoned by W. H., and stiffly apologising for not having been servile to him), rises and is clinched plainly in the final couplet; we are reminded of the references to the roving eye glancing round for new conquests; Shakespeare includes the whole ambiguity in his enthusiasm; the worth and sin, the beauty and painting, are all delightful to him, and too subtle to be grasped.

A Valediction, of weeping weeps for two reasons, which may not at first sight seem very different; because their love when they are together, which they must lose, is so valuable, and because they are 'nothing' when they are apart. There is none of the 'Platonic pretence Donne keeps up elsewhere, that their love is independent of being together ; he can find no satisfaction in his hopelessness but to make as much of the actual situation of parting as possible ; and the language of the poem is shot through with a suspicion which for once he is too delicate or too preoccupied to state unambiguously, that when he is gone she will be unfaithful to him. Those critics who say the poem is sincere, by the way, and therefore must have been written to poor Anne, know not what they do.

Let me powre forth

My teares before thy face, whil'st I stay here,

For thy face coins them, and thy stampe they beare,

And by this Mintage they are something worth.

For thus they be Pregnant of thee.

Fruits of much grief they are, emblemes of more.

When a tear falls, that thou falst which it bore.

So thou and I are nothing then, when on a divers shore[29]

'Allow me this foolishness; let me cry thoroughly while I can yet see your

29 The three verses of the poem are quoted separately.and examined

face, because my tears will be worth nothing, may, in fact, not flow at all, when once I have lost sight of you.' ' Let me plunge, at this dramatic moment, into my despair, so that by its completeness I may be freed from it, and my tears may be coined into something more valuable.'

The metaphor of coining is suitable at first sight only ' because your worth and your beauty are both royal,' but other deductions from it can be made. In that his tears will not reflect her face unless he stays here it may imply ' because it is only when I am seeing your beauty that it matters so much to me ; I only shed valuable tears about you when I am at your side.' There is a shift of the metaphor in this, brought out by line 3, from the tears as molten metal which must be stamped with her value to the tears themselves as the completed coin because,' then, 'you are so fruitful of unhappiness ' ; and in either case, far in the background, in so far as she is not really such a queenly figure, 'because you are public, mercenary, and illegal[30].'

In each of the three verses of the poem the two short middle lines are separated only by commas from the lines before and after them; Professor Grierson on the two occasions that he has corrected this has accurately chosen the more important meaning, and unnecessarily cut off the less. In this verse, for thus they be may be a note to give the reasons why the tears are something worth, or may be parallel to for thy face coins them, so that it leads on to the rest of the stanza. Going backwards, ' Let me pour out at once the tears I shall have to shed sooner or later, because if I do it now they will reflect your face and become valuable because they contain you ' ; going forwards, ' Let me pour forth my tears before your face, because they are epitomes of you in this way, that they are born in sorrow, and are signs that there is more sorrow to come after.' Pregnant because they are like her, in that they fall and are emblems of grief, and give true information about her (as in 'a pregnant sentence'), because they are round and large like a pregnancy, because they hold a reflection of her inside them, and because, if they are wept in her presence, they will carry her more completely with them, and so do him more good. It is this last obscure sense, that he is getting rid of her, or satisfying her, or getting his feeling for her into a more manageable form, by a storm of emotion in her presence, that gives energy to the metaphor of pregnancy, and logic to the second alternative — the idea that she normally causes sorrow.

---

30 I doubt now whether Donne would have minded leaving these conceivable implications lying about, even if the poem were in fa(S written for his wife. He might well have feared that she would throw 'up her reckless marriage.

Corresponding to these alternative meanings of for thus, that thou means 'the fact that you' and 'that particular case of you.' ' The tears are emblems of more grief by foreshowing, when they fall, that you will fall who were the cause of them ' (if which refers to a person it should be the subject of bore), or, beginning a new sentence at when, 'when a tear falls, that reflection of you which it carries in it falls too ' (which now refers to a thing and so can be the object).

And corresponding to these again, there is a slight variation in the meaning of so, according as the last line stands alone or follows on from the one before. 'These tears by falling show that you will fall who were the cause of them. And therefore, because you will fall when we are separated, when we are separated we shall both become nothing,' or 'When the reflection of you is detached from my eye and put on a separate tear it falls ; in the same way we shall ourselves fall and be nothing when we are separated by water.'

All these versions imply that their love was bound to lead to unhappiness; the word fall expects unfaithfulness, as well as negation, from her absence ; then means both'when we are separated,' as if they were much the same thing; and nothing (never name her, child, if she be nought, advised Mrs. Quickly) says the same of himself also, when a channel divides them deeper, but no less salt, than their pool of tears.

On a round ball,

A workeman that hath copies by, can lay

An Europe, Afrique, and an Asia,

And quickly make that, which was nothing, All,

So doth each teare Which thee doth weare,

A globe, yea world by that impression grow

Till my tears mixed with thine do overflow

This world, by waters sent from thee, my heaven dissolved so.

The first four lines are defining the new theme, and their grammar is straightforward. Then the teare may be active or passive, like the workman or like the ball on the face of it, it is like the ball, but so doth may treat it as like the workman. For doth may be a separate verb as well as an auxiliary of grow, while, in any case, grow may either mean 'turn into' or 'grow larger.' The globe and the world may be either the teare or thee. The other meanings of impression (p. 166) would be possible here. Either, then, ' In the same way each tear that wears you, who are a whole world yourself or at least the copy of one, grows into a world, 'or ' And so does every tear that wears you ; each tear, that is, grows, so as to include everything, or to produce a great deal more water'; it is only this second, vaguer meaning which gives a precise meaning to till, and suggests, instead of a mere heap of world-tears, such a flood as descended upon the wickedness of the antediluvians.

Which thee doth weare suggests by the order of the words a more normal meaning, that her tears are jewels and she is wearing them; this is inverted by the grammar, so as to leave an impression that she is uniquely and unnaturally under the control of her tears, or even has no existence independent of them.

The last line but one may stand alone, with overflow meaning simply 'flow excessively,' or 'flow into each other,' so as to spoil each other's shape, and then the last line, by itself, means, ' In the same way, the necessities of this, the real, world have dissolved my precarious heaven by means of, or into, tears.' Or making world the object of overflow, it may mean, according as this world is the real world or the tear, either ' we produce more and more tears till we drown the world altogether, and can no longer see things like ordinary people,' or 'my tear reflects you and so is a world till one of your tears falls on it, spoils its shape and leaves only a splash'; it is she who has made the world which is his heaven, and she who destroys it. The rest of the line then says, ' in the same way my happiness in our love has been dissolved, by this meeting with your tears,' making heaven the subject of the intransitive verb dissolved. But my heaven may be in apposition to thee dissolved may be a participle; and so may be not 'in the same way' but 'so completely, so terribly'; it is not merely his memory and idea and understanding of her, it is the actual woman herself, as she was when they were happy together, who is dissolving under his eyes into the tears of this separation ; dissolved, it has already happened. The waters are falling that were above the firmament; the heaven and crystalline spheres, which were she, are broken; she is no longer the person he made her, and will soon be made into a different person by another lover. These broken pieces of grammar which may be fitted together in so many ways are lost phrases jerked out whilst sobbing, and in the reading, 'so my heaven dissolved this world,' which though far in the background is developed in the following stanza, there is a final echo of unexplained reproach.

O more than Moone,
Draw not up seas to drowne me in thy spheare,
Weep me not dead, in thine armes, but forbeare
To teach the sea, what it may doe too soone,
Let not the winde
Example finde,
To do me more harm, then it purpose th,
Since thou and I sigh one another's breath,
Whoe'er sighs most, is cruellest, and hasts the other's death.

She is Mooney with a unifying reference to the first line of the poem, because she draws up the tides of weeping both from him and from herself, a power not necessarily to her credit, but at any rate deserving adoration; the moon, too, is female, inconstant, chaste because though bright cold, and has armes in which the new moon holds the old one. Some of the lyrical release in the line may be explained as because it is deifying her, and remembering the Sidney tradition, even now after so many faults in her have been implied, and are still being implied. She is more than Moone because she is more valuable to him than anything in the real world to which he is being recalled ; because she has just been called either the earth or the heavens and they are larger than the moon; as controlling tides more important or more dangerous than those of the sea; as making the world more hushed and glamorous than does moonlight; as being more inconstant, or as being more constant, than the moon; as being able to draw tides right up to her own sphere ; as shining by her own light; and as being more powerful because closer.

In thy spheare may be taken with me 'don't drown me, whether with my tears or your own, now that I am still fairly happy and up in your sphere beside you ; don't trouble to draw up the seas so high, or be so cruel as to draw up the seas so high, that they drown me now, since to-morrow they will drown me easily, when I am thrown down into the world'; may be taken alone, as ' your sphere of influence,' your sort of drowning, ' don't you go drowning me ; I have the whole sea to drown me when I take ship to-morrow'; or may be taken with Moone 'you, far in your sphere, high and safe from sorrow in your permanence and your power to change, do not drown a poor mortal who is not in your sphere to whom these things matter more deeply.'

The machinery of interpretation is becoming too cumbrous here, in that I cannot see how these meanings come to convey tenderness rather than the passion of grief which has preceded them, how they come to mark a particular change of tone, a return towards control over the situation, which makes them seem more vividly words actually spoken. It is a question of the proportions in which these meanings are accepted, and their interactions ; it is not surprising that the effect should be what it is, but I do not know that it could have been foreseen. Perhaps it is enough to say that the request, in its fantastic way, is more practical, and draws its point from the immediate situation.

Weep me not dead means: 'do not make me cry myself to death; do not kill me with the sight of your tears; do not cry for me as for a man already dead, when, in fact, I am in your arms,' and, with a different sort of feeling, 'do not exert your power over the sea so as to make it drown me by sympathetic magic; there is a conscious neatness in the ingenuity of the phrasing, perhaps because the same idea is being repeated, which brings out the change of tone in this verse. What it may doe too soone since the middle lines may as usual go forwards or backwards, may be said of the sea or of the winde if of the winde the earlier syntax may be 'forbeare in order to teach the sea to be calm ' ; this gives point to the crude logic, which has in any case a sort of lyrical ease, of ' do not weep, but forbeare to weep. The sea is going to separate them; it may be going to drown him; and so it may drown him, for all he cares, when he has lost her. The winde purposeth to blow him from her, and if she doesn't stop sighing she will teach it to do more harm and upset the boat. One may notice the contrast between the danger and discomfort of this prospect, also the playfulness or brutality of the request, and the cooing assured seductive murmur of the sound doe too soone; by this time he is trying to soothe her.

I always think of this poem as written before Donne's first voyage with Essex, which he said he undertook to escape from 'the queasy pain of loving and being loved'; the fancy is trivial but brings out the change of tone in the last two lines. In itself the notion is a beautiful one, 'our sympathy is so perfect that any expression of sorrow will give more pain to the other party than relief to its owner, so we ought to be trying to cheer each other up,' but to say this is to abandon the honest luxuriance of sorrow with which they have been enlivening their parting, to try to forget feeling in a bright, argumentative, hearty quaintness (the good characters in Dickens make the orphan girl smile through her tears in this way); the language itself has become flattened and explanatory: so that he almost seems to be feeling for his hat. But perhaps I am libelling this masterpiece ; all one can say is that its passion exhausts itself; it achieves at the end the sense of reality he was looking for, and some calm of mind[31].

This poem is ambiguous because his feelings were painfully mixed, and because he felt that at such a time it would be ungenerous to spread them out clearly in his mind; to express sorrow at the obvious fact of parting gave an adequate relief to his disturbance, and the variety of irrelevant, incompatible ways of feeling about the affair that were lying about in his mind were able so to modify, enrich, leave their mark upon this plain lyrical relief as to make it something more memorable.

I hope I have now made clear what the fourth type is like when it really gets under way; I shall add some much slighter cases which seemed illuminating.

> What if this present were the world's last night ?
>
> Mark in my heart, O Soule, where thou dost dwell.
>
> The picture of Christ crucified, and tell
>
> Whether that countenance can thee affright,
>
> Teares in his eyes quench the amasing light.
>
> Blood fills his frownes, which from his pierc'd head fell.

---

31 It seems at least possible that they may choose to do each other less harm than they could he seems therefore to have cured himself of some of the earlier suspicions. I still think that all this analysis is correct.

And can that tongue adjudge thee unto hell,

Which prayed forgivenesse for his foes fierce spight ?

No, no; but as in my idolatrie

I said to all my profane mistresses,

Beauty, of pitty, foulness onely is

A sign of rigour; so I say to thee.

To wicked spirits are horrid shapes assign'd.

This beauteous form assures a piteous mind.

(Donne, Holy Sonnets xiii.)

In one's first reading of the first line, the dramatic idea is of Donne pausing in the very act of sin, stricken and swaddled by a black unexpected terror: suppose the end of the world came now ? The preacher proceeds to comfort us after this shock has secured our attention. But looking back, and taking for granted the end's general impression of security, the first line no longer conflicts with it. ' Why, this may be the last night, but God is loving. What if it were ? ' In the first notion one must collect one's mind to answer the Lord suddenly, and Donne, in fact, shuffles up an old sophistry from Plato, belonging to the lyrical tradition he rather despised, and here even more absurdly flattering to the person addressed and doubtful as to its general truth than on the previous occasions he has found it handy. Is a man in the last stages of torture so beautiful, even if blood hides his frowns ? Never mind about that, he is pleased, we have carried it off all right; the great thing on these occasions is to have a ready tongue[32].

A similar doubt as to emphasis runs through the Apparition and almost leaves one in doubt between two moods ; an amused pert and fanciful contempt, written up with more elaboration than it deserves, so as to give him an air of being detached from her and interested in literature; and the scream of agony and hatred by which this is blown aside.

32 I leave in my expression of distaste for the poem, but it nas little to do with the ambiguity in question.

Then thy sicke taper will begin to winke

is a bumping line full of guttering and oddity, but brisk with a sense of power over her. This has reached a certain intensity by the time we get to

thinke

Thou call'st for more.

And in false sleepe will from thee shrinke.

with the stresses in the line almost equal ; Crashaw uses a similar rhythm to convey a chanting and mystical certainty.

And in her first ranks make thee room,

Donne's version conveys: 'I am speaking quite seriously, with conviction, but with personal indifference, to this toad.'

And then poore Aspen wretch neglected thou

All in a cold quicksilver sweat wilt lye

A veryer ghost than I.

The stress is on neglected', 'you would be glad to get me back now if you could.' But

since my love is

I had rather thou shouldst painfully repent

Than by my threatenings rest still innocent.

What a placid epigrammatical way of stopping, we are to think, and how trivial the affair is made by this final admission that she is innocent ! he would not say that if he cared for her any more.

But after all, the first line calls her a murderess, and the way most people read the poem makes the poet more seriously involved ;

Then thy sicke taper will begin to winke

('As does mine now; you have left me ill and exhausted,' and the last part of the line gabbles with fury.)

And in false sleepe will from thee shrinke

('As you, if I can credit it, as you have shrunk from me with a disgust which I shall yet turn to terror.')

And then poore Aspen wretch, neglected thou

(It is almost a childish cry; 'I find it intolerable to be so neglected.')

A veryer ghost than I

('Than I am now,' not 'than I shall be then'); that his love is spent has become pathetically unbelievable ;

I had rather thou shouldst painfully repent

'(As I am repenting, in agony'); and innocent has become a scream of jealous hatred at her hypocrisy, of an impotent desire to give any pain he can find.

The meaning of an English sentence is largely decided by the accent, and yet one learns in conversation to put the accent in several places at once ; it may be possible to read the poem so as to combine these two ways of underlining it. But these last two cases are curious in that the alternative versions seem particularly hard to unite into a single vocal effect. You may be intended, while reading a line one way, to be conscious that it could be read in another; so that if it is to be read aloud it must be read twice; or you may be intended to read it in some way different from the colloquial speech-movement so as to imply both ways at once. Different styles of reading poetry aloud use these methods in different proportions, but perhaps these two last examples from Donne respectively demand the two methods in isolation. The following example from Hopkins shows the first case being forcibly included in the second.

Margaret, are you grieving

Over Goldengrove unleafing ?

Leaves, like the things of man, you

With your fresh thoughts care for, can you ?

Ah, as the heart grows older

It will come to such sights colder

By and by, nor spare a sigh
Though world of wanwood leafmeal lie ;
And yet you will weep and know why.
Now no matter, child, the name.
Sorrow's springs are the same.
Nor mouth had, no, nor mind express'd.
What heart heard of, ghost guess'd :
It is the blight man was born for,
It is Margaret you mourn for.

Will weep may mean : ' insist upon weeping, now or later,' or 'shall weep in the future.' Know in either case may follow will like weep 'you insist upon knowing, or you shall know,' or may mean : ' you already know why you weep, why you shall weep, or why you insist upon weeping,' or thirdly, may be imperative, ' listen and I shall tell you why you weep, or shall weep, or shall insist upon weeping, or insist upon weeping already.' Mr. Richards, from whom I copy this (Practical Criticism p. 83), considers that the ambiguity of will is removed by the accent which Hopkins placed upon it; it seems to me rather that it is intensified. Certainly, with the accent on weep and will can only be the auxiliary verb, and with the accent on will its main meaning is 'insist upon.' But the future meaning also can be imposed upon this latter way of reading the line if it is the tense which is being stressed, if it insists on the contrast between the two sorts of weeping, or, including know with weepy between the two sorts of knowledge. Now it is useful that the tense should be stressed at this crucial point, because it is these two contrasts and their unity which make the point of the poem.

It seems difficult to enjoy the accent on are which the poet has inserted; I take it to mean: 'Sorrow's springs, always the same, independent of our attitude to them and our degree of consciousness of them, exist,' permanently and as it were absolutely.

The two sorts of knowledge, intuitive and intellectual, form ambiguities again in the next couplet; this may help to show they are really there in the line about will. Mouth and mind may belong to Margaret or somebody else ; what heart heard of goes both forwards and backwards; and ghost, which in its grammatical position means both the profundities of the unconsciousness and the essentially conscious spirit, brings to mind both immortality and a dolorous haunting of the grave. 'Nobody else's mouth had told her, nobody else's mind had hinted to her, about the fact of mortality, which yet her own imagination had already invented, which her own spirit could foresee.' 'Her mouth had never mentioned death; she had never stated the idea to herself so as to be conscious of it; but death, since it was a part of her body, since it was natural to her organs, was known at sight as a portent by the obscure depths of her mind.' My point is not so much that these two are mixed up as that the poet has shown precisely by insisting that they were the same, that he knew they were distinguishable.

A much fainter example of the sort of ambiguity in question is supplied by one of Pope's great passages about dowagers, which possesses in a high degree the sensuous beauty that is supposed to have been beyond his powers :

As hags hold sabbats, not for joy but spite.

So these their merry miserable night ;

So round and round the ghosts of beauty glide,

And haunt the places where their honour died.

See how the world its veterans rewards.

A youth of frolics, an old age of cards.

Fair to no purpose, artful to no end,

Young without lovers, old without a friend ;

A fop her passion, and her prize a sot;

Alive ridiculous, and dead forgot.

(Essay on Women, Ep, 11. 245.)

An impression of febrile and uncontrollable hatred is given to the terrible climax of this passage by the flat, indifferent little words, fop, sot, which, if they are to fill out the line, to give it weight, as its meaning and position demand, cannot be dropped with the analytical contempt with which they appear on the printed page; must be hurled at a person conceived as in front of you, to whom you know they are intolerable. Never was the couplet more of a rocking-horse if each line is considered separately; but all the inertia of this flatness is needed to give him strength; never was the couplet given more delicacy of modulation than is here imposed by the mere weight and passion of the sense conveyed. What is so compelling about the passage is the combination within it of two sharply distinguished states of mind ; the finicking precision with which the subject-matter is handled; the pity, bitterness, and terror with which the subject-matter must be conceived.

In the third type, two such different moods would both be included, laid side by side, made relevant as if by a generalisation ; in the fourth type they react with one another to produce something different from either, and here the reaction is an explosion.

I spoke of ' sensuous beauty,' thinking of the second couplet quoted, to which a more verbal analysis can be applied. The dowagers may glide round and round because they are still dancing, or merely, since they are fixed to the card-table in the next couplet, because they go on and on, in rotation, to the same drawing-rooms. In this way they may at once be conceived as still dancing and yet as at an age when, in those days, they would have had to stop. They are first spoken of as ghosts of their dead beauty, and will then be thought of as still dancing, since such ghosts would still be echoing what they had done in life ; but in the next line they are ghosts of their dead honour, haunting a place only, and that not so much the ballroom as the card-table. (These places, however, are practically the same, so there is an independent ambiguity as to whether they lost their honour by cheating at the card-table or making assignations in the ballroom.) The result of this is that the two lines cannot run as simply as they claim to do ; ghosts means something different for each line, and you must in each case translate the line back into something said about old ladies, or the transitions will not work. But one is accustomed to this process of immediate translation only in verses of flowery and graceful ornament, so that it is a parody of the manner in which a gallant compliment would have been paid

to the ladies, and has a ghastly air of being romantic and charming.

I must not deny that the ghost of a dead beauty might haunt the place where her honour had died, as she might haunt the place where anything that interested her had happened. If you read it like this, there is a touch of that form of wit which caps a sentence with the unexpected word ; ' you might think she was most distressed at losing her beauty; but no, it's her conscience that troubles the old woman, and well it may.' However, I find it very difficult to read the lines like this; they stand too completely parallel and apart, and read like one blow after another.

Or you may say from this parallelism that beauty and honour are treated as necessary corollaries of one another, the two names being used in the two lines only for variety (as if from the old dictionary interest in synonyms); so that ghosts of beauty are the same as ghosts of honour, and had necessarily to lose their properties in the same place. Beauty and honour, then, are identical, so that we find ourselves, to our justifiable surprise, in Spenser's fairy-story world of sensuous idealism. There is a sort of subterranean resonance in the verses from the clash of this association ; with a feverish anger, like the screws of a liner racing above water. Pope finds himself indeed hag-ridden by these poor creatures; they excite in him feelings irrelevantly powerful, of waste, of unavoidable futility, which no bullying of its object can satisfy.

Wordsworth was not an ambiguous poet; the cult of simplicity moved its complexity back into the subconscious, poisoned only the sources of thought, in the high bogs of the mountains, and stated as simply as possible the fundamental disorders of the mind. But he sometimes uses what may be called philosophical ambiguities when he is not sure how far this process can tolerably be pushed. In the third type we found minor uses of ambiguity for jokes; the fourth type includes its electoral applications. Thus the degree of pantheism implied by some of Wordsworth's most famous passages depends very much on the taste of the reader, who can impose grammar without difficulty to uphold his own views.

For I have learnt

To look on nature, not as in the hour

Of thoughtless youth; but hearing oftentimes

The still, sad music of humanity,

Nor harsh nor grating, though of ample power

To chasten and subdue. And I have felt

A presence that disturbs me with the joy
Of elevated thoughts ; a sense sublime
Of something far more deeply interfused,
Whose dwelling is the light of setting suns,
And the round ocean and the living air.
And the blue sky, and in the mind of man :
A motion and a spirit, that impels
All thinking things, all objects of all thought,
And rolls through all things.

(Tintern Abbey.)

It is not sufficient to say that these lines convey with great beauty the mood intended; Wordsworth seems to have believed in his own doctrines and wanted his readers to know what they were. It is reasonable, then, to try to extract from this passage definite opinions on the relations of God, man, and nature, and on the means by which such relations can be known.

There are several points of difficulty in the grammar when one tries to do this. It is not certain what is more deeply interfused than what. It is not certain whether the music of humanity is the same as the presence', they are separated by the word and a full stop. We may notice, too, that the word in seems to distinguish, though but faintly, the mind of man from the light, the ocean, the air and the sky this tends to separate the motion and the spirit form from the presence and the something', but they may, again, all be identical with the music. Wordsworth may then have felt a something far more deeply interfused than the presence that disturbed him; we seem here to have God revealing himself in particular to the mystic, but being in a more fundamental sense immanent in his whole creation[33]. Or the something may be in apposition to the presence (the sense equal to the joy;); so that both are ' more ' deeply interfused than the music of humanity, but apparently in the same way. This version

33 Or one may stand for paganism (the local deity of a bit of lake scenery, say) and the other for the more puzzling doctrine (far more deeply interfused) on which Wordsworth would support it.

only conceives God as immanent in his creation, and as affecting the poet in the same way as he affects everything else; or as only imagined by the poet as immanent in creation, in the same way as the music of humanity is imagined as immanent. Thus, the first version is Christian, the second in part pantheistic, in part agnostic. Again, the something may possibly dwell only in the natural objects mentioned, ending at sky the motion and the spirit are then not thought of at all as interfused into nature, like the something they are things active in the mind of man. At the same time they are similar to the something; thus Wordsworth either feels them or feels a sense of them. With this reading the voice would rise in some triumph at the words mind of man; man has a spirit immanent in nature in the same way as is the spirit of God, and is decently independent from him. Or the something may also dwell in the mind of man, and have the motion and the spirit in apposition to it; under this less fortunate arrangement a God who is himself nature subjects us at once to determinism and predestination.

So far I have been examining grammatical ambiguities, but the last three lines also admit of doubt, as to the purpose of what seems an irrelevant distinction. Whether man or some form of God is subject here, he distinguishes between things which are objects or subjects of thought, these he impels; and things which are neither objects nor subjects of thought, through these he merely rolls. (I am not sure what is the logical status of the

things not the objects of thought about which Wordsworth is thinking here ; after all, he is not thinking very hard, so it may be all right.) The only advantage I can see in this distinction is that it makes the spirit at once intelligent and without intelligence; at once God and nature ; allows us to think of him as the second, without compromising his position as the first[34].

---

34 Critics have disliked the meanness and fussiness of this passage, and I wish that I had something wise and reconciling to say after all these years. Miss M. C. Bradbrook wrote that the norms after the full stop are all obviously in apposition, because the theme is the transcendence of the subject-object relationship. It is, I suppose, almost certain that Wordsworth meant the grammar to nm on like this. But surely, even if clauses are in apposition, they must be supposed to be somehow distinguishable, or why do they have to be said one after another ? One could give a much more sympathetic account of the philosophical background of Wordsworth, and no doubt if I. A. Richards Coleridge on Imagination had been already published I would have written differently. But the more seriously one takes the doctrine, it seems to me, the more this expression of it seems loose rhetoric.

And, indeed, whether or not a great deal of wisdom is enshrined in these lines, lines just as muddled, superficially speaking, may convey a mode of using their antinomies, and so act as creeds. The reason why one grudges Wordsworth this source of strength is that he talks as if he owned a creed by which his half statements might be reconciled, whereas, in so far as his creed was definite, he found these half-statements necessary to keep it at bay. There is something rather shuffling about this attempt to be uplifting yet non-denominational, to put across as much pantheism as would not shock his readers. I must protest again that I enjoy the lines very much, and find, like everybody else, that I remember them; probably it was necessary for Wordsworth to shuffle, if he was to maintain his peculiar poetical attitude. And, of course, by considering the example in this chapter, I have shown that I regard the shuffling as a deeply rooted necessity, not conscious at the time when it was achieved. But, perhaps, this last example may show how these methods can be used to convict a poet of holding muddled opinions rather than to praise the complexity of the order of his mind. To the more fruitful sorts of muddle I must proceed in my next chapter.

V

An ambiguity of the fifth type occurs when the author is discovering his idea in the act of writing, or not holding it all in his mind at once, so that, for instance, there is a simile which applies to nothing exactly, but lies half-way between two things when the author is moving from one to the other[35]. Shakespeare continually does it :

Our Natures do pursue

Like Rats that ravyn downe their proper Bane

A thirsty evil, and when we drinke we die.

(Measure for Measure i. ii.)

Evidently the first idea was that lust itself was the poison ; but the word proper introduced as meaning 'suitable for rats,' but also having an irrelevant suggestion of 'right and natural,' and more exact memory of those (nowadays phosphorus) poisons which are designed to prevent rats from dying in the wainscot, produced the grander and less usual image, in which the eating of the poison corresponds to the Fall of Man, and it is drinking water, a healthful and natural human function, which it is intolerable to avoid, and which brings death. By reflection, then, proper bane becomes ambiguous, since it is now water as well as poison.

Ford is fond of the same device, possibly from imitation :

Giovanni. Now, now, work serious thoughts on baneful plots;

Be all a man, my soul ; let not the curse

---

35 This is at least ambiguous in the sense that the reader is puzzled by it; but the definition does not assert that there would be alternative reactions to the passage when completely grasped, or that the effect necessarily marks a complex nut integral state of mind in the author. I could claim, I think, that the confusion technique needs separate treatment, and it is put late in the book as showing much logical disorder.

Of old prescription rend from me the gall

Of courage, which enrolls a glorious death:

If I must totter like a well-grown oak, ;

Some undershrubs shall in my weighty fall

Be crushed to splits; with me they all shall perish.

('Tis Pity' V. iii. end.)

Gall is first used as 'spirit to resent insults,' the bitterness which is a proper part of the complete man. (We have galls: Othello, IV. iii. 93.) By the next line galls have suggested oak-galls (the reactions of an oak to irritations), and the idea of proper retaliation is transferred to its power of falling on people, whether they are guilty of wrongs against it or not. But in between these two definite meanings the curious word enrolled seems a blurring of the focus ; he is thinking of his situation itself, rather than either metaphor, and keeping up the metaphorical language rather as a matter of form.

A glorious death may be enrolled on the scroll of fame, so that the word could stand by itself ; or, looking backwards, one may gain strength for a glorious death by being bathed in, sustained by, a spurt of bitterness, so that gall has been rent (now with the opposite consequences) from its boundaries in the orderly mind, by being rolled in, or round about by, gall or, looking backwards, it may be the oak itself which rolls down, both to death and upon its victims. You may say this is fanciful, and he was only looking for a word containing the letter 'r' which kept up the style, but in that case it is these associations which explain how that particular word came into his mind. I do not claim that one should admire this turgid piece of writing merely because it is explicable.[36]

This form of ambiguity was fairly common in the nineteenth century; there is an example in the Shelley Skylark about which Mr. Eliot started a discussion. I am afraid more points were brought out than I remembered.

The pale purple even

Melts around thy flight ;

Like a star of Heaven,

36 A trivial example from Dryden omitted.

In the broad daylight
Thou art unseen, but yet I hear thy shrill delight –
Keen as are the arrows
Of that silver sphere
Whose intense lamp narrows
In the white dawn clear.
Until we hardly see, we feel that it is there.
All the earth and air
With thy voice is loud.
As, when night is bare.
From one lonely cloud
The moon rains out her beams, and Heaven is overflowed.

Mr. Eliot claimed not to know what the sphere was; one would take it to be the star as a matter of grammar. But the simile goes tumbling on into the next verse ; the bad rhyme clear – there – air may serve as evidence of this. The sphere is then the moon ; both moon and star are made fainter by the morning. There are two syntaxes for the verse: 'your delight is as keen as are the arrows of the sphere,' and 'though the arrows of the sphere are so keen (as to carry a long way), yet even when we are so far off as to 6e out of shot we still feel the presence of its beauty.' The last line may mean : ' We feel that your delight is there for a long time, until, in fact, we can hardly see you,' or 'whose lamp narrows till we can scarcely be said to see it, till we can more truly be said to feel that it is there.' All these are well enough suited to the first simile, in which the lark out of sight but still audible as a series of silvery notes, is compared to a star, which is spherical and whose light is silvery, out of sight in the daytime but still faintly sounding the music of the spheres. The arrows are then the bird's separate piercing notes and the star's separate twinkles, whether conceived as searching the poet's heart or as rays drawn on an optical diagram. In this simile we jump from daylight to dawn to illustrate as process what was before considered as achieved ; as the lark becomes smaller, then invisible, as the star grows smaller, then goes out, so the poet is rapt into an ecstasy which purifies itself into nescience, and faints from the full clarity of beauty. In the new simile, therefore, the time of completion is not day but night and it is for this reason that the lark begins the first verse quoted by going up in the evening, (Mr. Eliot complained that Shelley had mixed up two of these periods; it seems less of an accident when you notice that he names all four.) The bird is now like the moony either when just emerging from a cloud so that there is still a process though the sphere is now becoming more, not less, visible ; or when behind a cloud so that though it leaves the earth in darkness (as the bird is out of sight) it can be recognised by its light on the edges of other clouds as something which is overflowing (being too great an ecstasy for) their upper surfaces. For this version bare means dark,' and is contrasted with overflowed. Or, taking bare as ' empty,' though the moon itself is not in sight the whole sky is glimmering with moonlight which has touched the invisible mists of the upper air ; the moon has overflowed its limitations, and takes effect mysteriously, like the poet, like the principle of beauty, even on those who cannot directly apprehend it. For the bird is a symbol of the poet; so is the cloud the poet and the moon behind it his inspiration ; one of the basic assumptions of Shelley's poetry is that the poet stands in a very peculiar relation to ordinary people; he is an outcast and an unacknowledged legislator, and probably dying as well.

Of the meanings of arrows those involving a series of shots may seem less suited to the moon than to the star, as the moon does not twinkle ; but they are helped out by the word rains, by the idea of the moon suddenly emerging from the cloud to give a brief overwhelming illumination, and by the idea of Diana as the huntress. This last, indeed, may be regarded as the point of the new simile; her beauty is too keen and too unattainable, so as to destroy the humanity which apprehends it. And the transition from one simile to another itself produces an effect which must be conceived in terms of this belief ; one is forced to swoon, in an ecstatic and febrile way, not rooted upon the earth, from flower to flower, and to find all exquisite and all unsatisfying. 'How exciting all these beautiful things are ! here is another beautiful thing, which all my readers will think beautiful.'

The poem was probably written under the influence of the Keats Nightingale Ode, and for it to seem straightforward one must hold the main tenets of the Romantics. The skylark, I should have said before, is a very precise symbol of Shelley's view of the poet; it rises higher and higher, straight upwards, alone, always singing, always in effort, till becoming exhausted somewhere out of sight of the normal world it tumbles back in silence, and resumes a humble, isolated, and invisible existence somewhere in the middle of a field. But on to this view of the bird as a symbol of the spiritual life, which thinks of it as struggling and dying, is grafted another view which thinks of it as outside human limitations; as free from pain and the satiety which follows mortal ecstasy, and indeed, like the nightingale, as immortal. From this point of view the rising of the skylark is an apotheosis of nature and unquestioned animal satisfaction (as at once more and less than human, and so in either case free from our inadequacy), which is shown either rising to Heaven, because nature is superior to the complex and disorderly human processes which apprehend it (the natural is divine), or near it that is, rising to the stars or the moon and so to one of the crystalline spheres (the natural is perfect). Its song, therefore, becomes something absolute, fundamental, outside time, and underlying all terrestrial harmony. (Surely it was unappreciative of Mr. Eliot to call that extremely packed line 'shabby.')

Such beauty is never wholly known by human limitations, and as it grows more it must grow less visible. The sphere narrowing in daylight, then, is like the narrowing of the poet's iris or eyelids, in the ecstasy of Romantic appreciation, like that fainting of the temporal mind in the very act of recognition of the eternal and absolute beauty, which Shelley has elsewhere compared to the fading of a red-hot coal. 'Now more than ever were it rich to die'; 'thou wert not born for death, immortal Bird.' The lark is dawning into its day of joy just as the day of common earth is fading, and, to complete the reversal, the mind which has darkened, ' forlorn,' from the vision of natural beauty, may then dawn again into an intellectual apprehension of it. The grammatical disorder of the verses is a very proper expression of the doctrine they convey.[37]

Another point Mr. Eliot has raised against Shelley is susceptible of the same sort of explanation :

The world's great age begins anew,

The golden years return.

---

37 There seems no need to claim any ' grammatical disorder ' ; the sphere can be taken simply as the Morning Star. However, the example shows, I think, that the' technique of tumbling from one simile to another is likely to produce this type of ambiguity.

The earth doth like a snake renew

Her winter weeds outworn ;

Heaven smiles, and faiths and empires gleam

Like wrecks of a dissolving dream.

(Hellas)

Mr. Eliot said that snakes do not renew their cast skins, and do not cast them at the end of winter; and that a seventeenth century poet would have known his own mind on such points. Weeds means both 'garments,' especially those of widows, like the old and dried snake-skin, and 'vegetation,' especially such coarse and hardy plants as would last through the winter, till something more interesting came up in the spring. Evidently it is the second half of the pun which justifies the bad natural history; the Snake is relevant as gleaming as a classical symbol of fertility and earth-spirits, and as effecting a transition to widows[38]. I agree very heartily with what Mr. Eliot was saying at the time, and certainly these meanings are not so much united as hurried on top of each other, but it is, after all, a pun, almost a conceit. At the same time the thought seems excessively confused; this muddle of ideas clogging an apparently simple lyrical flow may be explained, but is not therefore justified; and it is evident that a hearty appetite for this and the following type of ambiguity would apologise for, would be able to extract pleasure from, very bad poetry indeed.

In so far as an ambiguity sustains intricacy, delicacy, or compression of thought, or is an opportunism devoted to saying quickly what the reader already understands, it is to be respected (in so far, one is tempted to say, as the same thing could not have been said so effectively without it, but, of course, in poetry the same thing could never have been said in any other way). It is not to be respected in so far as it is due to weakness or thinness of thought, obscures the matter in hand unnecessarily (without furthering such incidental purposes as we have considered) or, when the interest of the passage is not focussed upon it, so that it is merely an opportunism in the handling of material, if the reader will not easily understand the

38 The snake gleams in its new skin ; the old skin looks dull, and yet that seems to be compared to the faiths and empires (since they are wrecked). Or are they seen as burgeoning in the new spring while known to be temporary ? This, I think, is the interesting part of the confusion.

ideas which are being shuffled, and will be given a general impression of incoherence. The ideas in the Shelley Skylark (if my interpretation is right) were obvious to Shelley, were, in fact, the main cause of the excitement he was translating into lyrical terms, but if they were to appear at all they required to be explained and kept in his conscious mind. The question is here one of focus; and it is in modem poetry, when the range of ideas is great and the difficulty of holding the right ones in the mind becomes acute, that we discover examples of the most advanced types of this series, and that ambiguity is most misused.

One might regard as an extreme case of the transitional simile that 'self-inwoven' simile employed by Shelley, when not being able to think of a comparison fast enough he compares the thing to a vaguer or more abstract notion of itself, or joints out that it is its own nature, or that it sustains itself by supporting itself.

With mighty whirl the multitudinous orb

Grinds the bright brook into an azure mist

Of elemental subtlety, like light.

(Prometheus Unbound iv.)

The matter of the vision is so highly informed, so ethereal, that it can be compared to the Pure Form of which it is the matter.

Like to a child o'erwearied with sweet toil . . .

The spirit of the earth is laid asleep,

And you can see its little lips are moving

Within the changing light of their own smiles

Like one who talks of what he loves in dream.

(Ibid,)

The last comparison is merely a statement of what he is.

So came a chariot in the silent storm

Of its own rushing splendour. . . .

me sweetest flowers delayed not long . .

Me, not the phantom of that early

Form Which moved upon its motion, . . .

(The Triumph of Life,)

The Form is its own justification ; it sustains itself, like God, by the fact that it exists. Poetry which idolises its object naturally gives it the attributes of deity, but to do it in this way is to destroy the simile, or make it incapable of its more serious functions. Shelley seldom perceived profitable relations between two things, he was too helplessly excited by one thing at a time, and that one thing was often a mere notion not conceived in action or in an environment. But, even with so limited an instrument as the short-circuited comparison, he could do great things.

And others mournfully within the gloom

Of their own shadow walked, and called it death.

(Ibid)

My definition also gave ' not holding all the idea in one's mind at once' as a criterion. Any fortunate muddle would be included in this, such as occurs in the course of digesting one's material. Shakespeare's Ariachne (Troilus v. 4), for Arachne and Ariadne, those two employers of thread, is a shining example.

I saw fair Chloris walk alone

When feathered rain came softly down,

Like Jove descending from his tower

To court her in a silver shower.

(Anon., Oxford Book)

Chloris herself was evidently not in the tower of Danae, because she was out walking in the snow; besides, the possession of towers is a sufficiently male characteristic; and there must be something from which the snow is to fall. Altogether the tower may just as well be given to Jupiter and this makes sure that the reader will remember the right story. There is a delicious air of being every day and humble in that the shower is not gold but silver after all, no one could deny it was as good as that. In so far as the snow is feathered another myth is brought into the situation, and she is Leda as well as Danae. All this is what the Freudians would call transference; and being a psychological rather than a linguistic matter, one is not surprised to find that, in a more deeply-rooted, less gay and conscious form, it was of great use to the poets of the nineteenth century.

The following odd and delicious example treats what I believe was a conscious pun as if it was an accident, and leaves piled up in a 'sweet disorder' what the conceit would have found it hard to enclose.

The Rose was sick and smiling died ;

And, being to be sanctified,

About the bed there sighing stood

The sweet and flowery sisterhood :

Some hung the head, while some did bring,

To wash her, water from the spring.

(Herrick, The Funeral Rites of the Rose)

The comparison with maids of honour is not being worked out in any detail, and they fetch water from the spring merely because it is a fresh and pastoral sort of place to fetch it from. But surely, in the background, the spring is also the springtime; they fetch from the spring, which is the morning of the year, the dews of morning; they wash her with the dew of their own, freshness, in that they are the flowers of spring; are, indeed, therefore (so brief is life) already dead before her, and experienced in the matter; and if the water is dew they wash her with their tears.

The thing is not worked out coherently because Herrick is almost afraid to touch creatures of such delicacy; only in the most tangent, the most unselfseeking, medium will they allow him to observe them; and only in these hinted conceits, floating, treasured and uncertain, can he satisfy himself as if by capture what is so painfully unattained.

Swinburne uses this wider variety of the fifth type for a sort of mutual comparison which (unlike the mutual comparisons in the third type) is not interested in either of the things compared; he merely uses the connections between them to present the reader with a wide group of his stock associations. The mixed epithets of two metaphors are combined as if in a single statement not intended to be analysed but to convey a ' mood ' :

Night falls like fire ; the heavy lights run low,

And as they drop, my blood and body so

Shake as the flame shakes, full of days and hours

That sleep not neither weep they as they go.

Ah yet would God this flesh of mine might be

Where air might wash and long leaves cover me.

Where tides of grass break into foam of flowers,

Or where the wind's feet shine along the sea.

(Laus Veneris.)

' The coming of night is like the falling of fire ' ; the sun becomes a red, glowing, exhausted ball on the horizon, day is going out, the fire, as it burns down, glows hotter, and all the heat natural to the firmament is being brought down (as if the ceiling was weighing on me) and crushed into my temples. But when the flame shakes our attention is transferred to a lamp ; it is lighting up time; the indoor Victorian-furnished Venusberg becomes hotter, stuffier and more enclosed, more irritating to sick headache and nervous exhaustion, and the gas-jet will have to be popping from now on. Or the flame may be a symbolical candle ; it gutters in its socket which, low in its last struggles, it scorches, and rises and falls in popping and jerking disorder, like the throbbing and swooning of headache, and casts leaping and threatening shadows on the walls. Full because it has ended the time it is capable of, and because in its shaking it seems to be measuring seconds, magnified by a sickbed fixity of attention into hours; not sleeping or weeping of the poet's insomnia and emotional exhaustion, because of its contrast with, and indifference to, his weeping and the approaching sleep of his death, and because in the story, this mood is fixed into an eternity outside the human order, in which tears are pointless, and the peace even of death unattainable[39].

39 The first verse belongs to this chapter all right, but it is the second verse which gives a straightforward example of Swinburne's of mutual comparison.

In the next verse, air might wash like water, and leaves might cover like the sea or the grave; then by direct implication grass and flowers are compared to waves; then the wind's feet shining along the sea whitening the tops of the waves, is compared, the other way round, to grass and flowers and, as a fainter implication, to grassy mounds with white tombstones on them. The sea, in Swinburne, shares with earth the position of great sweet mother, is cleaner, fresher, and more definitely dead. Nor must one forget the feet, so beautiful upon the mountains, of him that brings good tidings of the Lord.

When Swinburne comes off he is a very full and direct writer; it is no use saying these verses show interest in mere sound, or pattern of verbal cadence. It would be true, perhaps, to say that he feels it more important to keep up his effect of texture than that, in any particular case, the meanings, the chord of associations, should come through. But in a literary, not perhaps in a stage, sense, this hypnotised detachment is a powerful dramatic weapon. The various impulses when Tannhauser is before the Pope in *Laus Veneris;* his wish for help, and hopelessness, his impression that something kind was said (as if he knew it ought to have been, or heard later of the miracle, or simply the reader knew that the miracle occurred) and yet that 'perhaps it can't have been said, I know I heard him tell me not to seek mercy till the rod budded,' and the further hopelessness justifying the dramatic accident (which embodies it) of his never hearing of the miracle, 'what if it does bud, it would be a stranger thing for me to change my nature (even though, if I could change it, I might yet obtain mercy)' — ^all this, by the very disorder of memory implied in the technique itself, is passed as a single unit into the reader's mind.

There is a kind of working model (from its bare simplicity and efficiency) of this technique in the famous chorus of Atalanta in Calydon :

> Time with a gift of tears
>
> Grief with a glass that ran.

This pretends to be two elements of a list with their attributes muddled, but is in fact a mutual comparison between the water clock and the tear bottle.

People are oddly determined to regard Swinburne as an exponent of Pure Sound with no intellectual content. As a matter of technique, his work is full of such dissolved and contrasted reminiscences as need to be understood; as a matter of content, his sensibility was of the intellectual sort which proceeds from a process of analysis. His view of the relations between sadism and normal sexuality, for instance, whether or not it is particularly realistic, is always being laid before the reader (by contrasted adjectives and so forth) as if he understood it himself by very intellectual means. So careful have his readers been not to analyse him that I might almost quote

> All shrines that were vestal are flameless.
>
> But flame has not fallen from this
>
> (Dolores,)

as an example of a subdued pun ; though in itself it is a perfectly solid metaphysical conceit.

I believe, then, that later English poetry is full of subdued conceits and ambiguities, in the sense that a reader has to know what the pun which establishes a connection would have been if it had been made, or has to be accustomed to conceits in poetry, so that, though a conceit has not actually been worked out, he can feel it as fundamental material, as the justification of an apparent disorder. In the same way such poetry will often imply a direction of thought, or connection of ideas, by a transition from one sleeping metaphor to another. Later nineteenth-century poetry carried this delicacy to such a degree that it can reasonably be called decadent, because its effects depended on a tradition that its example was destroying.

But, of course, even if it be true that the nineteenth-century technique was arrived at, historically speaking, in this way, so that it is in part the metaphysical tradition dug up when rotten, still that is no reason to think there is no other way to read it. One might deduce from what I have said that Shelley could only be enjoyed by persons intimately acquainted with the past history of English poetry, which is far from true. And, for other reasons, it would be hard to make the statement good, to map out such effects, or to show that they were important when you had done so; I can only hope that my last examples will have made il plausible. It may, however, be illuminating to approach the matter historically, and show how the later metaphysical poets came to take the conceit for granted, came to blur its sharp edge till they were writing something like nineteenth-century poetry.

There is a sort of mental association which gains strength because it has been crystallised into a pun elsewhere; thus Marvell's phrase about Charles the First

He nothing common did or mean

Upon that memorable scene ;

But with his keener eye

The Axes edge did try

(Horatian Ode)

seems to be remembering the Latin acies 'eyesight' and 'sharp edge.' Crashaw's phrase about the Virgin and Child,

She 'gainst those Mother-Diamonds tryes

The points of her young Eagles' Eyes,

may rely on the same association, but at a further remove as the word axe is not used. You may say that the resulting poetry is not dependent on this word ; whether on the reader's knowledge of it or on his belief that it existed. But even so it may be dependent on his making the association which had produced the word, and which the word itself had then strengthened.

A similar situation occurs within the English language when a word has contracted in meaning since its use in a poem :

[a successful lover is happy]

But soon those Flames do lose their light

Like Meteors of a Summer's night.

Nor can they to that region

To make impression upon Time

(Marvell, The Unfortunate Lover)

Impression meant an assault, a meteor and the noxious effects of the night air, as well as the modern meaning which gives 'to make time take some notice of them and be respectful.' Thus the word originally read as a pun, whereas it now seems a subdued conceit, in itself flat and puzzling, but to which we have been made accustomed by a later fashion. This is rather interesting, because it suggests that it was a change in the language itself, a limitation of its ambiguity, which produced the later fashion; poetry came automatically to be read in a different way. It is less fanciful to point out that, after the word had altered, the poetry, though read in a different way, remained substantially the same; you have now in some degree to invent the subsidiary meanings of impression for yourself, but this is not impossible. 'Time is a Platonic idea lodged in the highest heaven, whereas meteors can only reach the lowest of the spheres; in the same way the fires of love, though they are not denied to be heavenly, yet cannot snatch from the more exalted heavens any of that immortality, any of those powers over fate, which by being heavenly they seem to claim, and which since they are heavenly many people claim for them.' Climb and the context force the meaning 'assault' on to impression; what is lost is the wit, and the courage which could be witty when it was saying such a thing, of the meaning 'meteor.' (It was always, of course, in the background; it would not make sensible grammar.)

It is tactful, when making an obscure reference, to arrange that the verse shall be intelligible even when the reference is not understood. Thus many conceits are prepared to be treated as subdued conceits, though in themselves they have been fully worked out. Consider as the simplest kind of example

The brotherless Heliades

Melt in such amber tears as these.

(Marvell, The Nymph Complaining.)

If you have forgotten, as I had myself, who their brother was, and look it up, the poetry will scarcely seem more beautiful ; such of the myth as is wanted is implied. It is for reasons of this sort that poetry has so much equilibrium, and is so much less dependent on notes than one would suppose. But something has happened after you have looked up the Heliades; the couplet has been justified. Marvell has claimed to make a classical reference and it has turned out to be all right; this is of importance, because it was* only because you had faith in Marvell's classical references that you felt as you did, that this mode of admiring nature seemed witty, sensitive, and cultured. If you had expected, or if you had discovered, that Marvell had made the myth up, the couplet might still be admired but the situation would be different; for instance, you would want the brother to be more relevant to the matter in hand. Lyly continually invents fabulous beasts for his own stylistic convenience, and this gives him a childish, didactic, and exquisite air, merely because one gives his statements an unusual degree of disbelief. This is, of course, legitimate, and in an odd way courtly, because it treats the reader as a patron of learning without threatening to assume things that he ought already to know. More definitely it is a colloquial or prose device, intended to convey its point at a single reading; all that is relevant about the beast must be said at once, because from the nature of the case it is impossible to find out any more about him. But from a writer whose references are to be relied upon one expects a use of them which will repay study; one expects a simile with reserves of meaning and at any rate the first type of ambiguity.

I have suggested here a few ways in which conceits might become vaguer than they need be; I shall now consider a couple of vague conceits by Marvell, which fall below the standard of precision that the metaphysical set themselves, and try to explain how in effect they are so powerful. One difficulty about this is that I must assume they are peculiar, whereas the history of English literature has been such that to a modern reader they will seem more normal than the style from which they diverge. I must try, then, to show also that lines which approach towards the nineteenth-century 'simplicity' are, in fact, more complicated than the normal metaphysical conceit, though their machinery and its strangeness are less insistent, and though they move as though something simple was being conveyed. Marvell is a convenient person for this plan; as a metaphysical poet who had not forgotten the Elizabethans he is sensitive to a variety of influences, and one can watch the conceit at the beginning of its decay. From the elegy for the death of the Lord Hastings:

The gods themselves cannot their Joy conceal

But draw their Veils, and their pure Beams reveal:

Only they drooping Hymeneus note,

Who for sad Purple tears his Saffron coat,

And trails his Torches through the Starry Hall

Reversed, at his Darling's Funeral.

An extreme, a direct, an unambiguous beauty wells up in these lines; the young man has died on the eve of his wedding; night has fallen. But apparently this is conveyed by comparing some funeral custom with something, possibly astronomical, seen in the sky; the mood of comparison is caught before it has worked itself out; instead of the sharp conceit at which Marvell excelled we ^ are given the elements which were to have been fitted together, but flowing out, and associated only loosely into an impression of sorrow ; something, perhaps something very apocalyptic and reassuring, seems to have been meant, but we cannot think of it; and a veil of tenderness is cast over the dissatisfaction of the mind.

This impression, that it is a Romantic Revival piece of writing, is given by regarding Marvell as one of the metaphysical poets, and then failing to find their particular sort of precision in his methods. But if you regard him as a disciple of Milton, there is nothing indefinite about the image; saffron is merely the colour of a marriage, purple of a mourning, robe; you are meant to see Hymen an allegorical figure, performing a simple symbolical movement, with all his stock epithets about him. It is no longer necessary to interpret the first two lines, so that they mean 'night fell and the stars came out,' the gods appear as in a story about them. No doubt Milton or Spenser would have intended the epithets to be beautiful for a variety of reasons, but such extra meanings would be grouped loosely about an allegory to be imagined in its own terms. It would not be necessary (as it is if you expect a conceit) to wonder whether Hymen has any official standing as a star, or whether he has become identified with the sun for a moment, or how this could be justified; or to remember that Hymen, even when unshadowed by the darkness of death, was beloved of Vesper, and impatient for the nightfall. But then again, it is easier to feel that Marvell is describing a sunset watched alone in the open than the picture of a concretely imagined mythological figure; one feels, for some reason, that he has observed intensely what he has described only in this cursory and unplausible way, as yellow deepening into purple, above a horizon of black with red isolated flares. The lines have thus a curious and impalpable form of ambiguity, in that they are drawing their energy from three different literary conventions at once.

Only they drooping Hymeneus note,

Who for sad Purple tears his Saffron coat,

Whatever he may be, he is considered in the puzzled and fanciful way that one reserves for foreigners and the natural world ; we must watch patiently the strange pageant of his actions and force upon them any interpretation we can imagine. Only means fromthe point of view of the allegory 'the only thing that prevents their perfect rejoicing,' but as a matter of nature-study only the brightest stars, and they not fully unveiled, can be there to note the solemn celebrations of the nightfall. The next line contrasts its active and vehement verb tears with the 'tears' of weeping, then pronounced the same way (and the coats of a sunset are indeed formed of its tears), with the inactive sorrow of drooping, with the ritual dignity of the mythological figure, and with the slow far-reaching gradations of the colour-changes in the sky. If the saffron and purple noted by stars are indeed a sunset (we are not told so) there is another quieting influence from the sun's regularity; from a sense that he may safely reverse his operations (dangerous and extravagant as this seems with most sorts of torch) in that his setting is only the reversal of his rising; from a sense of order and perhaps of resurrection in the death of the hero.

And trails his Torches through the Starry Hall

Reversed, at his Darling's Funeral.

Hymen may always trail his torches, and on this occasion be trailing them, with no less pomp, reversed, or he may at this painful news be trailing them in the sense of dragging them behind him, extinguished, not being used for anything, in his dejection. In either case the torches have to be interpreted as something to do with the sunset, something up in the sky, like the Stars they must be the same sort of thing, or why is it considered so striking hat they should be different? Torches when reversed are liable to go out, smoke more, and are wasting themselves; never are they less like the perfect or eternal stars \ and in that we find them up in the sky we are set free ourselves, with a sense of being made at home in the sunset, to float out into the upper air[40].

I feel some word of apology or explanation is needed as to why such a particularly fantastic analysis has to be given to lines of so direct a beauty, which seem so little tortured by the intellect, which are, in fact, early

40 have cut nearly two pages of this analysis for the second edition, and indeed feel that the whole chapter is verbose. It seemed hard to make the points convincingly without evocative writing.

work, and rather carelessly phrased. The fact is that it is precisely in such cases, when there is an elaborate and definite technique at the back of the author's mind but he is allowing it to fall into the disorders that come most easily, when he has various metaphors in mind which he means to fit in somewhere, when the effect is something rather unintelligible but with a strong poetical colour, when the mere act of wondering what it means allows it to sink, in an uncensored form, into the reader's mind ; it is in just such cases that fifth type ambiguities are most likely to be found, and are most necessary as explanations.

A very similar effect, again produced by blurring of the metaphysical conceit, comes in Marvell's poem on Eyes and Tears,[41] The funeral elegy on Lord Hastings moved rather in the world of Milton, whereas these verses are excellent and complete conceits, so that here there is no doubt the crux must be approached from the metaphysical point of view.

How wisely Nature did decree.

With the same Eyes to weep and see.

That, having viewed the object vain,

They might be ready to complain.

And, since the Self-deluding Sight

In a false Angle takes each hight ;

These tears that better measure all,

Like wat'ry Lines and Plummets fall.

It is among such verses as these that one finds :

What in the World most fair appears,

Yea, even Laughter, turns to tears ;

And all the Jewels which we prize

Melt in these pendants of the Eyes.

---

41 I now think this example a mare's nest —not in the details of the analysis but in the aim that they amount to a blurring of the conceit. It is true, however, I think, that the lines would easily be enjoyed by nineteenth century critics who thought conceits merely quaint.

The chief impression here surely is not one of neatness but of parts which do not quite fit; and since the verse 'carries it off' with such an air of gracious achievement the mind is blurred and puzzled into a reflective state, and the second couplet sticks in your head. Jewels, of course, are relevant as typical of what appears most fair, as a symbol of the lust of the eye ; but why or how does a jewel melt in a pendant ? The definiteness of the good conceit suddenly escapes us, and yet it is no use saying this produces a failure of the poetry; on the contrary, the lines seem suddenly to have become more serious and generalised.

Melt in may mean 'become of no account beside tears,' or 'are made of no account by tears,' or ' dissolve so that they themselves become tears,' or 'are dissolved by tears so that the value which was before genuinely their own has now been assumed by and resides in tears.' Tears from this become valuable in two ways, as containing the value of the jewels (as belonging to the world of Cleopatra and hectic luxury) and as being one of those regal solvents that are competent to melt jewels (as belonging to the world of alchemists and magical power). Which suggests, more than 'that' would have done, that not all jewels are prized, and only those prized melt in, or into, pendants. Eked out by this, but independent of it, there is a hint that it is eyes, especially a loved woman's, which shine and are jewels; why should eyes have pendants, the word prompts us, if they are not jewels themselves ? Eyes, too, are brightest when suffused with tears, not for shedding, and of happiness; which yet, says the poet, shall fall from their jewel, turn to sorrow, and become pendants.

Thus we have now some more meanings for melt in : ' in the melting of these eyes into pendants, which is a type of the world, we see the melting of all jewels into nothing, or into lesser stones of no value,' or 'in that these pendants coming from her eyes melt, and turn out to be water, we see that there is no permanence in those values that flow from the sources of the world,' or ' her eyes have been jewels with tenderness, but such jewels melt; those tears shall fall and be despair.'

One may notice that the jewels which we prize ate thought of as Eyes all the more easily because, in so far as they are not, the most striking thing about the reflection made by the couplet is that it is so untrue :

that jewel in your ear . . .

Shall last to be a precious stone

When all your world of beauty's gone,

(Carew.)

represents not only the facts of the case but the more usual sentiment about it; and the couplet makes up for its lack of 'wit' by the claim on one's attention contained in its paradox. But the reason that this claim seems justified, as the verse enters the mind, is that it contains the materials of many true conceits, pruned into the background, left vague, and packed closely.

The reader may plausibly object that a poet cannot expect his readers to make up conceits for themselves, and that, in so far as I have been doing so, I have been making up a poem of my own. But no, I have been quoting; what is assumed by these verses is a wide acquaintance on the part of the reader with the conceits about tears that have been already made.

Perhaps I have overstated the extent to which the conceit has been dissolved in this example; the one about Lord Hastings, I think, has no simple point, but in this case the idea of a jewel melting in a tear is sharp enough, and carries most of the feeling But, even if you regard it as a simple and successful conceit, there are yet crowding at its back this multitude of associations, taking effect in a different way, which are almost as strong as the main conceit and threaten to displace it in the mind or at least make it unnecessary. Marvell was admired both by his own generation and by the nineteenth century; one may suspect that this was because they were able to read him in different ways. If the previous example from Marvell was the bursting of the conceit, this is its final and most mellow ripeness, the skin thin and stretched to its utmost, the seeds ready to be scattered. By the last example of this chapter it has been made into jam.

The distinction may not seem clear between this example and, say, Donne's Valediction in the last chapter. There one had to accept a conceit, by itself, and the ambiguities to be discovered were deductions from it : whether as to the reasons which must justify its implied comparison or as to the judgments which would make those reasons valid. I put the result into the fourth type because of the ordered complexity of judgment which the ambiguities of language implied. Here the conceit is only one element in the total effect, may indeed be no more than the facade which holds the effect together and makes it seem sensible ; the ambiguities are to be discovered in more or less disorderly reactions between the words themselves, and I put it in the fifth type as a case of fruitful disorder.

Vaughan, as the disciple of Herbert, and precursor of Wordsworth, naturally employs in the same way this swoon of the conceit into the suggestion of conceits, into this vaguer and apparently more direct, more evocative and sensory, mode of appeal. The following pantheistic quatrain, for instance, is at once wit and nature-study.

So hills and valleys into singing break ;

And though poor stones have neither speech nor tongue,

While active winds and streams both run and speak.

Yet stones are deep in admiration.

(The Birds)

Compared to speech and speak, tongue and run seem to be paired by sound rather than by sense ; till one remembers that tongues may be said to 'run on,' and that streams possess tongues in that they are running. It is by means of this verbal echo, which last century critics would have regarded as a matter of Pure Sound, that the subdued puns are passed into the mind. And deep may refer to speechlessness, or to the solid rock which is below the soil; so that the verse as a whole is in part a conceit upon stones in general, as one of the four elements; in part, as evocative description, it gives the boulders on the hillside, struck dumb in the presence of the precipices, and in a giant silence waiting for their fall.

Put on, put on, your best array.

Let the joyed road make holiday.

And flowers, that into hills do stray,

Or secret groves, keep the highway.

(Palm Sunday).

Parts of nature outcast and retiring, like Jesus, are to be brought, on this day of his showing forth, into the agora. On the one hand, there is a conceit on the connection of nature and the cult hero; on the other, an implied description hf the solitary wanderings of the Christ.

Such was the bright world, on the first seventh day,

Before man brought forth sin, or sin decay. . . .

When Heaven above them shined like molten glass

While all the planets did unclouded pass.

And springs, like dissolved pearls, their streams did pour,

Never marred with floods, nor angered with a shower.

(Ascension Day.)

On the one hand, it is an exalted and sensuous view of nature; on 'the other, perhaps from the gong-like note as of Dryden, which suggests a more precise and striking interpretation, we feel that before the Fall the whole mechanism of the spheres, a celestial orrery, a circumterrestrial clockwork, was seen going in the sky. It is these evanescent but powerful suggestions (like Milton's two-handed engine) that Vaughan gains by blurring the outline and losing the energy of the conceit of Herbert.

And in this last example the fading multiplicity of the conceit seems to have glimmered out of sight altogether. ' He trembles,' said Johnson, 'upon the brink of meaning.'

God's saints are shining lights; who stays

Here long must pass

O'er dark hills, swift streams, and steep ways

As smooth as glass.

('Joy of my life while left me here.')

One does not separate them in one's mind; it is the Romantic Movement's technique ; dark hair, tidal water, landscape at dusk, are dissolved in your mind, as often in dreams, into an apparently direct sensory image which cannot be attached to any of the senses.

VI

An ambiguity of the sixth type occurs when a statement says nothing, by tautology, by contradiction, or by irrelevant statements; so that the reader is forced to invent statements of his own and they are liable to conflict with one another. We have already considered examples of contradiction which yield a direct meaning, and these might be regarded as in this class ; thus Moses, according to the Authorised Version, told the Lord that 'Thou hast not delivered thy people at all,' but ' Delivering thou hast not delivered ' is the more direct translation in the margin. ' Though you said you would,' or 'No doubt from your point of view you are delivering us all the time, but it does not seem much to us,' or ' I do not presume to say you are not delivering your people, but I find myself puzzled and unable to say that you are.' In Hebrew this, presumably, is a polite idiom, and cannot fairly be put into the sixth type because its meaning is not in any doubt; the device is in a sense real and active, but it is not conceived as a contradiction.

Contradictions of the same kind, however, when they are used as jokes, fall more definitely into this type, because the reader is meant to be conscious of them as such. The paragraph which describes the appearance of Zuleika Dobson is a pretty example.

> Zuleika was not strictly beautiful.

' Do not suppose that she was anything so commonplace; do not suppose that you can easily imagine what she was like, or that she was not, probably, the rather out-of-the-way type that you particularly admire ' ; in this way (or rather, in the gambit of which this is a parody) jealousy is placated, imagination is set free, and nothing has been said (what is this strict type of beauty, anyway ?) which can be used against the author afterwards.

> Her eyes were a trifle large, and the lashes longer than they need have been.

Not knowing how large the trifle may be, the reader has no means of being certain whether he would be charmed or appalled. ' To me, from an academic point of view, this face is all wrong; but never mind me, boys; don't let me spoil your fun.' Her brow was not discreditable her hair, we are positively told, was curly. 'I must say I find something very excessive about all this; but you, of course, would have been impressed.'

> The mouth was a mere replica of Cupid's bow.

He is becoming petulant; after not strictly beautiful it is no kindness to construct her out of familiar models; flashy-looking creature had the same face as every one else, only twice as much of it. The eulogy now rises out of apparent understatement into warm but ambiguous praise :

> No apple-tree, no wall of peaches, had not been robbed, nor any Tyrian rose-garden, for the glory of Miss Dobson's cheeks. Her neck was imitation-marble. Her hands and feet were of very mean proportions. She had no waist to speak of.

The negatives in the first sentence throw a prim pattern over its lush fullness, force one to think 'no, the tree had not,' and give it, as a doubt in the background, exactly the opposite meaning, as by an Italian or vulgar-English double negative. In the second, of course, her neck could only imitate marble, but was it imitating imitation-marble ? the doubt reminds us of the appalling possibilities in imitating many perfectly genuine marbles, and perhaps of the imitation-marble environment of her early struggles. And then, since mean may be medium, small or without quality; since a waist is at once flesh and the absence of flesh; we are left in doubt whether the last two sentences mean that her beauty was unique and did not depend on the conventional details, or that these parts of her body were, in fact, not good enough to be worth mentioning, or that they were intensely and fashionably small.

This contradiction as to the apparent subject of the statement seems very complete; it is not obvious what we are meant to believe at the end of it. But it cannot be said to represent a conflict in the author's mind ; the contradiction removes the reader from the apparent subject to the real one, and the chief ' meaning ' of the paragraph, apart from the criticism in its parody, is 'please believe in my story; we have got to take it sufficiently seriously to keep it going.' I hope I need not apologise, after this example, for including Mr. Beerbohm among the poets.

I shall consider what may reasonably be called two ambiguities by contradiction, in the love scene between Troilus and Cressida; but one must speak in this tentative way because, when readers can easily extract meaning from a sentence, there is a sort of irrelevance about saying that its main grammar has none; the fact might be true but not important. And I said that a reader should be conscious of a contradiction if it is to be of the sixth type ; but in complex cases the reader is not so much conscious of the contradiction as of the way it fails so as to have meaning. Thus the contradictions are likely to be well embedded in their setting, and not of a simplicity suitable for demonstration.

Partly conscious of the difference between them, and feeling that she must bid for his sympathy, Cressida begins the scene by giving herself away; she has always wanted Troilus, she held off 'lest he would play the tyrant,' to lengthen the time of wooing when at least she was definitely wanted, and make as sure of him as possible. It is said in the hope that he, too, will turn out to be a conscious and calculating person, living not by one consistent ideal but by the manipulation of several; she is not sure how much she is saying, or how much she can afford to say. It leads her to confusion, shame at her lack of simplicity, and an innocent fear that she has been trying to take advantage of him (helplessly, having got into the wrong style, she confesses that too) when he remains noble and romantic, silent and puzzled; when she is answered only by that heroic loyalty which will so easily turn to contempt of her, which springs from a secret belief that one can get anything one sets one's heart on, which poor Cressida, in the humility of her opportunism, can echo only in her tantrums. She tries to get away from him.

Tro. What offends you Lady?

Cress. Sir, mine owne company.

Tro. You cannot shun your selfe.

Cress. Let me goe and try:

I have a kinde of selfe recides with you :

But an unkinde selfe, that it selfe will leave,

To be anothers foole. Where is my wit?

I would be gone : I speake I know not what.

Tro. Well know they what they speak, that speak so wisely.

(iii. ii. 141.)

They are wise too who know what has been spoken. I call it a contradiction on the assumption that the kinde of selfe which is fixed is the same as the unkinde selfe which will leave ; the pun amounts to one contradiction, the two statements as to mobility another, and there is a third as to whether she has left herself already or is trying to do so now. She may mean ; ' I can leave myself since I have done so already ; part of me has gone over to your side, and is unkind to me because it makes me talk so foolishly,* or 'the self I have given you is unkind because it is able to leave you, able to retire into its own privacy, able to take another lover. But we may also regard the two selves as different; the point of the paradox is the assumption of difference within a term dedicated to unity. 'Part of me will always be fixed in you ; but I have also an unkind self which does not know what it is about, wants to leave the kind self with you for the moment and get away to be alone. This needs a further interpretation of another's fool I think she feels ' Part of me I have already given you ; but there is another part of me which I am unnaturally trying to give as well; I have been trying to submit myself to you more than I have the generosity to do ; I have been trying to obtain a greater intimacy from you than you have the wit to sustain. Hence, 'I have an ungenerous self which will cease to be ungenerous by becoming another's fool, when I submit myself wholly to a lover; or remembering the fool was a domestic critic, ' I have a store of unkindness in me which may yet be brought out against you to mock at you.

Perchance my Lord, I shew more craft then love.

And fell so roundly to a large confession,

To Angle for your thoughts: but you are wise,

Or else you love not : for to be wise and love,

Exceedes mans might, that dwels with gods above.

I call this second example, following on from the first, a contradiction, because the generalisation which is added to show the force of the antithesis makes it a false one. 'Either you are wise or you do not love, because you cannot love if you are wise. There is some difference between the alternatives, so that the antithesis is not actually illogical; if a man is wise we know he does not love, but if he does not love the dictum tells us nothing as to whether or not he is wise. Logically, then, the force of or else is ' at any rate ; she moves down to a less sweeping deduction from his silence. But this is far-fetched, and the remark has an air of saying something directly; perhaps one takes or else to mean 'in other words,' and the generalisation as a statement that the two things are much the same. But since the two things are, in fact, placed as alternatives, we are forced to see that there is some doubt about the matter, and put a double interpretation upon both love and wisdom.

You are wise ' you love in the wholesale, self-dedicating, self careless (because self-confident) way approved by theory'; you are wise (with admiring reproach) ' because, loving as I do, you will not confess it.' Wise means single-minded,' as one speaks of the wisdom of the beasts, or ' careful to appear so, and not to give yourself away'; perhaps, also, 'too well-balanced to be conscious of your duplicities.' Love is a heroic and selfless, or a pathetically unscrupulous passion. Or else you love not, ' If you are not so wise as to love simply you cannot love me at all, for no one could both love and be too politic to confess his complexity.' Or else you love not, ' If you are not keeping silent only out of caution you cannot love me at all, for no one could both love and be simple ; when you are really in love you cannot afford to be heroic and single-minded.' (If either of these meanings is there, both must be, because there is no reason why the two meanings should be distributed one way rather than the other.) She feels that, in one way or another, he must be very wise, if only by contrast with her own folly in talking to him as she has done.

The main logical structure of this exquisite song[42] is a contrast; take, but bring-, which involves a contradiction; and there is another in the idea of 'returning' a kiss :

Take, oh take thy lips away,

That so sweetly were forsworne.

---

42 It is sung for Mariana in the moated grange (Measure for Measure, Act. iv. i.) and so I assumed that the forswearer was a man, not a woman.

And those eyes : the break of day

Lights that doe mislead the Morne ;

But my kisses bring againe,

bring againe.

Seals of love, but seal'd in vaine, seal'd in vaine.

In that he must take his lips away he is already in her presence ; she is actually telling him to go, and keeping command of the situation; or if he is only present in her imagination, because she cannot forget him, still the source of her fantasy satisfaction is to pretend that he is already in her presence, that she is in a position to repel him, or pretend to repel him ; and her demand would be satisfied both by an expression of her resentment and by a forgetting of her desire. But he cannot be in her presence already, because he must come and bring again her kisses; and thus, when he is not present, she confesses that she wants more of them. But, again (if perhaps he is present, and she is sending him hick to fetch the things), he must not bring her new kisses, but only her old ones back, so as to restore her to her original unkissed condition. Notice that the metaphor from seals does not keep up this last pretence, which seems to be her main meaning; it is no more use giving back a seal when it has been broken than a kiss when you wish to revoke your kisses. It is these two contradictions, in short, which convey the ambivalence of her feeling for him. (And yet, after all, it is no use calling this a serious contradiction; we know what her total feelings are well enough.[43])

One can extract minor contradictions from the imagery. Either at the break of day : at dawn she can again see his beauty; in the morning he leaves her harshly and forgets his vows. Or like the break of day : he must take his eyes away even though, when they come, they give her world all the light it can now hope for; and in that they are like the sun of a day, one ought always to have expected that they would soon be taken. I think, too, there is a pun on break which gives it two opposite actions upon day; their coming is like daybreak because they restore her happiness, but he must take them away because they broke into, or broke up, the easy clarity of her carelessness; because they broke her heart either with their first beauty or

43 It is cleat p I think, that the song turns the conflict of feeling entirely ' into poetry,' however much you regard the ambiguity as inherently a dramatic one.

with their final harshness; and the word still hints, under all these muffling associations, at the loss of her virginity. They mislead the morn is in main idea a simple hyperbole; when your eyes arrive at a place nature thinks it is the sun rising.' But mislead is a word already well suited to the situation ; she was herself in a state of morning before he came to her, because of her youth, freshness, and lack of experience ; just as she was day in the previous line, either when she was happy in his love for her, so that the promise of her morning had been achieved, or before she met him, because of her sanity, safety, understanding of her own feelings, and freedom from the darkness of complex or unsatisfied desires.

One may call those statements contradictions which make the reader reflect that they are untrue, or that they conflict with the implications of the passage. Thus

Ah moon of my delight that knowest no wane,

The moon of heaven is rising once again ;

How oft hereafter rising shall she look

Through this same garden after me, in vain.

(Omar Khayyam.)

contains a contradiction; the point of the verse is the inevitability of death, and the first line says that one or other of the persons concerned is unchanging. (Fitzgerald seems to have invented the clause about not waning, by the way; it does not occur in some of the versions.) In part this is to be excused as the super-imposition of two time-scales, in part as a compensation mechanism, which holds in mind an untruth in order to find energy to recognise a truth. In part, I daresay, it should not be excused at all.

In place of stating a contradiction it is often possible to ask a question whose answer is both yes and no; this device is particularly frequent when an author is adopting a 'poetical' style, so that he often wants to say things of greater logical complexity than his method will allow. It makes less parade of its complexity than any other.

But who hath seen her wave her hand ?

Or at the casement seen her stand ?

Or is she known in all the land.

The Lady of Shalott ?

Yes and no. She is not known personally to anybody in all the land but everybody knows of her as a legend. Both these facts heighten the dramatic effect, and they are both conveyed by the single question.

Ambiguity of the sixth type by tautology (not by irrelevance) is likely to fulfil the following rather exacting conditions : there will be a pun which is used twice, once in each sensi, and the massive fog of the complete ambiguity will then arise from a doubt as to which meaning goes with which word. The following example from Herbert is of this sort. One should start with an earlier verse of the poem.

Whereas my birth and spirit rather took

The way that takes the town,

Thou didst betray me to a lingering book,

And wrap me in a gown.

I was entangled in the world of strife

Before I had the power to change my life.

(Affliction.)

Long as Herbert delayed in taking orders, the two halves of this verse, one saying he was betrayed into the life of contemplation, the other that he was entangled in the life of action, show him still doubtful which he would have preferred. Thus he seems to want to change his life even now, but it is hard to see in what direction.[44]

Yet though thou troublest me, I must be meek;

In weakness must be stout.

Well, I will change the service, and go seek

Some other master out.

Ah, my dear God, though I am clean forgot.

Let me not love thee, if I love thee not.

44 Probable the gown was Cambridge not the church ; he is recounting his life.

It is the last line which I call an ambiguity by tautology. In the first line, meek may mean that he must endure what God puts upon him; in the second, stout may mean that he must endure it bravely. Thus the third line, which shows that both these words carried some hint of revolt, is a surprise; we arrive in some doubt at the final couplet.

Forgotten, either by God or the world, either now or later, in consequence of seeking or of not seeking another master, of loving or of not loving God, To make the last line sensible (able to use these possible ambiguities), there must be some play, in the engineering sense, on the word love or only, perhaps, some displacement among the tenses. The only grammatical and sensible variation of tense would make the first love future, the second present: ' If I have stopped loving you, let me go; do not make me love you again in the future, so that I shall regret it if I return to the world. Allow me to be consistent, even though it means an entire loss of your favour.' But one may also distinguish between the love of God which is an arduous effort towards a goal and the loye of God which has achieved its goal, which being a mystical illumination has no doubts and is its own reward. Allotting these meanings in the order given, we have : ' Do not let me spend my life trying to love you, loving you in will and deed but not in the calm of which so few are worthy. Do not make me hanker after you if I would be better under some other master elsewhere ; even though this would mean you must forget me altogether.' It is a very reasonable deduction from the sexual metaphor used by devotional poets that God should in most cases be well scolded as a flirt; it seems always, however, to be done in language as veiled as that of my example. But the meanings may also be allotted the other way round : ' And yet, though you have already clean forgotten me, let me not love you in achievement if I do not love you in desire.' ' Damn me if I don't stick to the parsonage'; he has no worse imprecation than the first part of the line, and it is used to give force to the statement of purpose in the second[45].

---

45 Mr. F. L. Lucas took this treatment of Herbert's poem as a proof of the vulgarity of my whole mode of approach. No doubt it is flippantly written, but a purely logical point can be made more clearly if it is not muffled by a sympathetic tone. The matter I cannot understand anyone objecting to ; the line seems to me so beautiful when it is interpreted as I do that I would have picked out this passage as the only splendid and obvious success I had had the good luck to achieve.

There was an Archbishop Sharp who died with this couplet on his lips, and indeed, to a mind trained by dividing the word of God in the pulpit, to the febrile imagination, to the attention limited on to words remembered, of a sickbed, they might well open into extraordinary vistas of meaning.[46]

Ambiguity of the sixth type by irrelevant statements maintains a precarious existence between the first type and the seventh. It is not merely a statement with various implications, but a statement with various implications which conflict; nor is it an essential contradiction, but a contradiction on matters not central to the writer's interests at the moment, or a contradiction which is thought of as capable of being resolved. Like the first type it may be hunted among similes. Thus to say a thing is like gold may mean that it is glittering, strong, lifegiving, like the sun, young, virtuous, untrammelled, like the Golden Age, expensive and hence aristocratic, capable of being drawn and beaten into delicate ornaments, a worthy setting for jewels; or it may mean simply 'mercenary,' and a heavy symbol of wealth, suitable for storage.

Then rose the seed of Chaos, and of Night,

To blot out order, and extinguish light.

Of dull and venal a new world to mould,

And bring Saturnian days of lead and gold.

(Pope, Dunciad)

The Saturnian was the Golden Age ; Saturn was lead in astrology. Gold is intended to have the two sorts of meaning I have suggested, so that this is a fair example of the sixth type, in a very simple form. Evidently the contradiction is capable of being resolved; it is resolved into a joke. My next example is in every sense more serious.

It is the Cause, it is the Cause (my soul).
Let me not name it to you, you chaste Starres,
It is the Cause. Yet He not shed her blood.
Nor scarre that whiter skin of hers, then Snow,
And smooth as Monumental Alabaster :
(Othello V. ii.)

46 Be that as it may, the Archbishop was murdered and probably had little time.

The stress may be on it or on cause the capitals suggest the latter. This favours Dr. Johnson's meaning: 'It is not the act of murder that horrifies me here; it is the cause of it.' But regarding the stress as on it (an actor should stress both) we are made to wonder what it was that was causing the tempest in his mind; and are given only the 'irrelevant' statement that it was the cause. If it is necessary to find one word for what was in his mind, I should myself plump for blood but it is no use assuming, for the ease of mind of the chaste stars of criticism, that one cause can be assigned, and one thing it is the cause of. There is no primary meaning for lack of information, and the secondary meaning, therefore, holds the focus of consciousness, that we are listening to a mind withdrawn upon itself, and baffled by its own agonies. As primary meanings of it, however, thus thrust back among the assumptions, one might list his blackness, as causing her defection ; the universality of human lust (in both him and her), as causing her defection and his murder; her defection, as causing his horror and her death.

Yet Othello will not shed her blood, because that would be to display the animal now latent in her and be like the taking of a virginity. If she is chaste, it would be to stain her with the blood hidden even in her; if she is guilty but pitiful, it would be indelicately to display the hypocrisy of her beauty, which ought in decency, like a tombstone, to be preserved; if she is guilty, it would be to stain Othello himself with the blood in Desdemona, which is so new a horror to him. Before calling this fantastic one must consider how many other hints of that symbolism can be found in the course of the death-scene; the marriage-sheets which were to be laid on the bed; 'Aye, but not yet to die'; Othello's phrase about 'plucking the rose'; and the sword stolen from him as an emblem of cuckoldry. It is as a sort of parody of the wedding night, I think, that the scene is given its horror and Othello's violence is made to seem inevitable. But independently of this latent comparison in the whole scene, which different people will absorb in different ways, the meaning of the particular line depends on Elizabethan associations with blood; Webster may have been remembering it when he made the White Devil say it the other way round :

Oh, my worst sin was in my blood ;

Now my blood pays for it.

(v. vi.)

It is the same doubt, expressed by a similar 'irrelevance,' which gives their extraordinary quality to the next two lines. In the line praising the skin of the creature he is enjoying the straightforward relief of a Marlowan hyperbole, so as to give himself strength by reviving what she had meant to him; he escapes for a moment the clash between love and hatred by an irrelevant praise about which he has no doubt, so that the effect is as if he thought her innocent. In the line about the tombstone the rhythm takes on a hushed and reflective horror, and mutters like the talk of vergers down an aisle; 'It is fearful that her beauty should be such a lie ; it almost makes one doubt the whole story; under the calm of this effigy (already judged) one looks for an inscription accusing her murderer, and yet within it is all uncleanness and already rotten.

You might say that this is a fundamental indecision on the point at issue, and should be put into the seventh type. But the point at issue is as to whether he will kill her,^ and there the decision is already made. Taking this for granted, so that it overshadows the speech, he is trying to believe it, trying to order his feelings about her in accordance with it, trying to make it seem tolerable in his mind.

The strength of vagueness, in fact, is that it allows of secret ambiguity; it seems to have forced itself on nineteenth-century poets when they felt they needed ambiguity, but would have considered its more discoverable forms improper. If I may once more attempt to give reasons for this fact, it may spring from their respect for logical punctuation, from their admiration for simple ecstasies (it was no longer courtiers and administrators who wrote poetry), from their resulting admiration for smoothness of lyrical flow, and from the fact that the language had become less fluid, a less subtle mirror of the mind (though a more precise mirror of the scientific world), since the clarifying labours of the eighteenth century. This cult of vagueness produced the nonsense writers like Lear and Lewis Carroll (the Carpenter was a Castle; the Walrus, who could eat so many more oysters because he was crying into his handkerchief, was a Bishops in the chessboard scheme. It was the cult of vagueness which saved their extraordinary author from thinking himself a satirist); and the dowagers of Oscar Wilde's plays, who by the gentle indifference of their vagueness could give insults beside which violence must pale. My next example shows the extreme beauty which such a technique can sustain.

One of the finest poems of W. B. Yeats is an example of an ambiguity of the sixth type, under the sub-heading 'irrelevant statements.'

Who will go drive with Fergus now.
And pierce the deep wood's woven shade,
And dance upon the level shore ?
Young man, lift up your russet brow.
And lift your tender eyelids, maid.
And brood on hopes and fears no more.
And no more turn aside and brood
Upon Love's bitter mystery;
For Fergus rules the brazen cars,
And rules the shadows of the wood,
And the white breast of the dim sea,
And all dishevelled wandering stars.

There is another poem in the volume explaining about Fergus. He appears as a king, who has left the judgment-hall, and the pleasures of the Court, and the chariot races by the seashore, who has grown weary of active life, and has sought out a Druid to be given the bag of dreams. The Druid warns him that

No woman loves me, no man seeks my help.
Because I be not of the things I dream.

Fergus, insisting, is given the dreams and awakes to what they imply, the intellectual or contemplative life, so that

now I am grown nothing, being all.
And the whole world weighs down upon my heart,

and so that he cries out

Ah ! Druid, Druid, how great webs of sorrow
Lay hidden in the small slate-coloured bag !

One may notice the way a foreign idiom is implied by the two uses of how: 'how great were the webs' and 'how the webs of sorrow lay hidden.'

The first poem, of course, assumes this story, but now may mean before or after the transformation. If after, the first line means: 'Now that the awful example of Fergus is in front of you, surely you will not be so unwise as to brood?'; to drive with him would be to wander through the woods like a ghost, as he does ; the dancing would be that of the fairy child who danced upon the mountains like a flame and stole away the children. Or 'Now who will be so loyal as to follow him?' or 'Can you be so cruel as to abandon him now ? ' ; or with a different feeling : 'Now that Fergus knows everything, who will come and join in his meditations; who will share his melancholy and his knowledge; which of you will pierce the mystery of the forest and rejoice in sympathy with the whole of nature ? ' If before, so that the force of now is : ' There is still time to drive with Fergus, as he is still a king in the world,' or 'There is still time to give a warning, as the fatal thing has not yet happened'; then the first line gives: 'Who will come out with the great figures of the Court, and join in their sensible out-of-door pleasures?'

If before, the second verse means: 'You need not brood, because Fergus is guardian of commonsense ; he is a strong man to drive war-chariots, as you should be ; he owns all the territory on which magic takes place ; he will keep it under decent control; there is no need for you to worry about it.' If after: 'Do not brood; be warned by Fergus, who though still king, still technically in command of war-chariots, is true ruler only of the dim appurtenances of magic dreams,' or, since there is no mistaking the triumph of the line about cars into whatever melancholy the verse trails away, 'Remember that though Fergus is a great poet or philosopher or what not, though he drives some mythological chariot of the Muses,' of whose details I am afraid I am ignorant, 'yet even he, because these victories involved brooding, is reduced to the dim and ghostly condition of the last three lines.'

I said that an example of the sixth type must say nothing, and this poem says: 'Do not brood.' But the words have little of the quality of an order ; they convey rather : ' How strange and sad that you should still be brooding ! ' ; and one may interpret variously the transition from advice to personal statement, from such of an imperative as was intended to the mere pain of loss, in the repetition of no more. ' I in that I am Fergus, can no more turn aside from brooding,' is a sort of false grammar by juxtaposition, which may be felt in the line, and there is a suggestion that they must now lose their dreams, as they have already lost the real world, without getting anything in exchange for either, 'All has grown bitter, and who can join in either activity of Fergus any longer?' One might finally distinguish the erotic brooding of the young persons from the philosophical brooding of Fergus, which as hoping for nothing is at once grander and more empty; no doubt this distinction is only intended faintly, since it is part of the wisdom of the language of the poet that it treats these two as of the same kind. But, in so far as it is intended, it allows of an opposite meaning for 'Do not brood' — ' Do ndl Brood in this comparatively trivial fashion but go and drive with Fergus, who will teach you to brood about everything, who will teach you to wander, untouchable, and all-embracing, in an isolation like that of the stars.'

The wavering and suggestive indefiniteness of nineteenth century poetry is often merely weak. When, as here, it has a great deal of energy and sticks in your head, it is usually because the opposites left open are tied round a single strong idea; thus here, on the one hand, the condition of brooding is at once to be sought out and to be avoided; on the other, the poet, 'nothing, being all,' contemporaneously living all lives, may fitly be holding before him both the lives of Fergus, and drawing the same moral from either of them.

In a sense the sixth class is included within the fourth. In the fourth class several feelings, several reactions to a complex situation, are united by the writer, and can be accepted as a unity by the reader. The criterion for the sixth class is more verbal; the same result may be achieved, but it must be by an evasive mode of statement. Thus the last example of my fourth chapter belongs by rights either to the fifth or to the sixth; I gave a rather nagging and irrelevant analysis of one of the great passages of Wordsworth, and complained that his theological statements were either so muddled or so evasive as not to disturb people of many shades of theological opinion. In a sense this is only to say that it is a sort of generalisation from theological opinions; Wordsworth is concerned with the resultant sentiments rather than the source of belief from which they are drawn. So one cannot say that he is contradicting himself, even by implication, because the theological ideas he has to invoke are not, so to speak, what he wants to make a statement about. I put it at the end of the fourth chapter, partly because in this sense the example is not a contradiction, and partly as a transition, to show how the same methods could be used for a different case.

But the criterion for the sixth class is not merely verbal, in contrast with the psychological criterion of the fourth; indeed, if a poet is using language properly, it ought to be impossible to maintain such a distinction. So here, as cause or result of their verbal form, the examples of the sixth class convey an evasive frame of mind ; they show the author feeling that he will lose the attitude he is expressing if he looks at it too closely. Of course, the same verbal form may be used for an opposite reason, because he takes the solution of his contradiction for granted, and feels sure that he will be understood; I should not call this a genuine ambiguity in the sense with which I am concerned, and must claim not to have selected such examples for this chapter.

But these two sorts of resolvable contradiction are alike in this : they assume that the reader understands a great deal already, and that he is able to guess by sympathy the way the contradiction must be resolved. They are both then similar to the nineteenth century form of modishness, which worked by implying it was obviously too exhausted (by its wealth of experience, or by the inadequacy of everything in sight at the moment) to say or feel anything very positively, and that you were a fool if you didn't already understand what it was taking for granted. (The corresponding thing at present is to express quite strong feelings, in a placid way, but feelings such as would only have occurred to a very active and widely informed sensibility, so that to the auditor they seem impressively inappropriate.) In its way such an evasiveness is a confession of weakness ; and it is chiefly by this lack of positive satisfaction in the contradiction, by this feeling that one could say the things more clearly but had much better not, that I should distinguish advanced examples of the sixth class from the definite statements of contradictions in the seventh.[47]

Most of the early examples in the seventh chapter belong to the sixth, if read as seems to be intended; I am putting them in the seventh to show the scale as a whole.

---

47 The Herbert example in this chapter, which fits the logical criterion neatly, does not seem to fit the psychological one, as it is certainly not weak. But you could call it evasive ; because Herbert in writing about himself keeps a certain reserve.

The sixth type is related to the seventh much as the third is related to the fourth; in each case the earlier on my scale is more conscious because more superficial. W. B. Yeats' poem contains both types; the doubt as to the meaning of now was, I take it, a 'device,' employed for compactness and to display the poet's assumptions, and suchlike; the doubt as to the merits of brooding which I suggested later, is a 'mood,' or enshrines the poet's permanent attitude to the word. It might be argued that the first doubt is of the sixth type, but the second of the seventh. To a consideration of the seventh I shall now proceed.

VII

An example of the seventh type of ambiguity, or at any rate of the last type of this series, as it is the most ambiguous that can be conceived, occurs when the two meanings of the word, the two values of the ambiguity, are the two opposite meanings defined by the context, so that the total effect is to show a fundamental division in the writer's mind. You might think thht such a case could never occur and, if it occurred, could not be poetry, but as a matter of fact it is, in one sense or another, very frequent, and admits of many degrees. One might say, clinging to the logical aspect of this series, that the idea of 'opposite' is a comparatively late human invention, admits of great variety of interpretation (having been introduced wherever there was an intellectual difficulty), and corresponds to nothing in the real world ; that —a .bis contrary to a for all values of b ; that words in poetry, like words in primitive languages (and like, say, the Latin altus, high or deep, the English let, allow or hinder), often state a pair of opposites without any overt ambiguity; that in such a pair you are only stating, for instance, a scale, which might be extended between any two points, though no two points are in themselves opposites; and that in searching for greater accuracy one might say ' 2 per cent, white ' and mean a very black shade of grey. Or one might admit that the criterion in this last type becomes psychological rather than logical, in that the crucial point of the definition has become the idea of a context, and the total attitude to that context of the individual.

A contradiction of this kind may be meaningless, but can never be a blank; it has at least stated the subject which is under discussion, and has given a sort of intensity to it such as one finds in a gridiron pattern in architecture because it gives prominence neither to the horizontals nor to the verticals, and in a check pattern because neither colour is the ground on which the other is placed; it is at once an indecision and a structure, like the symbol of the Cross. Or it may convey an impression of conscious ornamentation such as the Sumerians obtained, in the earliest surviving civilised designs, by putting two* beasts in exactly symmetrical attitudes of violence, as in supporting a coat-of-arms, so that whatever tendencies to action are aroused in the alarmed spectator, however he imagines the victim or the huntsman to have been placed, there is just the same claim on his exclusive attention, with a reassuring impossibility, being made on the other side, and he is drawn taut between the Wo similar impulses into the stasis of appreciation. You might relate it to the difference of sound heard by the two ears, which decides where the sound is coming from, or to the stereoscopic contradictions that imply a dimension.[48]

Opposites, again, are an important element in the Freudian analysis of dreams ; and it is evident that the Freudian termin* ology, particularly the word 'condensation,' could be employed with profit for the understanding of poetry. Now a Freudian opposite at least marks dissatisfaction ; the notion of what you want involves the idea that you have not got it, and this again involves the 'opposite defined by your context,' which is what you have and cannot avoid. In more serious cases, causing wider emotional reverberation, such as are likely to be reflected in language, in poetry, or in dreams, it marks a centre of conflict; the notion of what you want involves the notion that you must not take it, and this again involves the 'opposite defined by your context,' that you want something different in another part of your mind. Of course, conflict need not be expressed overtly as contradiction, but it is likely that those theories of aesthetics which regard poetry as the resolution of a conflict will find their illustrations chiefly in the limited field covered by the seventh type.

The study of Hebrew, by the way, and the existence of English Bibles with alternatives in the margin, may have had influence on the capacity of English for ambiguity; Donne, Herbert, Jonson, and Crashaw, for instance, were Hebrew scholars, and the flowering of poetry at the end of the sixteenth century corresponded with the first thorough permeation of the English language by the translated texts. This is of interest because Hebrew, having very unreliable tenses, extraordinary idioms, and a

---

48 It may be said that the contradiction must somehow form a larger unity if the final effect is to be satisfying. But the onus of reconciliation can be laid very heavily on the receiving end. One could, of course, also introduce much philosophical puzzling about the reconciliation of contradictions. The German tradition in the matter seems eventually based on Indian ideas, best worked out in Buddhism. But I daresay there is more than enough theorising in the text here already.

strong taste for puns, possesses all the poetical advantages of a thorough primitive disorder.

I invoke primitive languages on the authority of Freud (Notebooks vol. iv. No. lo), and cannot myself pretend to understand their mode of action. The early Eg5rptians, apparently, wrote the same sign for 'young' and 'old,' showing which was meant by an additional hieroglyphic, not to be pronounced, which may have taken the place of gesture in conversation. (This claim is anyway partly borne out by the standard dictionary of Ancient Egyptian.) They ' only gradually learnt to separate the two sides of the antithesis and think of the one without conscious comparison with the other.* When a primitive Egyptian saw a baby he at once thought of an old man, and he had to learn not to do this as his language became more civilised. This certainly shows the process of attaching a word to an object as something extraordinary; nobody would do it if his language did not make him; and if one considers the typical propositions which can be applied to a baby, other than those as to its age, the opposite applies less to an old man than to a man in the prime of life. Evidently there are two ways in which such a word could be constructed. It may mean, for instance, 'no good for soldiers, because of age; it may have been thought of in connection with some idea which regarded the very young and the very old in the same way. Thus one speaks of the two ends of a stick, though from another point of view one of them must be the beginning. Or it may be important to remember that the notion of age excites conflict in almost all who use it; between recognising the facts about oneself, and feeling grown-up or feeling still young and strong.

In so far as the opposites are used to resolve or to soften a conflict, so that an ageing man is not forced suddenly to find that a new and terrible word will apply to him, or can speak of himself as a young man by an easy and forgivable alteration of tone, to this extent there seems nothing peculiarly primitive about the sentiment, or the delicacy which allows it to be phrased; it has, perhaps, something primitive in its weakness of hold on external truth, and its honesty in voicing desires. And this form of the identity of opposites is not at all what one would expect from other properties of primitive languages; from the African grammars which insist on dealing with each case on its own merits ; from the vocabulary of the language of Terra del Fuego, which requires a separate noun for each thing that English would name by permuting nouns and adjectives;

from the thousand different words in Arabic which describe the different sorts of camel. Indeed, Arabic is a striking case of the mental sophistication required to use a word which covers its own opposite, because, though it possesses many such words, they are of a late origin and were elaborated as a literary grace. The many examples one can find in English (a 'restive' horse, for instance, is a horse which is restless because it has been resting for too long) are almost all later developments in the same way. So that I believe myself, though this is only a useful prejudice with which to approach the subject, that though such words appeal to the fundamental habits of the human mind, and are fruitful of irrationality, they are to be expected from a rather sophisticated state of language and of feeling.

It seems likely, indeed, that words uniting two opposites are seldom or never actually formed in a language to express the conflict between them; such words come to exist for more sensible reasons, and may then be used to express conflict. Thus the Egyptian dictionary has much less doubt about the identity of 'dead white' and 'dead black,' a case for which it would be hard to invent a plausible conflict, than about the identity of 'young' and 'old.' One reason is that people much more often need to mention the noticeable than the usual, so that a word which defines a scale comes to be narrowed down more and more to its two ends; the English 'temper' is an example of this. Another reason is that of relational opposites one cannot be known without the other; to know what a ruled person is you must know whether the ruler is a general or an archbishop. Thus a word which names both parts of a relation may be more precise than a word which only names half of it. Another reason is that, in complicated matters, you may know that there are two difficult cases which ought to be distinguished, but being anxious on the point you find it hard to remember which is which ; to the senses they ma5 »be opposite, but they excite the same feelings. Thus primitive painters make lines parallel when they know that they are so in fact ; but rather less primitive painters make them meet, equally often, on the horizon and at the eye of the observer. There was no conflict in their minds between these two ways of making lines converge; there was only a general anxiety as to the convergence of lines. In so far, in short, as you know that two things are opposites, you know a relation which connects them.

This discussion is in some degree otiose because I really do not know what use the Egyptians made of their extraordinary words, or how 'primitive' we should think their use of them if we heard them talking; whereas I have, at any rate, a rough idea of how the words are being used in the examples which follow. I have been searching the sources of the Nile less to explain English verse than to cast upon the reader something of the awe and horror which were felt by Dante arriving finally at the most centrique part of earth, of Satan, and of hell.

Quando noi fummo l, dove la Coscia

Si volge appunto in sul grosso dell anche.

La Duca con fatica e con angoscia

Volse la testa ov egli avea le zanche.

We too must now stand upon our heads, and are approaching the secret places of the Muse.

When a contradiction is stated with an air of conviction it may be meant to be resolved in either of two ways, corresponding to thought and feeling, corresponding to knowing and not knowing one's way about the matter in hand. Grammatical machinery may be assumed which would make the contradiction into two statements; thus 'p and – may mean: 'If a–a1 then); if a=a2y then –p). If Ci and 2 are very different from one another, so that the two statements are fitted together with ingenuity, then I should put the statement into an earlier type ; if and 2 are very like one another, so that the contradiction expresses both the need for and the difficulty of separating them, then I should regard the statement as an ambiguity of the seventh type corresponding to thought and knowing one's way about the matter in hand. But such contradictions are often used, as it were by analogy from this, when the speaker does not know what a1 and he satisfies two opposite impulses and A2 a sort of apology, admits that they contradict, but claims that they are like the soluble contradictions, and can safely be indulged; by admitting the weakness of his thought he seems to have sterilised it, to know better already than anyone who might have pointed the contradiction out ; he claims the sympathy of his audience in that 'we can none of us say more than this,' and gains dignity in that even from the poor material of human ignorance he can distil grace of style. One might think that contradictions of this second sort (corresponding to feeling, and not knowing one's way about the matter in hand) must always be foolish, and even if they say anything to one who understands them can quite as

machines have explained the glories of England that shall come after, the king replies, as from the throne :

Wisely you have, whatever will please, reveal'd,

What wou'd displease, as wisely have conceal'd.

The remark is sharp but not damping; is quite different from the generous depression of Johnson which is a development from it; shows a power of understanding a situation while still feeling excited; and is not the sort of thing anyone would have the courage to say on such an occasion nowadays.

Such a mode of expression comes nearer to verbal ambiguity when it may be analysed in terms of the incidental conveniences of language, such as sound-effects, and thus put into the first type.

I taught my silkes, their whistling to forbeare,

Even my opprest shoes, dumb and speechlesse were.

(Donne, Elegy, iv. 51.)

Dumb and speechlesse have the same meaning, but their sound describes the silence and the noise, respectively, to which his attention is directed.

It is worth noting that opprest is a pun, and taught a metaphor ; because he is in a mood of adventure and general ship which makes him personify his property, as men have named their swords, through a heightened interest in their qualities and a sharper sense of participation in their actions.

But oh, too common ill, I brought with me

That, which betrayed me to mine enemy.

Everything he has brought into this alien house is his own invading army; it is a personal betrayal when he is discovered through his perfume :

Onely, thou bitter sweet, whom I had laid

Next mee, mee traiterously hast betraid.

— a metaphor drawn from political textbooks, about the spy in the council-chambers of princes; in the same way oppress means both 'even when I put my weight upon them' and 'podf good creatures, what a trial it must have been for them not to cry out before my path, and proclaim the greatness of their master ! '

I taught my treads evenly and cautiously; silkes and again whistling give the rustle of the rich cloak, which for two strides has swung loose, as he tiptoes down the passage. Forbeare, both from its even and compelling sound, from its quieting and repressive meaning, from the finality of its rhyme with their, and from the renewed emphasis this rhyme gives to the rhythm of his strides, shows him catching the thing again, and hushing it.

Forbeare, then, is normal onomatopoeia, but speechless , or a word like 'hush,' is not; on the contrary, its sound is a noise that will carry some distance. You make it partly from an excitement that finds relief in contrast, partly because it suggests the sounds you are afraid of and are listening for, partly in order to make a noise which your confederates will hear even when it is said softly, partly because, if only from being an unlikely sound for you to choose, it may easily be mistaken for a natural sound by your enemies.

The second line illustrates both principles. Dumb and the pause before it, also were as rhyming with forbeare, give you the shoe put down in silence ; opprest, shoes, and speechless make it squeak in a surrounding 'hush.' 'Even now, you see, the fools have not heard,' or 'This is what I am not letting it do' ; by the placing of these sibilants we are brought to see at once the silence and caution of his advance, and, in contrast with it, the triumph and expectation with which he approaches her bedroom.

And again, in part because of the vagueness of the definition, one may regard even quite casual expressions of relief, or the throwing off of anxiety, or what not, as of the seventh type. Thus Macbeth, faced suddenly with the Thaneship of Cawdor and the foreknowledge of the witches, is drowned for a moment in the fearful anticipation of crime and in intolerable doubts as to the nature of foreknowledge. Then, throwing the problem away for a moment (he must speak to the messengers, he need not decide anything till he has seen his wife) –

> Come what come may.
>
> Time, and the Houre, runs through the roughest Day.

Either,' if he wants it to happen: 'Opportunity for crime, or the accomplished fact of crime, the crisis of action or of decision, will arrive whatever happens; however much, swamped in the horrors of the imagination, one feels as if one could never make up one's mind. I need not, therefore, worry about this at the moment' ; or, if he does not want it to happen : ' This condition of horror has only lasted a few minutes ; the clock has gone on ticking all this time ; I have not yet killed him ; there is nothing, therefore, for me to worry about yet.' These opposites may be paired with predestination and freewill: 'The hour will come, whatever I do, when I am fated to kill him, so I may as well keep quiet ; and yet if I keep quiet and feel detached and philosophical all these horrors will have passed over me and nothing can have happened.' And in any case (remembering the martial suggestion of roughest day), 'Whatever I do, even if and when I kill him, the sensible world will go on, it will not really be as fearful as I am now thinking it, it is just an ordinary killing like the ones in the battle.'

Time and the Houre together take the singular, and yet you can parcel out the two opposites between them, as by making the hour the hour of action and time the rest of time, or detachment, so that they are opposites. These give the two opposed impulses, towards control, whether control over situation by committing the murder or over suggestion by not committing it, and towards yielding, whether yielding to fear so as not to act or to suggestion so as to act (Macbeth, i. iv. 134 uses the phrase yield to suggestion). Corresponding to these two there is a transitive or intransitive meaning of runs through , time and the hour force the day to its foregone conclusion, as one runs a man through with a dagger, or time and the hour are, throughout the day, after all, always quietly running on. The remark does not seem as ambiguous as it is because it is a shelving of indecision rather than an expression of it.[49]

And this, from the same play, is of the same sort.

Macbeth

Is ripe for shaking, and the powers above

Put on their instruments. Receive what cheer you may,

49 I realise that this analysis seems too elaborate, and yet I cannot see what else (what less) the line means if it is taken seriously as meaning anything.

The Night is long, that never finds the Day.

(Act IV. end.)

'Villains are punished in the end' is the cheerful part of the meaning; but not till the end of the play; we have no reason to suppose that this night is a short one or will end just yet. Receive what cheer you may, followed by a comma as in the Folio, should be imperative: 'Be as cheerful as you can,' or could mean: 'However cheerful you may be there is a long night before us.' Death is a long night that will never find day, and we will bring that darkness on Macbeth if we can ; but on the other hand he may bring it on us.

The total effect is cheerful enough, but not because these opposites are ill-balanced; the overtone is a stoical sense that one cannot alter the length of a night, and that human affairs are too brief and uncertain for it to be worthwhile becoming agitated about them.

No less complete opposites are a normal property of the language of faint and distant innuendo :

In her youth

There is a prone and speechless dialect

Such as move men.

(Measure for Measure, i. ii. 185.)

This is the stainless Isabel, being spoken of by her respectful brother. Prone means either 'inactive and lying flat' (in retirement or with a lover) or 'active,' 'tending to,' whether as moving men, by her subtlety or by her purity, or as moving in herself, for pleasure or to do good. Speechlesse will not give away whether she is shy or sly, and dialect has abandoned the effort to distinguish between them. The last half-line makes its point calmly, with an air of knowing about such cases; and, indeed, I feel very indelicate in explaining Claudio's meaning. It is difficult to put the workings of the mind into a daylight which alters their proportions without an air either of accusation or of ribaldry; he is making no moral judgment of his sister's character, and only thinking that as a weapon against Angelo she is well worth being given a try.

And, for an extreme but illuminating example of the triviality with which this class is compatible, consider

Blood hath bene shed ere now, i' the olden time.

Ere humane Statute purg'd the gentle Weale ;

(Macbeth, iii. iv. 75.)

where gentle might just as well be, and suggests, 'ungentle,' because the weal is conceived as 'ungentle' before it purged and gentle afterwards.

In general, an adjective by showing where it is to be applied, and assuming it makes a genuine distinction, can always imply its opposite elsewhere. But there is usually a crux as to where it is to be implied, and by whom; all that can strictly be deduced from the use of an adjective with a noun is that the author believes that, at some place and some time, someone might not have used the same adjective with the same noun. So that this form of implication, though normal to the idea of an adjective, takes effect only when the context brings it out.

Even when there is a more serious difference between the two meanings, it often does not matter which of two 'opposites' is taken, because the sentence already contains a paradox which includes both of them. For these and similar reasons, poetry has a surprising amount of equilibrium; bowdlerisation, for instance, is often comically helpless to alter the spirit of a passage.

I remember some critic saying that the whole attitude to life which crystallised out round Pope, all that jaunty defiance against mystery and disorder, all that sense of personal rectitude, in that it is virtue enough to have been sensible, all that faith in the ultimate rationality, even the ultimate crudity, of the world, were summed up in the lines which introduce the Essay on Man, Let us –

Expatiate free o'er all this scene of man;

A mighty maze ! But not without a plan.

To those who think this a just piece of criticism it must always seem curious that Pope originally wrote

A mighty maze, and all without a plan,

and then altered it to its present form because his friends told him this conflicted with his religious views. (A case, perhaps, such as was contemplated a few lines later :

Laugh where we must, be candid where we can

But vindicate the ways of God to man.

My point is that this is not really a joke against the critic, because the two lines are very nearly the same; a maze is conceived as something that at once has and has not got a plan so that, whichever you say, you are merely expanding the notion already stated.

A maze may be said to have no plan when it was designed with a plan to start with, but the plan has since been lost, or at any rate is not being shown to you. Or it may be said to have no plan when it is merely an untidy set of walks, and there are a variety of ways of getting to the centre. Or it might (these are the meanings that Pope was not allowed) mean that there is no way of getting to the centre, or even no recognisable centre at all. But if this were known to be the case it would be useless to try and expatiate over the thing, and incorrect to call it a maze. Pope's original antithesis was nearer that between art and nature than that between a Christian's hope and despair; it was jaunty and secure because he implied it was worth looking about, whether the maze had a plan or not; and because, in either case, it was possible to understand a great deal about the scene of man merely by not falling into absurdities. Or one may regard the contradiction between having and not having a plan so far as it went, as already implied, not only in the noun, but in the noun and adjective respectively: mighty 'this is a large and difficult matter, to which we must give all our attention,' but maze a quaint affair, stirring to the imagination perhaps but still mundane, something that would go well in one's private grounds if one were doing things on a grand scale, as would a Greek temple or the parish church for that matter, and though entailing tedium and inconvenience still a suitable occupation for a gentleman.

From this point of view, to admit it might not have a plan while taking for granted it was capable of having a plan made for it, this confession of doubt is the final expression of security ; shows the fading from consciousness of any further need for the encouragement of external faith; views from outside and has learnt not to imagine the isolation of the heart of man.

Misreading's of poetry, as every reader must have found, often give examples of this plausibility of the opposite term. I had at one time a great admiration for that line of Rupert Brooke's about

The keen

Impassioned beauty of a great machine,

a daring but successful image, it seemed to me, for that contrast between the appearance of effort and the appearance of certainty, between forces greater than human and control divine in its foreknowledge, which is what excites one about engines; they have the calm of beauty without its complacence, the strength of passion without its disorder. So it was a shock to me when I looked at one of the quotations of the line one is always seeing about, and found that the beauty was unpassioned, because machines, as all good nature-poets know, have no hearts. I still think that a prosaic and intellectually shoddy adjective, but it is no doubt more intelligible than my emendation, and sketches the same group of feelings.

Evidently the simplest way for the two opposites defined by the context to be suggested to the reader is by some disorder in the action of the negative; as by its being easily passed over or too much insisted upon. Thus in the Keats Ode to Melancholy

No, no; go not to Lethe ; neither twist

tells you that somebody, or some force in the poet's mind, must have wanted to go to Lethe very much, if it took four negatives in the first line to stop them. The desire to swoon back into pure sensation, abandonment of the difficulties of life, femininity (from the masculine point of view), or death from consumption is taken for granted in the reader, and this is powerful as a means of putting it there. And on the other hand, we must consider such effects as

My God, my God, look not so sharp upon me ;

Adders and serpents, let me breathe awhile;

Ugly Hell gape not: come not, Lucifer;

I'll burn my books. Ah Mephistophelis.

(Marlowe, Faustus.)

where there is no stress, as a matter of scansion, on the negatives, so that the main meaning is a shuddering acceptance, that informs the audience what is there. But behind this there is also a demand for the final intellectual curiosity, at whatever cost, to be satisfied :

> Let Ugly Hell gape, show me Lucifer;

so that perhaps, behind all his terror, it is for this reason that he is willing to abandon his learning, that he is going to a world where knowledge is immediate, and in those flames his books will no longer be required. Faustus is being broken ; the depths of his mind are being churned to the surface; his meanings are jarring in his mouth; one cannot recite Ugly Hell gape not as a direct imperative like 'stop gaping there'; and it is evident that with the last two words he has abandoned the effort to organise his preferences, and is falling to the devil like a tired child.[50]

Shakespeare's use of the negative is nearly always slight and casual ; he is much too interested in a word to persuade himself that it is 'not' there, and that one must think of the opposite of its main meaning.

> There's not a shirt and a half in all my company; and the half shirt is two napkins tacked together and thrown over the shoulders like a herald's coat without sleeves; and the shirt, to say the truth, stolen from my host at St. Alban's, or the red-nosed innkeeper of Daventry.

There lives not three good men unhanged in all England, and one of them is fat and grows old.

There's not three of my hundred and fifty left alive, and they are for the town-end, to beg during life.

One must bear Falstaff in mind when considering how Shakespeare came to write

> Mar. Tullus Aufidius, is he within your walls ?

---

50 A critic said that my interpretation here is wrong because the actor is meant to scream with horror not sound like a tired child. Certainly ' tired child' is a bit off the point. But the more the actor screams the stressed words the less the audience hears the unstressed words ' not ' ' not.'

In many languages new forms for expressing the negative have been introduced, because the old form being unstressed becomes progressively harder to hear. Hence the French pas etc. and the English do with the negative. This is clear evidence that the unstressed negative gets lost conveniently often. For that matter press correspondents regularly cable "he quaint and expensive grammatical form not repeat not.

ist Sen. No, nor a man that fears you lesse than he ;

'that's lesser than a little.

(Cor., i. iv. 13.)

The boast was to have been that nobody feared Marcius in the whole town, any more than the hero Aufidius feared him; the second line, at any rate, can have no other point; but on second thoughts that might have implied Aufidius feared him a great deal, since the town could not plausibly claim to be braver than its admitted leader. So more was changed to lesse the first line became a statement of Aufidius' courage; if you are puzzled for a moment by the negatives, fear you lesse evidently means that somebody is very brave ; the second line insists that somebody else is even braver ; and if the sentence is said quickly it certainly sounds like a sharp reply. At any rate it is doing its best with the difficulty of not implying the wrong thing, in that no obvious emendation is more sensible. Such muddles with negatives are common enough in Elizabethan writings ; like Spenser's

Thus did she watch, and weare the weary night

In waylful plaints, that none was to appease ;

Now walking soft, now sitting still upright,

As sundry chaunge her seemed best to ease.

Ne lesse did Talus suffer sleep to seaze

His eyelids sad, but watcht continually.

Lying without her door in great disease ;

Like to a spaniel wayting carefully

Lest any should betray his lady treacherously.

(Faerie Queene v. vi. 26.)

No more than Britomart did Talus allow sleep to seaze his eyelids sad; on the other hand, no less than Britomart did he suffer in great disease. And, ignoring this verbal attraction, the parts of the lines are thought of as quite separate pieces of ornamentation, laid on flatly; suffer sleep to seaze is translated into 'go to sleep — try to kdfep awake' without thinking about Ne lesse (='So too '). I have quoted the whole verse to show how impossible it would be to have any other reading, once you have got into the movement. It is important to bear in mind this attitude to grammar; once these floating and ill-attached parts of speech are crushed together into a pun (cease, as it were, to obey the pure gas laws) it is a matter, not of calculation, but of experiment, to see what corrections to the formula must be applied.

Perhaps the strangest case of Spenser's indifference to irrelevant meaning, lack of stress upon syntax, and readiness to push words quite flatly, without apology, into their place in the pattern, occurs during one of the descriptions of a dragon.

And at the point two stings infixed are

Both deadly sharpc, that sharpest steele exceedeth farre.

But stings and sharpest steele did far exceed

The sharpnesse of his cruell rending clawes.

(l. Xi. II-I2.)

Both these statements mean the opposite of what they say; steel — stings — claws are in ascending, not as a grammarian would suppose in descending, order of sharpness. It must seem an extraordinary degree of perversity which made exceedeth a singular verb, agreeing with the two stings thought of as a single weapon according to the usual Elizabethan practice, or with the abstract idea, not stated till the next verse, of their sharpness so that its only obvious subject is steel. But I doubt if Spenser gave it any attention; the main point of the lines is to compare stings with steel as of a similar degree of sharpness, and to say they are both exceedingly sharp.

I should connect a certain blankness in the meaning of this example with a much more rational failure on the part of Merth to say what she intended.

What bootes it all to have, and nothing use ?

Who shall him rewe, that swimming in the maine.

Will die for thirst, and water doth refuse ?

Refuse such fniitlesse toile, and present pleasures chuse.

(ii. vi. 17.)

Since the maine in Spenser is always the sea, the lady has chosen an absurdly bad example, at first sight only for the lake of the rhyme. But it is not the duty of a poet to put good arguments into the mouths of persons with whom he disagrees, and it is rather a profound evolutionary by-blow, which fits in very well with Spenser's sensuous idealism, that such a man does not drink the sea- water because it will hurt him and because it tastes nasty.

Shakespeare sometimes throws in a ' not ' apparently to suggest extra subtlety:

> Lenox. And the right valiant Banquo walked too late,
>
> Whom you may say (if 't please you) Fleans kill'd,
>
> For Fleans fled: Men must not walke too late.
>
> Who cannot want the thought, how monstruous
>
> It was for Malcolme, and Donalbaine
>
> To kill their gracious Father ?
>
> (Macbeth, in. vi.)

Who can avoid thinking, is the meaning; but the not breaks through the irony into 'Who must not feel that they have not done anything monstrous at all ? ' ' Who must not avoid thinking altogether about so touchy a state matter ? ' This is not heard as the meaning, however, the normal construction is too strong, and the negative acts as a sly touch of disorder.

There is an altered sign in Troilus serving a similar purpose :

> Pand. If ever you prove false one to another ... let all constant men be Troiluses, all false women Cressids and all brokers-between Pandars. (iii. ii. 216.)

The correction to ' unconstant ' is wrong because this was evidently said well on the front of the apron-stage, an address straight to the audience, which appealed to what everybody knew was going to be the story; he is pointing to each in turn, 'you know what we puppets stand for, it is a strong simple situation,' at the end of the scene.

It is not so much that 'not' was said lightly and might easily be ignored as that it implied a conflict (or why should you be saying one of the innumerable things the subject was not, instead of the one thing it was})y and it was upon this conflict, rather than upon the value of the passage as information, that the reader's sympathy devolved.

Stone walls do not a prison make,

Nor iron bars a cage ;

Minds innocent and quiet take

That for a hermitage.

(To Althea,)

The point of the poem is to describe those services that are freedom; constancy to a mistress, loyalty to a political party, obedience to God, and the limited cosiness of good company; thus to focus its mood, to discover what shade of interpretation Lovelace is putting on the blank cheque of a paradox, is in a sense to define the meaning of not in the first two lines. This is done to some extent by the grammar of the verse itself.

That may be 'the fact that they do not make a prison,' and we are then told that this notion withdraws the mind, as if to a hermitage from the anxieties of the world. But on the face of it, that is the cage or prison itself, and by being singular, so that it will not apply to walls or bars, it admits that they do, in fact, make even for quiet minds a prison and a cage. It is curious to read 'those' instead of that and see how the air of wit evaporates and generous carelessness becomes a preacher's settled desire to convince. If you read 'them' there is a further shift because the metre becomes prose ; the sentiment might be by Bunyan, and one wonders if it is at all true.

However, this experiment has hardly a fair chance, as there is another ambiguity which gives the verse recklessness, with an air both of paradox and of reserve. Take is a verb active in feeling though presumably here passive in sense; thus though it mainly says, 'such minds accept prison for their principles and can turn it into a hermitage,' there is some implication that 'such minds imprison themselves, escape from life, perhaps escape from their mistress, into jail, and cannot manage without their martyrdom.' It is the proximity of quiet which hushes this meaning, and keeps it from spoiling the proportions of the poem as a whole ; 'such persons, madam, were aware of the advantages of retiring from the world, and are accepting their misfortune with some philosophy.' There is another shade of meaning which is almost 'mistake,' as in 'cry you mercy, I took you for a joint-stool '; 'such minds may be so innocent that they know no difference between a prison and a hermitage'; for this they may be mocked or revered, but it is with irony that the poet includes himself among them; or 'so quiet that they pretend not to know the difference,' with a saintly impertinence that would have pleased George Herbert.

All these meanings are no more than slight overtones or grace- notes; the main meaning is sufficiently brave and is conveyed with enough fervour to stand alone ; thus, looking back to that, it may after all refer to walls and bars, and be attracted into the singular by the neighbouring hermitage.

I shall close the mild section of the seventh type with the most rational possible form of depraved negative, which puts something into your head while telling you it is not part of the picture. Thus Swinburne's

When the blood of thy foemen made fervent

A sand never moist from the main . . .

On sands by the storm never shaken

Nor wet from the washing of tides . . .

(Dolores.)

is not so much defining the sand of the arena as dragging in the sand of the sea, which has not so far been mentioned; by this simple device with negatives (Greek choruses are fond of it) he brings in the idea of Venus as born from the sea and, for himself if not for the reader, his whole pack of associations about the Great Sweet Mother.

Or for an even flatter use :

. . . behind her Death,

Close following pace for pace, not mounted yet

On his pale horse . . .

(Paradise Lost, x. 590.)

where, as saints in windows carry a gridiron, not for use, but because it is expected of them, or as the newspapers tell you there is no news to-day about the latest murder, so the pale horse is mentioned because people like to be reminded it is sometimes there.

There is another Shakespearean negative in one of the songs of Ophelia, an irrelevant little word in itself, which supports a faint but an elaborate reverberation of feeling; becomes, to an attent ear, a full ambiguity; and drapes about itself for a moment the whole structure of the play.

Oph. White his Shrow'd as the Mountaine Snow.

Que. Alas looke heere my Lord.

Oph. Larded with sweet flowers:

Which bewept to the grave did not go.

With true-love showres.

(Hamlet, iv. v.)

Evidently Pope was right in leaving out not from the point of view of the song considered as detached from the play.[51] Which may refer to the shroud the snow or tht flowers anyway true love showres contains a metaphor connecting them. The situations of flowers and the corpse may be either parallel or opposed with regard to mourners ; and it may be either flowers, if they are dewy, or human mourners, who weep, or do not weep, for the corpse.

It is easy to forget Ophelia's situation, and feel that she was a sweet pathetic creature, and it was somehow natural that she should be crazy. She has been told that because she obeyed her father her lover has gone mad ; her lover has certainly abandoned her with insults, and has certainly, with indifference, killed her father.

The Shrow'd then, is white because it covers one who is so noble and so valuable to her and because it is soon to be stained with corruption; it is glimmering before her mind's eye. Not may negate going or weeping. That the ear expects did go may mean that all nature wept for Polonius; that it gets did not go may mean he was interred in hugger-mugger (probably without any shroud); that it expects did go may mean Polonius is dead

51 I seem to have missed the point of the song taken alone. The apparent shroud of the snow is really a protection for the coming flowers of the spring, and therefore need not be wept. But this theological hope for the dead man of the song acts as a source of pathos while you consider the people Ophelia had in mind.

and buried; that it gets did not go may mean that, whether Hamlet wept for him or not, he went first into the lobby where he was safely stowed that it expects did go may mean that Hamlet is dead to her, that she feels he must really be dead and she ought to weep for him, and that he is going to England at the risk of his life ; that it gets did not go may mean that he is not really dead, that she must not weep for one who is alive and has so wronged her (the end of their love was not his death but his murder of her father), and that he is going to come back from England safely. She may alter the song through an echo of the misanthropy of her lover, from a feeling the flowers ought not to be mixed up with corpses, that the plucked flowers are the objects on a bier that ought really to be mourned for, though they are not. Or the dead man of the song may be Hamlet's father, so that the whole scene is a sort of satire against the Queen. I must consider the whole scene to insist upon this point.

Ophelia, when mad, is used as much to refer to other characters' histories as her own, being an inspired figure, or merely the reverberation of the play. The irony against the Queen is not intended, then, as in Ophelia's own mind; it is partly an isolated dramatic irony and partly a device to put us inside the guilty mind of the Queen, 'full of artless jealousy,' to whom 'each toy seems prologue to some great amiss.' She begins the scene by refusing to speak with her, but Ophelia enters with reverence, as an ambassador with news, or in ironical accusation.

(Enter Ophelia distracted.)

Oph. Where is the beauteous Majesty of Denmark?

There may be a meaning such as Hamlet has elaborated ; ' where is the vanished dignity of a world which has gone rotten?'; but she makes her exit with the same dignity[52].

Oph. How should I your true love know from another one?
By his Cockle hat and staffe and his Sandal shoone.

'How should I know which of your husbands is your true love, you whose reality escapes me. Which is the true pilgrim for his mistress's favour, the Ghost doomed for a certain time to walk the earth, the bloat King who has lost his peace of mind to win you, or your loving son you have just sent from me to his death in England ?

52 The point is that by dropping this initial brick she establishes herself with the audience as a figure who is expected to drop more important bricks later.

Que. Alas sweet Lady; what imports this Song?

Oph. Say you? Nay, pray you marke.

He is dead and gone Lady, he is dead and gone
At his head a grass-greene Turfe, at his heeles a stone.

'Pray you marke; the one you have killed already was the true one, and even the turf and stone will not keep him down. And it is my dead father, not Hamlet, who truly loved me.'

(Enter King.)

It is he who is walking now, not the Ghost, as the Queen's true love.

Que. Nay but Ophelia.

Oph. Pray you marke ;

and she sings the song I have quoted. From this point of view it is the Ghost whose Shrow'd is so white and the Queen's look here recalls : 'look here, upon this picture and on this.' In so far as old Hamlet went to the grave he did not go unwept but he went wept falsely by his Queen, also, perhaps, unwept by flowers without approval of nature, in that he died unshriven; in so far as he did not go to the grave he walked the earth, and so caused weeping.

But I am not sure that this is a complete example of the seventh type. There are too many implications, all 'rather distant, for a genuine pair of opposites to collide; one must distinguish between mere wealth of relevance to the setting (first type), mere disorder of preferences united in a single act of the sensibility (fourth to sixth types) and an impulse to state emphatically 'the two opposites defined by the context'; for this poor Ophelia, in the exhaustion of her wreckage, can hardly put in a claim. I have put the example here as a particularly elaborate use of the negative; it might have gone well enough among the dramatic ironies in the first chapter.

Keats often used ambiguities of this type to convey a dissolution of normal experience into intensity of sensation. This need not be concentrated into an ambiguity.

Let the rich wine within the goblet boil

Cold as a bubbling well

is an example of what I mean; and the contrast between cold weather and the heat of passion which is never forgotten throughout St. Agnes Eve. It is the 'going hot and cold at once' of fever. The same method is worth observing in detail when in the Ode to Melancholy it pounds together the sensations of joy and sorrow till they combine into sexuality.

> No, no: go not to Lethe, neither twist
>
> Wolf's-bane, tight-rooted, for its poisonous wine :
>
> Nor suffer thy pale forehead to be kissed
>
> By nightshade, ruby grape of Proserpine ;
>
> Make not your rosary of yewberries,
>
> Nor let the beetle nor the death-moth be
>
> Your mournful Psyche, nor the downy owl
>
> A partner in your sorrow's mysteries ;
>
> For shade to shade will come too drowsily,
>
> And dull the wakeful anguish of the soul.[53]

One must enjoy the didactic tone of this great anthology piece ; it is a parody, by contradiction, of the wise advice of uncles. ' Of course, pain is what we all desire, and I am sure I hope you will be very unhappy. But if you go snatching at it before your time, my boy, you must expect the consequences; you will hardly get hurt at all.'

'Do not abandon yourself to melancholy, delightful as that would be, or you will lose the sensations of incipient melancholia. Do not think always about forgetting, or you will forget its pain. Do not achieve death, or you can no longer live in its shadow. Taste rather at their most sharp the full sensations of death, of melancholy, and of oblivion.' But I have paraphrased only for my own pleasure ; there is no need for me to insist on the contrariety of the pathological splendours of this introduction.

Opposite notions combined in this poem include death and the sexual act, a pair of which I must produce further examples; pain and pleasure, perhaps as a milder version of this; the conception of the woman as at

---

53 The whole poem is quoted gradually.

once mistress and mother, at once soothing and exciting, whom one must master, to whom one must yield ; a desire at once for the eternity of fame and for the irresponsibility of oblivion; an apprehension of ideal beauty as sensual ; and an apprehension of eternal beauty as fleeting. The perfection of form, the immediacy of statement, of the Ode, lie in the fact that these are all collected into the single antithesis which unites Melancholy to Joy. Biographers who attempt to show from Keats's life how he came by these notions are excellently employed, but it is no use calling them in to explain why the poem is so universally intelligible and admired ; evidently these pairs of opposites, stated in the right way, make a direct appeal to the normal habits of the mind.

But when the melancholy fit shall fall

Sudden from Heaven like a weeping cloud.

That fosters the droop-headed flowers all.

And hides the green hill in an April shroud ;

Weeping produces the flowers of joy which are themselves sorrowful; the hill is green as young, fresh and springing, or with age, mould and geology; April is both rainy and part of springtime; and the shroud an anticipation of death that has its own energy and beauty, either is itself the fact that the old hill is hidden under green, or is itself the grey mist, the greyness of falling rain, which is reviving that verdure.

Then glut thy sorrow on a morning rose,

Or on the Rainbow of the salt sand wave,

Or on the wealth of globed peonies.

Either: 'Give rein to sorrow, at the mortality of beauty,' or ' defeat sorrow by sudden excess and turn it to joy, at the intensity of sensation.' Morning is parallel to April, and pun with mourning; the flowers stand at once for the more available forms of beauty, and for the mistress who is unkind.

Or if thy mistress some rich anger shows

Imprison her soft hand, and let her rave,

And feed deep, deep upon her peerless eyes.

She dwells with Beauty, Beauty that must die,

And Joy, whose hand is ever at his lips.

Bidding adieu, and aching Pleasure nigh,

Turning to poison while the bee-mouth sips;

Aye, in the very Temple of Delight Veiled

Melancholy hath her sovran shrine.

She is at first thy mistress, so that she represents some degree of joy, however fleeting; then, taking the verse as a unit, she becomes Veiled Melancholy itself ; veiled like a widow or holding up a handkerchief for sorrow, or veiled, like the hill under its green, because at first sight joy. Very and sovran, with an air of making a distinction and overcoming the casual prejudice of the reader, now insist that this new sort of joy is in part a fusion of joy and melancholy, sovran means either 'melancholy is here deepest,' or 'this new production is the satisfactory (and attractive) kind of melancholy'; and she is veiled because only in the mystery of her ambivalence is true joy to be found.

Though seen of none save him whose strenuous tongue

Can burst joy's grape against his palate fine ;

'Can burst the distinction between the two opposites; can discover the proud and sated melancholy to which only those are entitled who have completed an activity and achieved joy.'

His soul shall taste the sadness of her might

And be among her cloudy trophies hung.

If sadness here was taken as an attribute of melancholy only, as the only unambiguous reading must insist, we should have a tautology which no amount of historical allusion could make sensible; though melancholy meant Burton and Hamlet and sadness meant seriousness, it would still be like Coleridge's parody:

So sad and miff; oh I feel very sad.

She has become joy, melancholy, and the beautiful but occasionally raving mistress the grandeur of the line is unquestioned only because everybody takes this for granted.

Her trophies (death-pale are they all) are cloudy because vague and faint with the intensity and puzzling character of this fusion, or because already dead, or because, though preserved in verse, irrevocable. They are hung because sailors on escaping shipwreck hung up votive gifts in gratitude (Horace, iii. i.), or because, so far from having escaped, in the swoon of this achievement he has lost life, independence, and even distinction from her.

No doubt most people would admit that this is how Keats gets his effects, but the words are not obviously ambiguous because, in the general wealth of the writing, it is possible to spread out one to each word the meanings which are actually diffused into all of them.

I began this chapter with references to Freud; this last example may show how what is accepted as intelligible poetry may be considered as an association of opposites such as would interest the psycho-analyst. However, in the Keats Ode it is more obvious that opposites are being employed than that they are such as to interest the psycho-analyst; in the following examples from Crashaw it is more obvious that the psychoanalyst would be interested than that opposites are being employed. Crashaw's poetry often has two interpretations, religious and sexual; two situations on which he draws for imagery and detail. But are these both the context which is to define the opposites, or is he using one as a metaphor of the other, so that the ambiguity is of the first type, or each as a metaphor of each, so that it is of the third ? Is he deceiving us about either, or just making a poem (detached from life) out of both ? Is he generalising from two sorts of experience, or finding a narrow border of experience that both hold in common ? These questions can only be answered for particular poems, and then only by a very detailed attention to the attitude taken up by the poet. Thus I put a poem by Herbert, I gave to Hope a watch of mine, into the third type, because it applied to the courting both of God and of a mistress, and laid these two forms of experience side by side, thinking them different, but not thinking of them in a different way. (P. ii8.) An example from Crashaw on the same theme was treated as graceful but comparatively trivial. However, when Crashaw is not being directly witty on this theme the situation is more complicated. Though he lays them side by side and talks about both the two forms of experience are* as different as possible; one is good, the other evil. The 'context' here is that a saint is being adored for her chastity, and the metaphors about her are veiled references to copulation. Such a passage, then, must be placed in my seventh class, because the context defines the two situations as opposites; two opposed judgments are being held together and allowed to reconcile themselves, to stake out different territories, to find their own level, in the mind.

The great Hymn to the Name and Honour of the admirable Sainte Teresa is so innocently interpretable that I need only quote some passages to make this point clear.

She never undertook to know

What death with love should have to doe ;

Nor has she e'er yet understood

Why to show love, she should shed blood,

Yet though she cannot tell you why,

She can Love, and she can dy.

Scarce has she Blood enough to make

A guilty sword blush for her sake ;

Yet has she a heart dares hope to prove

How much lesse strong is death than love.

. . . she breathes all fire ;

Her weak breast heaves with strong desire

Of what she may with fruitless wishes

Seek for amongst her mother's kisses.

I am not saying that this is an ambiguity ; it is the overt metaphor of Christ as her spouse. But the treatment of the metaphor amounts to a strange mixture of feeling.

. . . some base hand have power to race

Thy Brest's chast cabinet, and uncase

A soul kept there so sweet, O no;

Wise Heaven will never have it so.

Thou art love's victime ; and must dy

A death more mystical and high. . . .

His is the dart must make the death

Whose stroke shall taste thy hallowed breath. . , .

O how oft shalt thou complain

Of a sweet and subtle pain.

Of intolerable joyes ;

Of a DEATH, in which who dyes

Loves his death, and dyes again.

And would for ever be so slain.

And lives, and dyes; and knowes not why To live.

But that he thus may never leave to dy.

Oh thou undaunted daughter of desires ; we may echo upon the poet his praise of the heroine.[54] How hard it is to keep this set of symbols far enough away from the no less charming set employed, not thirty years later, by Dryden:

The Youth, though in haste,

And breathing his last.

In pity died slowly, while she died more fast.

Till at length she cried.

Now, my dear, now let us go,

Now die, my Alexis, and I will die too.

(Marriage a la Mode.)

---

54 Crashaw could easily have laughed back at me here. He could have said that the English are always provincial, and that as a European scholar he was enriching me language with a normal piece of Counter-Reformation verse. But this claim for his own good sense would not, I think, make the convention he was using any less strange.

You might think I was being merely malicious in this collocation ; trying to defile a Holy Thought by making it into a Dirty Joke. But the two systems of thought are not as unlike as all that; Crashaw certainly conceived the bliss of the saints as extremely like the bliss which on earth he could not obtain without sin; and this certainly was a supply of energy to him and freed his virtue from the Puritan sense of shame. Dryden, in the same sort of way, is bringing a direct and unassuming attitude towards sexuality into relation with the heroic manner of his serious plays, in which people do indeed die for one another rather easily ; and the views of life contrasted in the song are no less oddly connected in the whole play it was written for. Of course, its main point is to be funny ; he is using the metaphor chiefly as a rag of decency and to laugh at the mystics. But it is also one of those mutual comparisons which benefit both parties ; the natural act is given dignity, the heroic act tenderness and a sort of spontaneity. Or if we can only consider it as a simple comparison, still by a sort of public feeling (like that which is the most real sentiment of his tragedies) he gives the subject a dignity which is the root of his gaiety; the joke is rather against human pretensions than human sentiments; there is no suggestion, after all, that they would not really have died for each other ; and the strongest resultant feeling, stronger than those of wit, of grace, and of impertinence, is a pathos not far from the central sentiment of Christianity. 'Pleasure is exhausting and fleeting; quelle est triste la jeunesse nothing is to be valued more than mutual forbearance; and it is harder to be happy, even under the most favourable circumstances, than anybody would have supposed.'

I have been talking as if Crashaw really thought the bliss of the saints was like that of the sexes, but, of course, this is too simple ; we only know that he feels and writes as if it were. One must consider, to understand such a use of language, not only what is being described but what terms the speaker has to describe it in; upon what basis of experience it is being conceived. One must not say that Crashaw described a sensual form of mysticism, only that he was content to use sexual terms for his mystical experiences, because they were the best terms that he could find. You may say, then, that this use of metaphor is not ambiguous at all, but it is certainly similar to ambiguity in a peculiar way; some people who think this a beautiful poem are reading it in a very different way from others who would agree with them.^ And to find reasons for the fact that any particular person reads it in any particular way, that he allows any particular settlement of territory between the two opposite modes of judgment, one would have to know a great deal about him. Indeed the way in which a person lives by vaguely-conceived opposites is the most important thing about his make-up ; the way in which opposites can be stated so as to satisfy a wide variety of people, for a great number of degrees of interpretation, is the most important thing about the communication of the arts. It is in this sort of way that I must justify my use of these odd passage as a culmination.

One feels, in fact, about much of Crashaw's verse, not that it is in itself particularly ambiguous, but that the ideas involved are so unfamiliar, are used in his judgments with such complexity that to think of it as ambiguous may be the right mode of approach. This epigram, for instance, is straightforward enough from its own point of view :

Suppose he had been Tabled at thy Teates,

Thy hunger feeles not what he eates :

Hee'l have his Teat eVe long (a bloody one)

The Mother then must suck the Son.

(Luke xi.. Blessed be the paps that thou hast sucked,)

This is to show the unearthly relation to earth of the Christ, and with a sort of horror to excite adoration. The antithesis assumes he was an ascetic even at the breast, and suppose he had half refuses to admit that he was once a baby, a parasite and an animal. Tabled, perhaps, also means 'taught,' whether the natural or the Judaic law; suppose would then mean that being ever virgin he never learnt it. The second couplet is 'primitive' enough; a wide variety of sexual perversions can be included in the notion of sucking a long bloody teat which is also a deep wound. The sacrificial idea is aligned with incest, the infantile pleasures, and cannibalism; we contemplate the god with a sort of savage chuckle ; he is made to flower, a monstrous hermaphrodite deity, in the glare of a short-circuiting of the human order. Those African carvings, and the more lurid forms of Limerick, inhabit the same world.

The grotesque seventeenth-century simile, of which this is a striking but in no way unique example, belongs to an age of collection of interesting oddities rather than to the scientific (eighteenth-century) age, with its limitations as to what is likely o be true and what it is sensible to say ; to an age when all kinds of private fancies were avowable on their own rights[55]. In considering what time would have called the 'curious' attitude of Crashaw here, we must remember the Cambridge Platonist who explained to the learned world that his breast smelt like violets, and the remarks on the same subject by Montaigne. One is sometimes driven to find ambiguities, or to become conscious of them, in mere surprise that such a thing should have been said ; whereas the fact is that that age was interested quite simply in such harmless reflections as a child might make to the embarrassment of the dinner-table. It is fair to give another example of this from Dryden, in which he now appears the more innocent and childlike of the two. (It is, of course,- an early work.) Upon the death of the Lord Hasting from smallpox :

> Blisters with pride swell'd, which thr'row's flesh did sprout
>
> Like Rose-buds, stuck i' th' Lilly-skin about.
>
> Each little Pimple had a tear in it,
>
> To wail the fault its rising did commit. . . .
>
> Or were those gems sent to adorn his Skin
>
> The Cabinet of a richer Soul within?

One is tempted to look around, as I did in the Crashaw quatrain, for some additional reasons, some strange causes at work, which would make the sorrowing parents feel satisfaction in this ; but the machinery of analysis would be irrelevant here ; they just thought it was 'curious,' and therefore graceful.

These steadying reflections must be borne in mind when we consider how the following quatrain came to be thrust into Crashaw's translation of the Dies Irae.

> O let thine own soft bowels pay
>
> Thy self; And so discharge that day.
>
> If sin can sigh, love can forgive.
>
> O say the word my Soul shall live.

---

55 In this and the following example I gather that Crashaw was not following contemporary models from Catholic European literature.

Something weird and lurid in their apprehension of the sacrificial system, a true sense of the strangeness of the mind's world, can continually be felt in the seventeenth-century mystics. I call it ambiguous, not from any verbal ingenuity of its own, but because it draws its strength from a primitive system of ideas in which the uniting of opposites (of saviour and criminal, for instance) is of peculiar importance. Of course, you may as well say it is ambiguous to use any idea which involves fundamental antinomies; the idea of relation itself, very likely; but I am here concerned only with ambiguities which are of literary interest and can be felt as complex when they are apprehended.

That day (of judgment) may either assume 'on' or be object of discharge. Discharge has

a variety of similar meanings centering round ^unload,' such as pay, prohibit, exonerate and dismiss; all these yield slightly different meanings. But evidently the main meaning, sustained by the pun, is 'and so discharge thy soft bowels'; it is a brave use of that Biblical metaphor or pliysiological truth, according to which the bowels are made active by sympathy and are the seat of compassion. I find it difficult to have any clear reaction to this other than 'what fun, all the Freudian stuff'; but there seems to be no doubt that it involves a curious ambivalence of feeling. The patriarchal view of the matter is not merely an exotic idiom; it is well known and felt to be serious ; but among people more civilised and anxiously delicate than they the metaphor is suppressed (in the New Testament it is already a relic of language), and the facts on which it is based are either ignored or recognised only, as in those rather schoolboy verses by Swift, as a culmination of horror at the nightmare of the human mechanism. Though Crashaw takes it in his stride he is deliberately invoking a clash much harsher than the previous one with Dryden (p. 221). Popular language only recognises a yearning of the bowels towards someone ('You are the sort of person one could afford to signalise love for in such a way') as a mark of contempt so terrible as to degrade also the contender. The same violent and deeply-rooted ambivalence is the point of that magnificent obscenity in the Dunciad (ii. 83) where Jupiter by receiving the petitions of humanity with a travesty of the ancient symbol of compassion makes the indifference of God disgusting and the subservience of man unendurable.

Crashaw seems to escape from these conflicts, and it may be that the oddity of the metaphor was only intended to give a sort of wit and point to the pun on discharge such as I have put in the third class, and thought peculiar to the eighteenth century. But the two opposite interpretations are active in the verse, though in so subdued a form ; he is viewing himself as wholly united and subdued to Gpd, made part of God's body, since this metaphor is tolerable ; and if we may rely on the idea of infantile modes of judgment it is as an extreme exercise of humility that he returns to them. ' Forgive me by a compassion as if for yourself ; regard me merely as part of the tribe with which you are united.'

So far I have regarded this pair of opposites as in some degree accidental, as a historical matter of the clash of two metaphors. Freud, however, would regard the pair as a natural unit, as the mark of a deep-seated conflict in the child between an infantile pleasure in defecating and the need to learn more adult pleasures. Assuming such a conflict, its opposites will always suggest One another : ' I must pay God with the most valuable thing possible ; therefore I must pay God with dung, because that is the most worthless thing possible. But his own dung is the most valuable sort conceivable, and matters of this kind have to be kept strictly private ; it will be much best, then, if I can induce him to pay himself with that.' To find an image for the purest love, for the generosity furthest from sexuality, he falls back on sexuality in its most infantile and least creditable form.

No context is more important than that which defines God and dung as opposites, and it is proper that they should have been brought into this chapter. But how Crashaw arrived at the quatrain I have been considering, what his public thought when they read it, I cannot pretend to know. Probably they just thought it curious and Biblical and let it go at that.

I shall end this chapter with a more controlled and intelligible example from George Herbert, where the contradictory impulses that are held in equilibrium by the doctrine of atonement may be seen in a luminous juxtaposition. But in such cases of ambiguity of the seventh type one tends to lose sight of the conflict they assume; the ideas are no longer thought of as contradictory by the author, or if so, then only from a stylistic point of view; he has no doubt that they can be reconciled, and that he is stating their reconciliation. So I shall first consider a sonnet by Gerard Manley Hopkins, The Windhover, to Christ our Lord, as a more evident example of the use of poetry to convey an indecision, and its reverberation in the mind.

I caught this morning morning's minion, kingdom of daylight's
dauphin, dapple-dawn-drawn falcon, in his riding
Of the level underneath him steady air, and striding.
High there ; how he rung upon the rein of a wimpling wing
In his ecstasy. Then back, back forth on swing
As a skate's heel sweeps smooth on a bowbend; the hurl and gliding
Rebuffed the big wind. My heart in hiding
Stirred for a bird, the achieve of, the mastery of the thing.
Brute beauty and valour and act, oh air, pride, plume, here
Buckle ; and the fire that breaks from thee then, a billion
Times told lovelier, more dangerous, oh my chevalier.
No wonder of it. Sheer plod makes plough down sillion
Shine, and blue-bleak embers, ah my dear.
Fall, gall themselves, and gash gold- vermilion.

I am indebted to Dr. Richards for this case ; he has already written excellently about it. I have little to add to his analysis, and use it here merely because it is so good an example.

Hopkins became a Jesuit, and burnt his early poems on entering the order; there may be some reference to this sacrifice in the fire of the Sonnet. Confronted suddenly with the active physical beauty of the bird, he conceives it as the opposite of his patient spiritual renunciation ; the statements of the poem appear to insist that his own life is superior, but he cannot decisively judge between them, and holds both with agony in his mind. My heart in hiding would seem to imply that the more dangerous life is that of the Windhover, but the last three lines insist it is no wonder that the life of renunciation should be the more lovely. Buckle admits of two tenses and two meanings: 'they do buckle here,' or ' come, and buckle yourself here' ; buckle like a military belt, for the discipline of heroic action, and buckle like a bicycle wheel, 'make useless, distorted, and incapable of its natural motion. Here may mean 'in the case of the bird,' or 'in the case of the Jesuit'; then 'when you have become like the bird, or 'when you have become like the Jesuit.' Chevalier personifies either physical or spiritual activity; Christ riding to Jerusalem, or the cavalryman ready for the charge; Pegasus, or the Windhover.

Thus in' the first three lines of the sestet we seem to have a clear case of the Freudian use of opposites, where two things thought of as incompatible, but desired intensely by different systems of judgments, are spoken of simultaneously by words applying to both; both desires are thus given a transient and exhausting satisfaction, and the two systems of judgment are forced into open conflict before the reader. Such a process, one might imagine, could pierce to regions that underlie the whole structure of our thought; could tap the energies of the very depths of the mind. At the same time one may doubt whether it is most effective to do it so crudely as in these three lines; this enormous conjunction, standing as it were for the point of friction between the two worlds conceived together, affects one rather like shouting in an actor, and probably to many readers the lines seem so meaningless as to have no effect at all. The last three lines, which profess to come to a single judgment on the matter, convey the conflict more strongly and more beautifully.

The metaphor of the fire covered by ash seems most to insist on the beauty the fire gains when the ash falls in, when its precarious order is again shattered ; perhaps, too, on the pleasure, in that some movement, some risk, even to so determinedly static a prisoner, is still possible. The gold that painters have used for the haloes of saints is forced by alliteration to agree with the gash and gall of their self-tortures ; from this precarious triumph we fall again, with vermilion, to bleeding[56].

In great contrast with this proud but helpless suffering is a doctrinal poem by George Herbert, which uses the same methods. In 'The Sacrifice,' with a magnificence he never excelled, the various sets of conflicts in the Christian doctrine of the Sacrifice are stated with an assured and easy simplicity, a reliable and unassuming grandeur, extraordinary in any material, but unique as achieved by successive fireworks of contradiction, and a mind

56 Nearly all this analysis is only putting in the background ; the test is buckle. What would Hopkins have said if he could have been shown this analysis ? It is, perhaps, the only really disagreeable case in the book. If 1 am right, I am afraid he would have denied with anger that he had mean ' like a bicycle wheel, and then after much conscientious self-torture would have suppressed the whole poem.

jumping like a flea. Herbert's poems are usually more ' personal ' and renaissance than this one, in which the theological system is accepted so completely that the poet is only its mouthpiece.

Perhaps this, as a releasing and reassuring condition, is necessary if so high a degree of ambiguity is to seem normal. For, to this extent, the poem is outside the 'conflict' thecuy of poetry; it assumes, as does its theology, the existence of conflicts, but its business is to state a generalised solution of them. Here, then, the speaker is Jesus, the subject doctrinal, and the method that strange monotony of accent, simplicity of purpose, and rarefied intensity of feeling, which belong to a scholastic abstraction, come to life on the stage of a miracle play.

They did accuse me of great villainy

That I did thrust into the Deitie ;

Who never thought that any robberie ;

Was ever grief like mine ?

Some said that I the temple to the floore

In three days razed, and raised as before.

Why, he that built the world can do much more.

Was ever grief like mine?

He is speaking with pathetic simplicity, an innocent surprise that people should treat him so, and a complete failure to understand the case against him; thus who in the third line quoted and he in the seventh make their point by applying equally to I and the Deitie, But before thinking the situation as simple as the speaker one must consider the use of the word rased to apply to the two opposite operations concerned ; and that the quotation from Jeremiah which makes the refrain refers in the original not to the Saviour but to the wicked city of Jerusalem, abandoned by God, and in the hands of her enemies for her sins.

Then they condemn me all, with that same breath

Which I do give them daily, unto death;

Thus Adam my first breathing rendereth :

Was ever grief like mine ?

Hark how they cry aloud still Crucify,

He is not fit to live a day, they cry;

Who cannot live less than eternally.

Was ever grief like mine ?

Me all 'they all condemn me, they condemn the whole of me (I am Jerfiisalem and include them), they condemn me unto the total death of which I am not capable, they condemn me and thus call down their own destruction, I give them breath daily till their death, and unto death finally shall I give them' ; so that rendereth includes 'repay me for my goodness' and 'give up the ghost,' both at their eventual death and in their now killing me. The same fusion of the love of Christ and the vindictive terrors of the sacrificial idea turns up in his advice to his dear friends not to weep for him, for because he has wept for both, when in his agony they abandoned him, they will need their tears for themselves.

Weep not dear friends, since I for both have wept

When all my tears were blood, the while you slept,

Your tears for your own fortunes should be kept.

Was ever grief like mine ?

In each case, of course, the stress of the main meaning is on the loving-kindness of Jesus; it is only because this presentment of the sacrificial idea is so powerfully and beautifully imagined that all its impulses are involved.

Now heal thyself. Physician, now come down ;

Alas, I did so, when I left my crown

And father's smile for you, to feel his frown.

Was ever grief like mine ?

The secondary meaning ('to make you feel ') is a later refinement, and the Williams manuscript reads 'to feel for you.'

The last verse of all contains as strong and simple a double meaning:

But now I die ; Now, all is finished.

My woe, man's weal; and now I bow my head:

Only let others say, when I am dead,

Never was grief like mine.

English has no clear form for the Oratio Obliqua. He may wish that his own grief may never be exceeded among the humanity he pities, 'After the death of Christ, may there never be a grief like Christ's ' ; he may, incidentally, wish that they may say this, that he may be sure of recognition, and of a church that will be a sounding-board to his agony; or he may mean mine as a quotation from the others 'Only let there be a retribution, only let my torturers say never was grief like theirs, in the day when my agony shall be exceeded.' (Better were it for that man if he had never been born.)

I am not sure how far people would be willing to accept this double meaning ; I am only sure that after you have once apprehended it, after you have felt this last clash as a sound, you will never be able to read the poem without remembering that it is a possibility. For the resultant meaning of this apparently complete contradiction, one must consider the way it is used as a religious doctrine; 'Christ has made all safe, a weight is off our shoulders, and it is for that very reason far more urgent that we should be careful. Salvation is by Faith, and this gives an intolerable importance to Works. O death, where is thy sting; because the second death is infinitely terrible.' You may say the pious Herbert could not have intended such a contradiction, because he would have thought it blasphemous, and because he took a 'sunny' view of his religion. Certainly it is hard to say whether a poet is conscious of a particular implication in his work, he has so many other things to think of; but for the first objection, it is merely orthodox to make Christ to insist on the damnation of the wicked (though it might be blasphemous, because disproportionate, to make him insist on it here without insisting more firmly at the same time on its opposite); and for the second objection, it is true George Herbert is a cricket in the sunshine, but one is accustomed to be shocked on discovering the habits of such creatures; they are more savage than they seem[57].

57 The poem makes the suffering and yearning Christ say ' I am the Lord of Hosts — ' who never yet whom I would punish missed — ' they in me deny themselves all pity — ' see how spite cankers things. The analysis is not digging up anything hidden. This, however, is not to say that Herbert would have passed it for print. It seems he sometimes had readers work passed or to him by the licensing authorities, and it would be natural for him to consider rather I ought to be published, not whether he ought to have been.

A memory of the revengeful power of Jehovah gives resonance to the voice of the merciful power of Jesus, even when verbal effects so pretty as these last cannot be found:

Herod in judgment sits, while I do stand ;

Examines me with a censorious hand.

I him obey, who all things else command.

Was ever grief like mine ?

Even in so quiet a line as the second, me is made to ring out with a triumphant and scornful arrogance – 'the absurdity of the thing – and there is a further echo from the former dispensation in that his attitude of deference before Herod is one would give full play to his right hand and his stretched-out arm; that he will be far more furious in judgment than his judges; that one would stand to exert, as well as to suffer, power.

Why, Caesar is their only king, not I.

He clave the stony rock when they were dry ;

But surely not their hearts, as I well try.

Was ever grief like mine ?

It is by its concentration that this is so powerful. The first line is part of his defence to his judges : ' I am not a political agitator.' In the bitterness of this apology, that his kingdom is not of this world, he identifies Caesar with Moses as the chosen leader of Israel ('Oh no, it was Caesar who gave them the water of life ; I am only an honest subject'), and by this irony both the earthly power of the conqueror and the legal rationalism of the Pharisees are opposed both to the profounder mercy of the Christ and to the profounder searching's of heart that he causes ; I may cleave their hearts with my tenderness or with their despair.

Ah, how they scourge me ! yet my tenderness

Doubles each lash ; and yet their bitterness

Winds up my grief to a mysteriousness.

Was ever grief like mine ?

Doubles because I feel pain so easily, because I feel it painful that they should be so cruel, because I feel it painful they should be so unjust, because my tenderness enrages them, because my tenderness (being in fact power) will return equally each stroke upon them, because I take upon myself those pains also. Mysteriousness because the bitterness in them or (for various reasons) due to them produces grief no one can fathom, or because it dramatizes that grief into a form that can show itself (as in initiation to the Mysteries) to a crowd (as the scourgers also are a crowd), wound up like a string to give out music, and echoing in the mind, repeatable, as a type of suffering.

Behold they spit on me in scornful wise

Who with my spittle gave the blind man eyes,

Leaving his blindness to mine enemies.

Was ever grief like mine ?

Leaving his blindness wilfully, the conceit implies, as a cruel judgment upon my enemies, that they should in consequence spit upon me and so commit sin. (Father, forgive them, for they know not what they do.) These two events are contrasted, but that they should spit upon me is itself a healing; by it they distinguish me as scapegoat, and assure my triumph and their redemption; and spitting, in both cases, was to mark my unity with man. Only the speed, isolation, and compactness of Herbert's method could handle in this way impulses of such reach and complexity.

Then on my head a crown of thorns I wear,

For these are all the grapes Zion doth bear,

Though I my vine planted and watered there.

Was ever grief like mine ?

So sits the earth's great curse in Adam's fall

Upon my head, so I remove it all

From the earth on to my brows, and bear the thrall.

Was ever grief like mine ?

The thorns of the curse upon Adam, the wild grapes of the wicked city against which Isaiah thundered destruction, and the crown of vine -leaves of the Dionysiac revellers (and their descendants the tragedians), all this is lifted on to the head of the Christ from a round world, similar to it, in the middle distance; the world, no longer at the centre of man's vision, of Copernican astronomy. The achievement here is not merely that all these references are brought together, but that they are kept in their frame, of monotonous and rather naive pathos, of fixity of doctrinal outlook, of heartrending and straightforward grandeur.

> They bow their knees to me, and cry. Hail, King!
>
> Whatever scoffs or scomfulness can bring
>
> I am the floor, the sink, where they it fling.
>
> Was ever grief like mine ?
>
> Yet since man's sceptres are as frail as reeds,
>
> And thorny all their crowns, bloody their deeds,
>
> I, who am Truth, turn into truth their deeds.
>
> Was ever grief like mine ?

I, out of my mercy making their sins as few as possible, reflect that I am indeed a king, and so worthy of mockery; because all kings are as inferior (weak, outcast, or hated) as this; because I am king of kings, and all kings are inferior to me ; or because from my outcast kingship of mockery all real kingship takes its strength (the divine right of kings, for instance, and the relief of popular irritation under lords of misrule). He has united Herod and Pilate, 'whose friendship is his enmity,' and his scarlet robe of princes shows that only his blood 'can repair man's decay.'

> Oh all ye who pass by, behold and see ;
>
> Man stole the fruit, but I must climb the tree.
>
> The tree of life, to all but only me.
>
> Was ever grief like mine ?

The first line now at last, with an effect of apotheosis, gives the complete quotation from Jeremiah. He climbs the tree to repay what was stolen, as if he was putting the apple back; but the phrase in itself implies rather that he is doing the stealing, that so far from sinless he is Prometheus and the criminal. Either he stole on behalf of man (it is he who appeared to be sinful, and was caught up the tree) or he is climbing upwards, like Jack on the Beanstalk, and taking his people with him back to Heaven. The phrase has an odd humility which makes us see him as the son of the house ; possibly Herbert is drawing on the medieval tradition that the Cross was^ made of the wood of the forbidden trees. Jesus seems a child in this metaphor, because he is the Son of God, because he can take the apples without actually stealing (though there is some doubt about this), because of the practical and domestic associations of such a necessity, and because he is evidently smaller than Man, or at any rate than Eve, who could pluck the fruit without climbing. This gives a pathetic humour and innocence (except ye receive the Kingdom of Heaven as a little child, ye shall in no wise enter therein); on the other hand, the son stealing from his father's orchard is a symbol of incest; in the person of the Christ the supreme act of sin is combined with the supreme act of virtue. Thus in two ways, one behind the other, the Christ becomes guilty; and we reach the final contradiction:

> Lo here I hang, charged with a world of sin
>
> The greater world of the two . . .

as the complete Christ ; scapegoat and tragic hero ; loved because hated; hated because godlike; freeing from torture because tortured ; torturing his torturers because all-merciful ; source of all strength to men because by accepting he exaggerates their weakness; and, because outcast, creating the possibility of society.

> Between two theeves I spend my utmost breath.
>
> As he that for some robberie suffereth.
>
> Alas ! what have I stolen from you ? Death :
>
> Was ever grief like mine ?

Herbert deals in this poem, on the scale and by the methods necessary to it, with the most complicated and deeply-rooted notion of the human mind.

VIII

I must devote a final chapter to some remarks about what I have been doing; about the conditions under which ambiguity is proper, about the degree to which the understanding of it is of immediate importance, and about the way in which it is apprehended.

For the first of these the preface to Oxford Poetry 1927, stated an opposition very clearly; that there is a 'logical conflict, between the denotary and the conrotatory sense of words; between, that is to say, an asceticism tending to kill language by stripping words of all association and a hedonism tending to kill language by dissipating their sense under a multiplicity of associations.' The methods I have been using seem to assume that all poetical language is debauched into associations to any required degree; I ought at this point to pay decent homage to the opposing power.

Evidently all the subsidiary meanings must be relevant, because anything (phrase, sentence, or poem) meant to be considered as a unit must be unitary, must stand for a single order of the mind. In complicated situations this unity is threatened ; you are thinking of several things, or one thing as it is shown by several things, or one thing in several ways. A sort of unity may be given by the knowledge of a scheme on which all the things occur; so that the scheme itself becomes the one thing which is being considered. More generally one may say that if an ambiguity is to be unitary there must be 'forces' holding its elements together, and I ought then, in considering ambiguities, to have discussed what the forces were, whether they were adequate. But the situation here is like the situation in my first chapter, about rhythm; it is hard to show in detail how the rhythm acts, and one can arrive at the same result by showing the effects of the rhythm upon the meaning of the words.

Some sort of parallel may be found in the way logical connectives (the statement of logical form in addition to logical content) are usually unnecessary and often misleading, because too simple. Omitting an adjective one would need 'therefore,' stressing the adjective 'although' ; both logical connections are implied if the sentences are just put one after another. In the same way, people are accustomed to judge automatically the forces that hold together a variety of ideas; they feel they know about the forces, if they have analysed the ideas ; many forces, indeed, are covertly included within ideas ; and so of the two elements, each of which defines the other, it is much easier to find words for the ideas than for the forces. Most of the ambiguities I have considered here seem to me beautiful ; I consider, then, that I have shown by example, in showing the nature of the ambiguity, the nature of the fences which are adequate to hold it together. It would seem very artificial to do it the other way round, and very tedious to do it both ways at once.[58] I wish only, then, to say here that such vaguely imagined 'forces' are essential to the totality of a poem, and that they cannot be discussed in terms of ambiguity, because they are complementary to it. But by discussing ambiguity, a great deal may be made clear about them. In particular, if there is contradiction, it must imply tension; the more prominent the contradiction, the greater the tension; in some way other than by the contradiction, the tension must be conveyed, and must be sustained.

n ambiguity, then, is not satisfying in itself, nor is it, considered as a device on its own, a thing to be attempted ; it must' in each case arise from, and be justified by, the peculiar requirements of the situation. On the other hand, it is a thing which the more interesting and valuable situations are more likely to justify. Thus the practice of 'trying not to be ambiguous' has a great deal to be said for it, and I suppose was followed by most of the poets I have considered. It is likely to lead to results more direct, more communicable, and hence more durable; it is a necessary safeguard against being ambiguous without proper occasion, and it leads to more serious ambiguities when such occasions arise. But, of course, the phrase 'trying not to be ambiguous' is itself very indefinite and treacherous; it involves problems of all kinds as to what a poet can try to do, how much

58 I was claiming here a purity I had failed to attain. Many of the analyses in the bookre, I should say, convincing, if at all, through consideration of forces known be at work in the poet's mind, not by the verbal details used in illustration of them. However, this doesn't affect the theoretical distinction.

of his activity he is conscious of, and how much of his activity he could become conscious of if he tried. I believe that the methods I have been describing are very useful to critics, but certainly they leave a poet in a difficult position. Even in prose the belief in them is liable to produce a sort of doctrinaire sluttishness; one is tempted to set down a muddle in the hope that it will convey the meaning more immediately.

As for the immediate importance of the study of ambiguity, it would be easy enough to take up an alarmist attitude, and say that the English language needs nursing by the analyst very badly indeed. Always rich and dishevelled, it is fast becoming very rich and dishevelled ; always without adequate devices for showing the syntax intended, it is fast throwing away the few devices it had ; it is growing liable to mean more things, and less willing to stop and exclude the other possible meanings. A brief study of novels will show that English, as spoken by educafled people, has simplified its grammar during the last century to an extraordinary degree. People sometimes say that words are now used as flat counters, in a way which ignores their delicacy; that English is coming to use fewer of its words, and those more crudely. But this journalist flatness does not mean that the words have simple meanings, only that the word is used, as at a distance, to stand for a vague and complicated mass of ideas and systems which the journalist has no time to apprehend. The sciences might be expected to diminish the ambiguity of the language, both because of their tradition of clarity and because much of their jargon has, if not only one meaning, at any rate only one setting and point of view. But such words are not in general use ; they only act as a further disturbing influence on the words used already. English is becoming an aggregate of vocabularies only loosely in connection with one another, which yet have many words in common, so that there is much danger of accidental ambiguity, and you have to bear firmly in mind the small clique for whom the author is writing. It is to combat this that so much recent writing has been determinedly unintelligible from any but the precise point of view intended.

Of the increasing vagueness, compactness, and lack of logical distinctions in English, the most obvious example is the newspaper headline. I remember a very fine one that went.

VIII

Italian Assassin Bomb Plot Disaster.

Here we have the English language used as a Chinese system of flat key-words, given particular meaning by noun-adjectives in apposition, or perhaps rather as an agglutinative system, one word one sentence, like Esquimo. I am told that American headlines, however mysterious, are usually sentences; the English method is more complete. Bomb and plot you notice can either nouns or verbs, and would take kindly to being adjectives, not that they are anything so definite here. One thinks at first that there are two words or sentences, and a semicolon has been left out as in telegrams : ' I will tell you for your penny about the Italian Assassin and the well-known Bomb Plot Disaster ; but the assassin as f far as I remember, was actually not an Italian; Italian refers to the whole aggregate, and its noun, if any, is disaster. Perhaps, by being so far separated from its noun, it gives the impression that the other words, too, are somehow connected with Italy that bombs ,plots , and disasters belong both to government and rebel in those parts; perhaps Italian Assassin is not wholly separate in one's mind from the injured Mussolini. This extended use of the adjective acts as a sort of syncopation, which gives energy and excitement to the rhythm, rather like the effect of putting two caesuras into a line ; but, of course, the main rhythm conveys : ' This is a particularly exciting sort of disaster, the assassin-bomb-plot type they have in Italy,' and there is a single chief stress on bomb.

Evidently this is a very effective piece of writing, quite apart from the fact that it conveys its point in a form short enough for large type. It conveys it with a compactness which gives the mind several notions at one glance of the eye, with a unity like that of metaphor, with a force like that of its own favourite bombs. Nor can I feel that it will be a disaster if other forms of English literature adopt this fundamental mode of statement, so interesting to the logician ; it is possible that a clear analysis of the possible modes of statement, and a fluid use of grammar which sets out to combine them as sharply as possible into the effect intended, may yet give back something of the Elizabethan energy to what is at present a rather exhausted language. The grammatical sentence is not the only form of statement in modem English, and I want to suggest that the machinery I have been using upon poetry is going to become increasingly necessary if we are to keep the language under control.

I am not sure that I have been approaching this matter with an adequate skeleton of metaphysics. For instance, Mr. Richards distinguishes\poem into Sense, Feeling, Tone, and Intention; you may say an interpretation is not being done properly (if the analyst has conquered the country, still he is not ruling it) unless these four are separated out into sub-headings and the shades of grammar that convey the contents of each sub-heading are then listed in turn. But the process of apprehension, both of the poem and of its analysis, is not at all like reading a list; one wants as far as clarity will allow to say things in the form in which they will be remembered when properly digested. People remember a complex notion as a sort of feeling that involves facts and judgments ; one cannot give or state the feeling directly, any more than the feeling of being able to ride a bicycle; it is the result of a capacity, though it might be acquired perhaps by reading a list. But to state the fact and the judgment (the thought and the feeling) separately, as two diflFerent relevant matters, is a bad way of suggesting how they are combined; it makes the reader apprehend as two things what he must, in fact, apprehend as one thing. Detailed analysis of this kind might be excellent as psychology, but it would hardly be literary criticism; it would start much further back; and a mere reader of the poem would have to read a great deal of it to get the information he wanted.

This notion of unity is of peculiar importance; not only, though chiefly, in poetry, but in all literature and most conversation. One may remember, rather as a comparison than as an explanation, what Pavlov found in the brains of his dogs; that stimulation of a particular region produced inhibition, almost immediately, over regions in the neighbourhood, and at the region itself a moment later. Thus to say a thing in two parts is different in incalculable ways from saying it as a unit; Coleridge says somewhere that the mind insists on having a single word for a single mental operation, and will use an inadequate word rather than two adequate ones. When you are holding a variety of things in your mind, or using for a single matter a variety of intellectual machinery, the only way of applying all your criteria is to apply them simultaneously; the only way of forcing the reader to grasp your total meaning is to arrange that he can only feel satisfied if he is bearing all the elements in mind at the moment of conviction; the only way of not giving something heterogeneous is to give something which is at every point a compound.

VIII

My third heading is more important, as to the way in which ambiguity is apprehended. I have continually employed a method of analysis which jumps the gap between two ways of thinking; which produces a possible set of alternative meanings with sotie ingenuity, and then says it is grasped in the preconsciousness of the reader by a native effort of the mind. This must seem very dubious; but then the facts about the apprehension of poetry are in any case very extraordinary. Such an assumption is best judged by the way it works in detail; I shall only try here to make it seem plausible.

We think not in words but in directed phrases, and yet in accepting a syntax there is a preliminary stage of uncertainty; 'the grammar may be of such or such a kind; the words are able to be connected in this way or in that.' Words are seen as already in a grammar rather as letters are seen as already in a word, but one is much more prepared to have been wrong about the grammar than about the word. Under some drugs that make things jump about you see any particular thing moving or placed elsewhere in proportion as it is likely to move or be placed elsewhere, in proportion to a sort of coefficient of mobility which you have already given it as part of your apprehension. In the same way, a plausible grammar is picked up at the same time as the words it orders, but with a probability attached to it, and the less probable alternatives, ready, if necessary, to take its place, are in some way present at the back of your mind.

In poetry much stress is laid on such alternatives; 'getting to know' a poet is largely the business of learning to control them. And as, to take another coefficient which the eye attaches to things, as you have an impression of a thing's distance away, which can hardly ever be detached from the pure visual sensation, and. when it is so detached leaves your eye disconcerted (if what you took for a wall turns out to be the sea, you at first see nothing, perhaps are for a short time puzzled as with a blur, and then see differently, so the reading of a new poet, or of any poetry at all, fills many readers with a sense of mere embarrassment and discomfort, like that of not knowing, and wanting to know, whether it is a wall or the sea.

It is these faint and separate judgments of probability which unite, as if with an explosion, to 'make sense' and accept the main meaning of a connection of phrases; and the reaction, though rapid, is not as immediate as one is liable to believe. Also, as in a chemical reaction, there will have been reverse or subsidiary reactions, or small damped explosions, or slow widespread reactions, not giving out much heat, going o» concurrently, and the final result may be complicated by preliminary stages in the main process, or after-effects from the products of the reaction. As a rule, all that you recognise as in your mind is the one final association of meanings which seems sufficiently rewarding to be the answer – 'now I have understood that it is only at intervals that the strangeness of the process can be observed. I remember once clearly seeing a word so as to understand it, and, at the same time, hearing myself imagine that I had read its opposite. In the same way, there is a preliminary stage in reading poetry when the grammar is still being settled, and the words have not all been given their due weight; you have a broad impression of what it is all about, but there are various incidental impressions wandering about in your mind; these may not be part of the final meaning arrived at by the judgment, but tend to be fixed in it as part of its colour. In the same way, there is a preliminary stage in writing poetry, when not all the grammar, but the grammar at crucial points of contact between different ideas, is liable to be often changed. There is a trivial but typical example of this in the two versions of the Crashaw Hymn for the Circumcision of our Lord,

All the purple pride of Laces

The crimson curtaines of thy bed ;

Guild thee not with so sweet graces ;

Nor set thee in so rich a red. (1646)

All the purple pride that laces

The crimson curtains of thy bed,

Guilds thee not in so sweet graces

Nor setts thee in so rich a red. (1652)

I have assumed that much could be extracted from the fact that one syntax rather than another was selected for a poetical statement; this example shows the limitations of such a method. For, clearly, the verse is altered very little by these quite considerable changes in the grammar; it would be easy in a rapid reading to think they had been the same. It does not make much difference whether laces the noun or the verb is used, because, though their meaning is different, each reminds the reader of the other. So for the corresponding change in guild it does not matter whether this is said to be done by the pride or by the upholstery which expresses it; whichever syntax is chosen, the reader thinks of the guilding as done, in their respective ways, by both. Thus each of these versions includes the other among its possibilities; probably there is a stage for most readers when they have not yet noticed which syntax is, in fact, used. This example of the complexity of the absorption of grammar in poetry may be convincing because so simple ; it shows, by the way, what I have said already, that a poetical effect is not easily disturbed by altering a few words.

One should also consider, not merely whether this generalising of the grammar at first occurs, but how scrupulously it is cleaned away ; how far, then, an attention to it will be profitable. Clearly, the critical principles of the author and of the public he is writing for will decide this to a considerable degree, and one has to bear them in mind in deciding whether a particular ambiguity is part of the total effect intended. (This is hardly a solemn warning, because they have to be borne in mind in any case.) Thus it is fair to hold the seventeenth century responsible for most of its ambiguities, because its taste seems to have been curiously free from such critical principles as interpose a judgment before the experience of accepting the poetry is completed. On the other hand, it would often be unprofitable to insist on the ambiguities of Pope, because he expected his readers to prune their minds of any early disorder as carefully as he had pruned his own. My eighteenth-century examples, therefore, have to depend on variations of grammar the authors would have thought trivial, puns which they had intended and thought intelligible, and variations of sense which spring from an effective superficiality in their thought. But, in the same way, one must often ignore ambiguities in the seventeenth century, because they would be irrelevant to the total effect intended and so were not absorbed.

Ben Jonson's most famous poem gives a puzzling example of this:

Drink to me only with thine eyes,

And I will pledge with mine ;

Or leave a kiss but in the cup

And ril not look for wine.

The thirst that from the soul doth rise

Doth ask a drink divine ;

But might I of Jove's nectar sup

I would not change for thine.

The last two lines say the opposite of what is meant; I must take some credit for not putting this well-known case into the seventh type of ambiguity.[59] But one has already decided from the rest of the verse that a simple lyrism is intended ; there are no other two-faced implications of any plausibility, and the word but after all, admits of only one form for the antithesis. This is not to say that the last two lines are an accident, and should be altered; you may feel it gives a touching completeness to his fervour that he feels so sure no one will misunderstand him. And indeed, you may take the matter more seriously, so as to regard these lines as a true statement of two opposites. You may say that the irrelevant meaning was one to which Jonson was much better accustomed; that he may have been echoing, for the purposes of lyrism, some phrase he had used already at the Mermaid, to express poetical rather than amorous ambition; that he might then not notice till too late about the grammar; that in this sort of lyric, whose business it is to be whole-hearted to an exhausting degree, a man would naturally draw on any generous enthusiasm he had already phrased to himself warmly; and that, at any rate, the lines are a true hyperbole, since Jonson did very seriously feel the thirst of the soul for the divine draught of poetry. All this may be true, and these facts very interesting to the biographer, but they have nothing to do with the enjoyment of the poem. Of course, such a distinction is hard to draw, and those who enjoy poems must in part be biographers, but this extreme example may serve to make clear that it is not all significant ambiguities which are relevant, that I am talking less about the minds of poets than about the mode of action of poetry.

This seems an important point, because I am treating the act of communication as something very extraordinary, so that the next step would be to lose faith in it altogether. It might seem more reasonable, when dealing with obscure alternatives of syntax, to abandon the claim that you are explaining a thing communicated, to say either that you are showing what happened in the author's mind (this should interest the

59 The last two lines, unlike the rest, are not a translation ; one can't settle the question that way.

biographer) or what was likely to happen in a reader's mind (this should interest the poet). This might be more tidy, but, like many forms of doubt, it would itself claim to know too much ; the rules as to what is conveyable are so much more mysterious even than the rules governing the effects of ambiguity, whether on the reader or the author, that it is better to talk about both parties at once, and be thankful if what you say is true about either.

The problem as to belief in poetry might well be mentioned here ; as to whether it is necessary to share the opinions of the poet if you are to understand his sensibility. Very often it is necessary to believe them in a behaviouristic sense; you have to be well enough habituated to them to be able to imagine their consequences ; thus you have to be a person who is liable to act as if they were true. Certainly, if this is so, it becomes puzzling that we should be able to enjoy so many poets. The explanation seems to be that in the last few generations literary people have been trained socially to pick up hints at once about people's opinions, and to accept them, while in the company of their owners, with as little fuss as possible ; I might say, putting this more strongly, that in the present state of indecision of the cultured world people do, in fact, hold all the beliefs, however contradictory, that turn up in poetry, in the sense that they are liable to use them all in coming to decisions. It is for reasons of this sort that the habit of reading a wide variety of different sorts of poetry, which has, after all, only recently been contracted by any public as a whole, gives to the act of appreciation a puzzling complexity, tends to make people less sure of their own minds, and makes it necessary to be able to fall back on some intelligible process of interpretation. Thus one finds it hard, in reading some passages of Keats, to realise that they were long enjoyed empirically, without the theoretical reassurance now given by the psycho-analysts ; the same applies to the ' anthropological ' writings of mystics, like those lines from Crashaw in my last chapter.

One's situation here is very like that of the visualiser who cannot imagine enjoying poetry without seeing the pictures on which he relies; any intellectual framework that seems relevant is very encouraging (as one sees from the cocksureness of the scientists) whether it actually 'explains' anything or not; if you feel that your reactions could be put into a rational scheme that you can roughly imagine, you become willing, for Instance, to abandon yourself to the ecstasies of the Romantic Movement, with a much lower threshold of necessary excitement, with much less fear for your critical self-respect. Thus it is very greatly' to the credit of the eighteenth century that it accepted Shakespeare ; indeed Dr. Johnson was much more sure that his humour was first-rate (nobody wants to feel a joke could be explained) than that his methods of rousing the more far-reaching sentiments of tragedy were to be admitted. The same machinery of reassurance, I suppose, is sought for in my use of phrases like ' outside the focus of consciousness,' without very definite support from psychological theory. To give a reassurance of this kind, indeed, is the main function of criticism.

Many people who would admit that there is a great deal of ambiguity in poetry, and that it is important, will consider that I have gone on piling up ambiguities on to particular cases till the 'whole thing' becomes absurd ; 'you can't expect us to believe all that.' I have, in fact, been as complete as I could in cases that seemed to deserve it, and considered whether each of the details was reasonable, not whether the result was reasonable as a whole. For these analytical methods are usually employed casually and piecemeal, with an implication that the critic has shown tact by going no further; if they are flung together into a heap they make, I think, rather a different impression, and this at any rate is a test to which it is proper that they should be subjected. If the reader has found me expounding the obvious and accepted at tedious length, he must remember that English literary critics have been so unwilling to appear niggling and lacking in soul that upon these small technical points the obvious, even the accepted, has been said culpably seldom.

This attitude, however, can be justified; the position of a literary critic is far more a social than a scientific one. There is no question of dealing finally with the matter, because, in so far as people are always reading an author, he is always being read differently. It is the business of the critic to extract for his public what it wants ; to organise, what he may indeed create, the taste of his period. So that literature, in so far as it is a living matter, demands a sense, not so much of what is really there, as of what is necessary to carry a particular situation 'off.' Detailed explanation, In the literary as in the social field, calls up a reaction of suspicion ; ' Why is he wasting our time, nagging us about this thing, when everybody knows it is all right What good will it do? In the same way, the analyst must be humbled by that story about Proust asking his duchesses why and how they came into a drawing-room like duchesses; they could not tell him, and the only result was to make them laugh when they saw him come into a drawing-room himself. It does not even satisfy the understanding to stop living in order to understand.

This social comparison or derivation may be worked out in some detail, and involves the problems of my first chapter. Thus the relation of Meaning to Pure Sound is very closely paralleled by the relation of Character to Looks; this may serve to show how very completely one may have to behave, in practice, as if the theory of Pure Sound was true. The fundamental source of pleasure about Looks is an apprehension of Character; a change in one's knowledge of the Character alters (by altering the elements selected) one's apprehension of the Looks. The Beauty resides in the Sound and the Looks; but these, being aesthetic constructions, are largely distillations (solutions into forms immediately conceivable) from the Meaning and the Character.

As to say that the Meaning (rather than the Sound) is what matters about poetry, so it seems very intellectual and puritanical to say that Character (rather than Looks) is what matters about people; un both cases those who do so can save the phenomena by invoking first pre-conscious and then instinctive modes of apprehension; in both cases they are using, for the satisfaction of the mind words belonging to the more intelligible part of a scale about the whole scale. And both involve the intellectual fallacy that regards the mind as something otherwise passive that collects propositions; or the assumption that truth is valuable in the abstract rather than as something digested so as to be useful. In both cases one can partly get over this by saying that it is less the Meaning that matters than 'what it means to you/ that it is less the Character itself that is apprehended than its possible relations with your own. And, of course, in both cases, the distinction which I am teasing so pitilessly is largely a verbal one which most people regard as indifferent; someone may say he reads Swinburne for the Sound and George Herbert for the Meaning, but he would not eagerly deny that he reads them both for Meaning conveyed in different ways ; a business man engaging a secretary may feel a distinction between Look and Character, but he would not find it absurd to call this a distinction between two sorts of character estimated in terms of Looks.

A reader may have regarded this parallel as a kind of theoretical joke; if so, it will have been misleading, because as a joke it involves a moral element and depends on an ambiguity. In both cases there is a noble-naughty scale (corresponding in part to the power of the thing to survive analysis if it could be analysed), and also an intellectual-instinctive scale (corresponding in part to the ease or difficulty with which such analysis could be performed) ; in both cases it is a naive intellectualism or Puritanism which mixes the two scales up together. I must confess it is not very far from this fallacy to make the assumption in the first bracket ; to say, as I did in my first chapter, that only bad poems are hurt by analysis (p. i6). There is no necessary reason why this should be true, and it is worth noticing an important class of readers for whom it is not.

Many works of art give their public a sort of relief and strength, because they are independent of the moral code which their public accepts and is dependent on; relief, by fantasy gratification; strength, because it gives you a sort of equilibrium within your boundaries to have been taken outside them, however secretly, because you know your own boundaries better when you have seen them from both sides. Such works give a valuable imaginative experience, and such a public cannot afford to have them analysed; the Crashaw poems in my last chapter may be examples of this state of things. And I suspect that the parallel of personal with poetical beauty still holds good; that there are some excellent people who rightly admire their neighbour's Looks, for valid reasons of Character, which they would find shocking if they could understand them.

Under these rather special circumstances one should try to prevent people from having to analyse their reactions, with all the tact at one's disposal ; nor are they so special as might appear. The object of life, after all, is not to understand things, but to maintain one's defences and equilibrium and live as well as one can; it is not only maiden aunts who are placed like this. And one must remember (since I am saying the best I can for the enemy) that, as a first approximation, or a general direction, to people who really do not know how to read poetry, the dogma of Pure Sound often acts as a recipe for aesthetic receptiveness, and may be necessary.

So that to defend analysis in general one has to appeal to the self-esteem of the readers of the analysis, and assume that they possess a quality that is at present much respected. They must possess a fair amount of equilibrium or fairly strong defences; they must have the power first of reacting to a poem sensitively and definitely (one may call that feminine) and then, having fixed the reaction, properly stained, on a slide, they must be able to turn the microscope on to it with a certain indifference and without smudging it with their fingers; they must be able to prevent their new feelings of the same sort from interfering with the process of understanding the original ones (one may call that 'masculine') and have enough detachment not to mind what their sources of satisfaction may turn out to be. ('Fixed' in the last sentence is a metaphor from printing snapshots; on second thoughts, it is better than the microscopical one, because after all a microscope is not available.) This quality is admired at present because it gives one a certain power of dealing with anything that may turn out to be true; and people have come to feel that that may be absolutely anything. I do not say that this power is of unique value ; it tends to prevent the sensibility from having its proper irrigating and fertilising effect upon the person as a while; a medieval sensibility may have been more total and satisfying than a modern one. But it is widely and reasonably felt that those people are better able to deal with our present difficulties whose defences are strong enough for them to be able to afford to understand things; nor can I conceal my sympathy with those who want to understand as many things as possible, and to hang those consequences which cannot be foreseen.

After this statement of preference I must return to what I have just called its fallacy, and discuss whether the scientific idea of truth is relevant to poetry at all. I have been trying to analyse verses which a great variety of critics have enjoyed but only described in terms of their effects ; thus I have claimed to show how a properly-qualified mind works when it reads the verses, how those properly-qualified minds have worked which have not at all understood their own working. It would be tempting, then, to say I was concerned with science rather than with beauty; to treat poetry as a branch of applied psychology. But, so far as poetry can be regarded altogether dispassionately, so far as it is an external object for examination, it is dead poetry and not worth examining; further, so far as a critic has made himself dispassionate about it, so far as he has repressed sympathy in favour of curiosity, he has made himself incapable of examining it.

This is not simply the old difficulty about what subjects can be treated by the scientific method; at least, it is here more difficult. For instance, one might apply the above argument to medicine; 'those bodies which can rightly be regarded dispassionately are not worth curing.' This may not seem very convincing, but it has been argued; it is the root of the objection to vivisection, and made the Russian Orthodox Church forbid the use of medical textbooks. However, there are, on the face of it, two ways of dealing with bodies; what is found as truth from bodies not considered valuable is found to work as goodness upon bodies that are so considered; and, even more important, the same body can effectively be considered both ways at once ; certainly there are difficulties such as appear in the doctor's objections to psycho-analysis, but the separation is possible. But poetry is not like bodies, because the act of knowing is itself an act of sympathising; unless you are enjoying the poetry you cannot create it, as poetry, in your mind. The scientific idea of truth is that the mind, otherwise passive, collects propositions about the outside world; the application of scientific ideas to poetry is interesting because it reduces that idea of truth (much more intimately than elsewhere) to a self-contradiction.

The human situation is oddly riddled with these antinomies, and, when they seem completely solved by intuition, there is not much object in separating them out; thus I have a vague impression that Proust has listed a great many reasons why it is impossible to be happy, but, in the course of being happy, one finds it difficult to remember them. Still, it seems proper here to consider how intuition ought to solve this antinomy, to say how the analysis of poetry can be useful, and indeed what it can be.

On the face of it, there are two sorts of literary critic, the appreciative and the analytical; the difficulty is that they have all got to be both. An appreciator produces literary effects similar to the one he is appreciating, and sees to it, perhaps by using longer and plainer language, or by concentrating on one element of a combination, that his version is more intelligible than the original to the readers he has in mind. Having been shown what to look for, they are intended to go back to the original and find it there for themselves. Parodies are appreciative criticisms in this sense, and much of Proust reads like the work of a superb appreciative critic upon a novel which has unfortunately not survived. The analyst is not a teacher in this way; he assumes that something has been conveyed to the reader by the work under consideration, and sets out to explain, in terms of the rest of the reader's experience, why the work has had the effect on him that is assumed. As an analyst he is not repeating the effect; he may even be preventing it from happening again. Now, evidently the appreciator has got to be an analyst, because the only way to say a complicated thing more simply is to separate it into its parts and say each of them in turn. The analyst has also got to be an appreciator; because he must convince the reader that he knows what he is talking about (that he has had the experience which is in question) ; because he must be able to show the reader which of the separate parts of the experience he is talking about, after he has separated them; and because he must coax the reader into seeing that the cause he names does, in fact, produce the effect which is experienced; otherwise they will not seem to have anything to do with each other. On the other hand, once the analyst has abandoned himself to being also an appreciator, he can never be sure that he has explained anything; if he seems to have explained something, it may be because he has managed to do the same unexplained thing over again. Thus, in finding several words to convey the mode of action of a single word in a poem, I do not, of course, claim that the new words are any more simple in their action than the old one; a word is of the nature of an organism, or of the nature of the part of an organism; not by a small series of propositions, but by a new piece of writing, must one sharpen a reader's apprehension of the way it is being used. And yet it is precisely the nature of a 'piece of writing' which is supposed to be undergoing analysis.

Mention of Sir Richard Paget's tongue-gestures, in my first chapter, led to an alarming notion; that it was no use trying to say how a poem came to take effect as it did because one could not say how much of the effect was being produced by sound effects, such as belong to the nature of language and have not yet been explained in sufficient detail. The answer is that such an explanation as I have attempted need not be complete because of the nature of its process; it should imply, by its own writing, both how much of the effect is produced by the one device explained and how much is left as at present inexplicable.

The process, then, must be that of alternating between, or playing off against one another, these two sorts of criticism. When you have made a quotation, you must first show the reader how you feel about it, by metaphor, implication, devices of sound, or anything else that will work; on the other hand, when you wish to make a critical remark, to explain why your quotation takes effect as it does, you must state your result as plainly (in as transferable, intellectually handy terms) as you can. You may say that this distinction is false, because in practice one must do both at once, but I think it is useful ; one can apply it, for instance, to that problem about how much one is to say the obvious which always seems to hamper the analytical critic.

Certainly, in appreciative criticism, where you are trying to show the reader how you feel about a poetical effect, it is important not to tease him ; it is annoying to read platitudes in such work because they interfere with the process, which is essentially that of repeating the original effect, in a plainer form. But in an analysis, whose object is to show the modes of action of a poetical effect, the author may safely insist on the obvious because the reader feels willing that the process should be complete. Indeed, it is then as arrogant in the author to hint at a subtlety as to explain it too fully; firstly, because he implies that those who do not know it already are not worth his notice; secondly, because he assumes that there is no more to know. For some readers may take the subtlety in question for granted, so they will think the hint must refer to something still more subtle.

Not to explain oneself at length in such a case is a snobbery in the author and excites an opposing snobbery in the reader; it is a distressing and common feature of modern aesthetics, due much more to disorientation and a forlorn sense that the matter is inexplicable (it is no use appealing to the reason of ordinary people, one has got to keep up one's dignity) than to any unfortunate qualities in the aestheticians. That is one of the reasons why the cult of irrationalism is such a bore ; analytical is more cheerful than appreciative criticism (both, of course, must be present) precisely because there is less need to agonise over these questions of tone.

t may be said that the business of analysis is to progress from poetical to prosaic, from intuitive to intellectual, knowledge; evidently these are just the same sort of opposites, in that each assumes the other is also there. But the idea of this doublet certainly enshrines some of the advantages of analysis, and it may be as well to show how I have been using it. You may know what it will be satisfying to do for the moment ; precisely how you are feeling; how to express the thing conceived clearly, but alone, in your mind. That, in its appreciation of, and dependence on, the immediate object or state of mind, is poetical knowledge. (It is true that poetry is largely the perception of the relations between several such things, but then it is the relations which are known poetically.) You may, on the other hand, be able to put the object known into a field of similar objects, in some order, so that it has some degree of balance and safety; you may know several ways of getting to the thing, other things like it b it different, enough of its ingredients and the way they are put together to retain control over the situation if some are missing or if the conditions are altered; the thing can be said to your neighbours, and has enough valencies in your mind for it to be connected with a variety of other things into a variety of different classes. That, from its administrative point of view, from its desire to put the thing known into a coherent structure, is prosaic knowledge. Thus a poetical word is a thing conceived in itself and includes all its meanings; a prosaic word is flat and useful and might have been used differently.

One cannot conceive observation except in terms of comparison, or comparison except as based on recognition; immediate knowledge and past experience presuppose one another; thus the question in any particular case must be largely as to what is uppermost in your mind. But this way of using the word-pair at least gives one an answer against those who say that analysis is bad for poetry; it often happens that, for historical reasons or what not, one can no longer appreciate a thing directly by poetical knowledge, and yet can rediscover it in a more controlled form by prosaic knowledge.

But even if we abandon the oppositions between thought and feeling, and attend to the intellectual notion of explanation, the situation is not much more encouraging. It is a matter of luck whether or not you have in your language or your supply of intellectual operations anything which, for a particular problem, will be of use ; and this may be true even in a field of known limitation, for instance, it is a matter of luck whether you can find a construction in Euclidean geometry (it would remain so even if you always could) ; whereas in Analytical geometry there will always be a way of setting about the proof of a proposition, if it is a recognisably geometrical one, but it is a matter of luck whether or not it is too complicated for human patience. And it is only by chance that these two matters of chance will work out the same in a particular case . Things temporarily or permanently inexplicable are not, therefore, to be thought of as essentially different from things that can be explained in some terms you happen to have at your disposal; nor can you have reason to think them likely to be different unless there is a great deal about the inexplicable things that you already know. Explanations of literary matters, to elaborate a perhaps rather trivial analogy, involving as they do much apparently random invention, are more like Pure than Analytical geometry, and, if you cannot think of a construction, that may show that you would be wise to use a different set of methods, but cannot show the problem is of a new kind.

I have been insisting on this because it seems important that people should believe that such explanations are possible, even if they have never yet been performed; but the analogy is useful in another way, through giving the notion of a construction. Continually, in order to paraphrase a piece of verse, it is necessary to drag in some quite irrelevant conceptions; thus I have often been puzzled by finding it necessary to go and look things up in order to find machinery to express distinctions that were already in my mind; indeed, this is involved in the very notion of that activity, for how else would one know what to look up ? Such machinery is necessary, partly so as to look as if you knew what you were talking about, partly as a matter of 'style,' and partly from the basic assumption of prose that all the parts of speech must have some meaning. (These three give the same idea with increasing generality.) Otherwise, one would be continually stating relations between unknown or indefinite objects, or only stating something about such relations, themselves unknown and indefinite, in a way which probably reflects accurately the nature of your statement, but to which only the pure mathematician is accustomed. So that many of my explanations may be demonstrably wrong, and yet efficient for their purpose, and vice versa.

The notion of a construction also shows the dangers of the process it describes. With a moderate intellectual apparatus one should be able to draw irrelevant distinctions without limit, and even those that are of linguistic interest need not be of interest to a reader of the poem. When a poem refers simply and unambiguously to a field it is usually possible to plant a hedge across the field, and say triumphantly that two contiguous fields were being described by an ambiguity. This may be of some use in that it shows the field to have extension, but one must not suppose that there is anything in a right apprehension of the field which corresponds to one's own hedge. Thus I think my seven types form an immediately useful set of distinctions, but to a more serious analysis they would probably appear trivial and hardly to be distinguished from one another. I call them useful, not merely as a means of stringing examples, but because, in complicated matters, any distinction between cases, however irrelevant, may serve to heighten one's consciousness of the cases themselves.

Since, however, I admit that the analysis of a poem can only be a long way of saying what is said anyhow by the poem it analyses, that it does not show how the devices it describes can be invented or used, that it gives no source of information about them which can replace that of normal sensibility, and that it is only tolerable in so far as it is in some way useful, I suppose I ought, in conclusion, to say what use I think it can be. It need not be any. Normal sensibility is a tissue of what has been conscious theory made habitual and returned to the pre-conscious, and, therefore, conscious theory may make an addition to sensibility even though it draws no (or no true) conclusion, formulates no general theory, in the scientific sense, which reconciles and makes quickly available the results which it describes. Such an advance in the machinery of description makes a reader feel stronger about his appreciations, more reliably able to distinguish the private or accidental from the critically important or repeatable, more confident of the reality (that is, the transferability) of his experiences ; adds, in short, in the mind of the reader to the things there to be described, whether or not it makes those particular things more describable. What is needed for literary satisfaction is not, 'this is beautiful because of such and such a theory,' but 'this is all right; I am feeling correctly about this; I know the kind of way in which it is meant to be affecting me.'

Of course, this distinction is not new, but it needs repeating; indeed, one often finds the surrealist type of critic saying that poetry would have been just the same if no criticism had ever been written. So Pope, for instance, would have written just the same if he had had no critical dogmas. Now it is unwise to say blankly that a theorist is talking nonsense (for instance, it is no use saying that all men are not equal) because he may consciously be making a paradox to imply a larger truth; thus, even here, there would be a little truth in saying that Pope could afford to forget his dogmas, so deeply had they become part of his sensibility. And certainly one is again faced with the problem about the hen and the egg; the dogma produces the sensibility, but it must itself have been produced by it. But to say that the dogma does not influence the sensibility is absurd. People only say it when they are trying to put the sensibility in a peculiar state of control over the dogma. The conflict between the scientific and aesthetic points of view, between which I have been trying to arbitrate, gives them a reason; people feel uncertain as to what sort of validity a critical dogma can have, how far one ought to be trying to be independent of one's own age, how far one ought to be trying to be independent of one's own preferences, and do not want their sensibility to be justified by reasons because they are afraid that once they start reasoning they will fall into the wrong point of view. Another such cause, arising out of this, has been mentioned already; it is only recently that the public, as a whole, has come to admire a great variety of different styles of poetry, requiring a great variety of critical dogmas, simultaneously, so as to need not so much a single habit for the reading of poetry as a sort of understanding which enables one to jump neatly from one style to another. This produces a sort of anxious watchfulness over the feelings excited by poetry; it is important not to forget what sort of poetry this is and so allow oneself to have the wrong feelings.

For such reasons, then, it is necessary for us to protect our sensibility against critical dogma, but it is just because of this that the reassurance given by some machinery for analysis has become so necessary in its turn. Thus I suppose that all present day readers of poetry would agree that some modern poets are charlatans, though different people would attach this floating suspicion to different poets ; but they have no positive machinery, such as Dr. Johnson thought he had, to a great extent rightly, by which such a fact could be proved. It is not that such machinery is unknown so much as that it is unpopular; people feel that, because it must always be inadequate, it must always be unfair. The result is a certain lack of positive satisfaction in the reading of any poetry; doubt becomes a permanent background of the mind, both as to whether the thing is being interpreted lightly and as to whether, if it is, one ought to allow oneself to feel pleased. Evidently, in the lack of any machinery of analysis, such as can be thought moderately reliable, to decide whether one's attitude is right, this leads to a sterility of emotion such as makes it hardly worthwhile to read the poetry at all. It is not surprising, then, that this age should need, if not really an explanation of any one sort of poetry, still the general assurance which comes of a belief that all sorts of poetry may be conceived as explicable.

I should claim, then, that for those who find this book contains novelties, it will make poetry more beautiful, without their ever having to remember the novelties, or endeavour to apply them. It seems a sufficient apology for many niggling pages.